Just for Two

JANET LAURENCE began her cookery training with her Swedish mother, a first class cook. She continued to learn as much as she could about food and cooking during an executive career that included many opportunities for travel and eating in first class restaurants. After marriage she began to cook professionally.

Janet has run a number of residential short cookery courses from her home in Somerset, covering basic family cooking to haute cuisine for entertaining. She demonstrates widely throughout the country, including regular appearances at John Tovey's Miller Howe in Windermere and Chenies Manor, Buckinghamshire. Her aim as a cookery writer is to present all that is interesting in cooking in easy to follow recipes. She has a deep interest in healthy eating.

She has written a weekly column for the *Daily Telegraph*, contributed to a number of publications including *Taste* and *Country Life* and is a member of the Guild of Food Writers. She also writes crime novels featuring her heroine Darina, a professional cook with a habit of getting mixed up in murder.

Just for Two

The Cookery Book for Two People

JANET LAURENCE

Hodder & Stoughton

LONDON SYDNEY AUCKLAND

This book is dedicated to

Winifred Carr

for many years Women's Page Editor of the *Daily Telegraph*,
without whose help and encouragement I
could never have become a cookery writer

British Library Cataloguing in Publication Data

Laurence, Janet
  Just for two.
  I. Title
  641.5

  ISBN 0-340-56904-2

Published by Hodder and Stoughton,
a division of Hodder and Stoughton Ltd,
Mill Road, Dunton Green, Sevenoaks, Kent TN13 2YA
Editorial Office: 47 Bedford Square, London WC1B 3DP

Photoset by Rowland Phototypesetting Ltd,
Bury St Edmunds, Suffolk

Printed in Great Britain by
St Edmundsbury Press Ltd, Bury St Edmunds, Suffolk

Designed by Trevor Spooner
Cover photograph by Steve Baxter

CONTENTS

INTRODUCTION

There are certain times in life when cooking means meals for two: setting up a flat with a friend; the early stages of marriage before a family comes along; rediscovering one's partner after the children leave home; living on one's own and entertaining friends singly rather than in a crowd.

It's all fun but problems soon arise. Most books' recipes cater for four or six and scaling down, besides being a chore, is not always easy. And recipes that are economical in time and effort for large numbers seem inappropriate when just cooking for two. But ideas for what to do with a chop quickly run out, cooking large casseroles and putting small portions in the deep freeze, if one's available, becomes boring and steak is beyond most daily budgets. Some people rely on convenience foods but, good as these can be, they lack the variety available to the home cook and are not cheap.

I know all about these problems as I've been coping with them for some time. When we entertained a lot it didn't seem to matter providing the odd meal for two, there were always left overs, or a couple of grilled chops or scrambled eggs seemed a nice change after more elaborate dishes. That way of life disappeared some time ago. And with my husband's retirement adding lunch to the daily menu, more and more demands were made on my ingenuity. I started collecting and devising recipes to help provide interesting food quickly and easily then thought there must be many more cooks coping with the same remorseless sequence of meals every week who would like some help. Some of the following recipes are based on favourites originally designed for more but many have been created particularly for two – and none calls for half an egg!

Most of the recipes are economical, many are budget conscious and the majority require very little skill. But every now and then such constraints are flung aside. For there are bonuses in cooking for two; the odd extravagance does not hit the purse in the same way as when catering for more nor does boning out two chicken or duck legs seem the same chore as double that quantity! And serving is much easier, food can go straight from stove to table to be eaten at its very best.

Along the way there are hints for maximising preparation time by looking ahead to another meal and though the recipes are for conventional cooking stoves, instructions for using a microwave oven are given wherever practical.

NOTES

QUANTITIES

The quantities given in all the recipes should feed two generously.

MEASUREMENTS

Follow the same measurements throughout a recipe as the metric/imperial/volume equivalents are not always exact. The spoon measurements are the standard metric ones of 1 teaspoon = 5 ml, 1 dessertspoon = 10 ml, 1 tablespoon = 15 ml (NB Australian tablespoons measure 20 ml, three Australian teaspoons are equivalent to the standard metric tablespoon used in this book).

The cup is the standard American volume measurement of 8 fl oz.

MICROWAVE

The testing of microwave ovens was standardised by the government in the summer of 1991. The new standards are identified by the initials "I.E.C." (these stand for "International Electrotechnical Commission"). As a result, the power output classification of some ovens has changed. If in doubt over yours, contact the manufacturers. The microwave versions of the following recipes have been tested in an oven equivalent to a 700 watt I.E.C.

If your oven has a lower power than 650 watts I.E.C., it will be necessary to increase timings, very roughly by half as much again for 400 watt I.E.C. ovens, by a quarter for 500–600 watt I.E.C. ovens. Start by underestimating cooking times, it is easy to give dishes a little longer and can be disastrous to overcook. Manufacturers are usually very happy to give guidance on converting times for their own particular ovens.

Microwave cooking is a skill that is still in its infancy and needs to be approached with circumspection. As a general rule, I have found that any recipe using poaching or steaming will work excellently in the microwave. When cooked with some liquid, fish, poultry and vegetables respond extremely well. Meats other than poultry are more tricky; some dishes don't work at all, others do, sometimes not quite as well as on a conventional stove but when using small quantities offer such a dramatic saving in time and effort the loss of a little quality is occasionally justified. Any reservations on quality have always been stated when giving the microwave instructions. Where no instructions appear it is because I have found its use is not justified, either because of the final result or because it offers no saving in time.

Salt and pepper are usually omitted when a dish is prepared for the microwave. This is for two reasons. First, because the microwave brings out much more flavour from the food than conventional cooking, less seasoning is necessary, with most vegetables I find it completely redundant. The second is because salt, unless completely dissolved in the food, can draw out liquid during cooking and pepper can develop an unpalatable strength.

Do observe standing times, they enable heat to equalise through the dish and finish cooking the food. Because microwave ovens vary in output and efficiency and ingredients are not always standard, cooks should use their intelligence when cooking meat, especially poultry. If your oven is not equipped with a turntable, give the food a quarter turn halfway through for the longer cooking items. If the dish is not quite cooked at the end of the stated standing time, give it a little extra time in the oven. When reheating any meat or fish dishes, ensure all the dish is bubbling hot before removing from the oven.

For those who are interested in expanding their knowledge of microwave cooking and do not already know it, I recommend *Microwave Gourmet* by Barbara Kafka, published by Barrie & Jenkins, paperback publisher Headline. A pioneering book, it converted me to using my microwave for many more dishes than I had thought possible. Her technique for covering most dishes tightly with cling film, thus conserving all the steam produced by the cooking food, is invaluable. But do be careful when unwrapping, always pierce the film first.

PRESSURE COOKER

A pressure cooker can save invaluable time and energy for many dishes which would normally call for long cooking on the stove or in an oven. I have found one which is much shallower than the normal, family-sized pressure cooker, reduces pressure very easily and the base of which doubles as an excellent sauté and frying pan. The Kuhn/Rikon Duromatic pressure cooker is available through: U.K. Kuhn-Rikon (UK) Ltd., P.O. Box 102, Wolverhampton WV6 8UT (0384) 400123, in USA and Canada from: Kuhn-Rikon Corporation, 120 Charlotte Place, Englewood Cliffs, N.R. 07632.

SYMBOLS

* Indicates preparation should be started several hours before cooking actually begins, usually to allow time for marinading. F means dish will freeze reasonably well. Freezing instructions have not been given for reasons of space, follow guidelines in any good freezer book. With very few exceptions, I believe dishes are much better eaten fresh than after a session in the freezer but there are times when it is necessary for preparation to be done so far ahead freezing is essential. A short time, such as a week or two, often have very little effect on food in which a longer period would produce noticeable deterioration.

INDEX

When cooking just for two, recipes often leave the cook with part of another ingredient, half a vegetable, for instance. Often this book will make a suggestion on how it can be used. But the index could provide other ideas.

SOUP OF THE EVENING –
OR ANY OTHER TIME

Soup for two can be very practical, it need not take long either to prepare or cook and can be substantial enough to form a complete meal.

Simplest of all is a soup made from a couple of large potatoes peeled and diced then covered with water, seasoned and simmered until the potatoes start to disintegrate. Stir well with a wooden spoon, hastening the disintegration process, and add a grated carrot or two, simmer for another 5 minutes or so, check seasoning, add a little milk if it's too thick, bash again with the spoon if necessary and serve with grated parsley on top. A spoonful of yoghurt or cream can also be added. A little chopped ham or bacon will improve both flavour and substance.

A small chopped onion sweated in a little oil makes a good base for any kind of vegetable soup. Stock can add flavour but isn't necessary, the vegetables will add their own distinctive contributions. Some left-over meat or fish can contribute protein and extra bulk, so will cooked pulses (and their stock is ideal for soup), add any you may have left over from some other dish. Most pulses need long soaking and cooking but a pressure cooker can save time and the process needs little attention so it's worth doing a quantity that can provide the basis for a soup, a casserole, a salad and a vegetable pâté, freezing those not required immediately. However, there is also a large range of pulses available in cans that are ready for instant use.

Garnishing need not offer great problems. A few freshly fried croûtons are the traditional crisp accompaniment but there are alternatives: a swirl of yoghurt or cream plus a few chopped herbs or grated cheese (blue cheeses add a distinctive flavour that goes well with creamy soups); a little grated vegetable can add crunch (sauté in olive oil or butter if you prefer but keep on the crisp side); or just some freshly chopped herbs.

Here are some soups requiring a slightly more structured approach.

F FISH SOUP WITH MUSSELS OR PRAWNS

A substantial soup designed to serve two meals. The basic soup is halved, the first part served with the mussels immediately, then the other half refrigerated and served next day with tomatoes and prawns. Or it can be frozen and eaten later. For preparation of the mussels, see MOULES MARINIÈRES in the SOMETHING FISHY section on page 27.

1.25 litres/2 pints/5 cups mussels, scrubbed and scraped
150 ml/5 fl oz/⅔ cup medium dry white wine
Approx. 500 g/1¼ lb mixed fish, including small whole whiting or dab, and remainder cod, monkfish or skate off the bone, plus bones if possible
2 unpeeled cloves garlic
1 medium onion   *1 stick celery* } *all finely chopped*   *1 medium carrot*
Bouquet garni
1.25 litres/2 pints/5 cups water
½ teaspoon sea salt and 6 black peppercorns
Few strands saffron
Garnish: Chopped parsley

Place mussels in a wide saucepan with the wine, cover and bring to the boil. Simmer for a minute or two, checking progress and removing mussels as soon as shells open, placing in a sieve over a jug or bowl. Discard any mussels that remain unopen after several minutes of cooking. Strain the mussel liquor, both that in the cooking pan and the bowl, through a fine sieve to remove any sand or dirt.

Wash fish and trimmings and place in a large saucepan with strained mussel liquor and all other ingredients except the mussels and the saffron. Bring briskly to the boil, removing scum as it rises, then simmer gently. After 5 minutes, start lifting out the fish as it is cooked. Remove flesh and return bones to the pot. Simmer for a further 10 minutes then raise heat to boiling point and cook for further 15 minutes.

Meanwhile, remove cooked mussels from their shells and peel away the "rubber band" running round each plus any bristly beard bits left.

At the end of the cooking time, remove any skin, then strain the soup, pushing as much debris through the sieve as possible. Set aside half, cool quickly and either refrigerate until next day or freeze.

TODAY:

Place saffron in a cup, add 3 tablespoons boiling water and stir well. Reheat soup in a clean pan to simmering point. Stir in the saffron. Check seasoning, add the flaked fish and the mussels and heat through for 2 minutes without bringing to the boil. Serve sprinkled with chopped parsley.

TOWARDS TOMORROW:

2 medium tomatoes, peeled, deseeded, flesh chopped
50–100 g/2–4 oz/¼–½ cup peeled prawns
Garnish: Chopped dill or parsley

Reheat soup to boiling point, add tomatoes and prawns, heat through, sprinkle with the chopped dill or parsley and serve.

CHOWDER

Chowder sustained generations of New Englanders battling with the seas off North America's Atlantic coast. Onions, potatoes, bacon and evaporated milk were all part of a ship's staple stores. Fish came fresh from the sea. There are many recipes for chowder, some add tomatoes, some use clams; the following is based on a traditional recipe I was given by a New England cook of the old school when my husband and I were staying with friends in Boston on our honeymoon. It may seem a little complicated but the base will provide another, quite different, soup for tomorrow; either version served with crusty bread could make a complete meal.

25 g/1 oz/1 tablespoon butter *1 large onion, finely chopped* *350 g/12 oz/2¼ cups potato, peeled and diced* *900 ml/1½ pints/4 cups milk* *Salt and freshly ground black pepper*	*basic soup base, can be halved if liked*
15 g/½ oz butter	

225 g/8 oz cod fillet
3 rashers streaky bacon, diced
4 tablespoons evaporated milk (or cream)
Garnish: Chopped parsley

Melt butter, add onion and cook gently until transparent. Add the potato and cook with onion for 2–3 minutes, then add the milk and season, bring rapidly to boil then lower heat and simmer gently, uncovered, for 10–15 minutes until potato is just cooked. Remove half, cool and refrigerate.

TODAY:

In a separate pan melt remaining butter then, when sizzling, add fish and brown. Remove fish and take off skin. Lower heat and add bacon, sautéing until cooked. (If by any miracle you have good, old-fashioned bacon, you can fry it first in a dry pan till it is crisp and has released its fat, then brown the fish in that, having removed the bacon first, omitting the butter altogether.) Add fish to soup mixture and simmer gently for a few minutes until cooked through, it will break up as you give the soup a stir. Add the evaporated milk or cream, check seasoning then serve in hot bowls with the bacon on top. The final garnish of parsley is not traditional but looks good.

TOWARDS TOMORROW:

Approx. 150 ml/5 fl oz/⅔ cup light stock or water
225 g/8 oz vegetables to choice, coarsely grated or diced quite small
Salt
50 g/2 oz salami or garlic sausage, diced (optional)
Garnish: Chopped parsley or mixed herbs

Cook prepared vegetables lightly in stock or water with no more than a pinch of salt if adding sausage, a little more if not. Add sausage and bring to boil, heat through then add the cooked basic mixture and bring to just below boiling point. Check seasoning then serve in bowls with chopped herbs as garnish.

CABBAGE AND GARLIC SAUSAGE SOUP

A whole cabbage, even a small one, is usually too much for two people but it can provide a vegetable dish for one meal and an unusual soup for another.

1 small onion, finely chopped
1 teaspoon caraway seeds
1 tablespoon good vegetable oil
1 Granny Smith or other tart, crisp apple, cored and grated
Approx. 175 g/6 oz/3 cups green cabbage, finely sliced or shredded
75 g/3 oz/¾ cup diced garlic sausage
750 ml/1¼ pints/3 cups water or light stock, including a little white wine if liked
Salt and freshly ground black pepper
Garnish: Thick natural yoghurt, preferably ewe's

Cook the onion and caraway seeds gently in the oil until transparent. Add apples, cabbage, sausage and water, season and bring to boil then simmer 10–15 minutes until the cabbage is tender and the sausage heated through. Because this soup is quickly cooked, there is no danger of the house smelling of cabbage for days! Add a big swirl of yoghurt before serving.

CREAM OF ARTICHOKE SOUP

Another soup with two alternative ways of finishing off that maximises preparation time. A little Gruyère or mild Cheddar cheese with some chopped walnuts provides a finish that both complements and contrasts with the smooth creaminess of the artichokes. For the second time around, finish with bacon and parsley for a completely different combination of flavours. Because the artichokes are sieved after cooking, there is no need to peel them, often a difficult job if half is not to disappear in the waste-bin with all the little knobs. Adjust the amount of milk to give the consistency you prefer, either thicker or thinner.

1 medium onion, finely chopped
1 tablespoon butter or oil
500 g/1¼ lb/4 cups scrubbed and sliced Jerusalem artichokes
Salt and freshly ground black pepper
450 ml/15 fl oz/2 cups chicken stock or water
Approx. 600 ml/1 pint/2½ cups milk

Cook onion very gently in butter or oil until transparent, add artichoke slices, season, cover with dampened greaseproof paper pressed down on top of vegetables; cook very gently for 15 minutes. Discard paper, add stock or water and simmer, covered, for 20 minutes or until vegetables are soft. Pass soup through a vegetable mill or process and sieve. Then stir in sufficient milk to provide good consistency. Check seasoning. Divide soup in half, cool one half rapidly and refrigerate or freeze.

TODAY:

40 g/1½ oz/2 tablespoons grated Gruyère or mild Cheddar cheese
1 tablespoon chopped walnuts

Reheat other half of soup to just below boiling, remove from heat, stir in grated cheese until melted, serve sprinkled with the chopped walnuts. A little cream can also be swirled on top if liked.

TOWARDS TOMORROW:

4 rashers smoked back bacon, diced
1 tablespoon good vegetable oil
Chopped parsley

Fry bacon in oil until crisp. Reheat soup to boiling point, check seasoning, remembering the bacon will be salty, add the bacon then serve sprinkled with parsley. A little cream can also be swirled on top if liked.

COOK'S TIP: Cooking with the dampened greaseproof paper keeps in and intensifies all the flavour of the vegetables, it really is worth the bother.

MICROWAVE OVEN: Place onion in large bowl, add oil, cover tightly and microwave on HIGH for 2 minutes. Add artichoke slices and four tablespoons stock, cover and microwave on HIGH for 8 minutes. Liquidise with more stock and sieve, or pass through a vegetable mill. It is now quicker to add remaining stock and milk and reheat on the hob than in the microwave. Finish as above.

15

PEA WITH MINT SOUP

Frozen peas produce a very quick and excellent soup with the help of a potato, spring onions and some fresh mint.

5 spring onions, trimmed, white and pale green part chopped
1 medium sized potato, peeled and diced
100 g/4 oz/1 cup peas, fresh or frozen
Large sprig mint
Salt, freshly ground black pepper, grating of nutmeg
½ teaspoon sugar
450 ml/15 fl oz/2 cups chicken stock or water or half a stock cube dissolved in boiling water
150 ml/5 fl oz/⅔ cup milk
Garnish: Cream or natural yoghurt, chopped fresh mint
Croûtons (optional)

Place spring onions, potato, peas, sprig of mint and other seasonings with the stock or water in a saucepan, bring to boil and simmer for 15 minutes or until the potato is soft. Remove mint, process, liquidise or pass soup through a food mill, reheat with the milk, check seasoning and serve garnished with a swirl of cream or yoghurt and the chopped fresh mint. Crisp croûtons are also very good with this soup.

COOK'S TIP: If using the stock cube, leave adding salt until the end, you may not need any, cubes are extremely salty.

CELERY AND APPLE SOUP

Another soup capable of different finishing touches. This has a fresh flavour that combines very well with Stilton cheese, while the addition of diced cooked lamb, chicken or ham to the other half makes a sustaining meal-in-a-bowl.

2 tablespoons light oil
225 g/8 oz/1½ cups celery (approx. half a head), trimmed and thinly sliced
4 eating apples, cored and diced

16

Salt and freshly ground black pepper

1 litre/1¾ pints/4½ cups water

Gently heat oil, add celery, apples and seasoning, press down a double layer of dampened greaseproof paper on top, cover and allow to sweat gently for 15 minutes. Uncover, add water, bring to boil then simmer until all ingredients soft, 15–20 minutes. Liquidise, or process and sieve, or pass through a vegetable mill. Divide into half, cool one half rapidly and refrigerate or freeze.

TODAY: WITH STILTON

50 g/2 oz/4 tablespoons grated Stilton cheese

Little cream (optional)

Celery leaves or chopped parsley

Reheat soup, adjusting consistency if liked. Check seasoning. Remove from heat, add Stilton cheese, stir to melt. Serve garnished with swirl of cream if liked and a celery leaf or two, or sprinkled with chopped parsley.

TOWARDS TOMORROW:

50–75 g/2–3 oz/4–6 tablespoons chopped cooked lamb, chicken or ham

Little cream (optional), chopped chives or parsley

Reheat soup, adjusting consistency if liked. Check seasoning. Add chopped meat, bring back to boil and simmer 5 to 8 minutes, until meat well heated through. Serve garnished with swirl of cream if liked and sprinkled with chopped chives or parsley.

Braise the other half of the celery head to accompany meat or fish, see the Vegetable dishes section on page 161.

COURGETTE AND CARROT SOUP

Most vegetables will make good soups, this one is particularly easy and very tasty. Again, the basic mix will make two soups, directions for a variation in the finish follow the recipe.

1 tablespoon oil
½ teaspoon cumin seed
3 spring onions, trimmed, white and green parts sliced
350 g/12 oz/4 cups courgettes, grated
225 g/8 oz/3 cups carrots, grated
Salt and freshly ground black pepper
750 ml/1¼ pints/3 cups water
Garnish: Little chopped green part of spring onions

Heat oil, when really hot, add cumin seed and sauté for 1 minute. Reduce heat, add spring onions and cook gently for 3–4 minutes. Add grated courgette and carrot and stir-fry for 3–4 minutes. Season, add water, bring to boil and simmer 15–20 minutes, until vegetables soft. The soup can be served as it is or liquidised, processed or passed through a vegetable mill. Divide in half, cool one half rapidly and refrigerate.

TODAY:

Serve first half of the soup garnished with the sliced spring onion tops. Cream or yoghurt can also be added.

TOWARDS TOMORROW:

Few flakes butter or little arachide/ groundnut/peanut oil
Few mushrooms, sliced
Little yoghurt (optional)
1 tablespoon pine kernels, toasted

Heat the butter or oil and sauté the sliced mushrooms until they are tender and all liquid evaporated. Toast the pine kernels separately, either in the oven, under the grill, or in a little oil in a frying pan. Heat the reserved soup, add the mushrooms, scatter the pine kernels on top and serve. A little yoghurt can also be added before the final touch of the pine kernels if liked.

CUCUMBER AND MINT SOUP

A traditional Lebanese cold soup that requires no cooking, ideal for the summer but even enjoyable at other times of the year with something hot to follow.

½ *large cucumber, coarsely grated*
Salt
150 ml/5 fl oz/⅔ cup cream or natural yoghurt
75 ml/2½ fl oz/5 tablespoons natural yoghurt
1 tablespoon tarragon vinegar
Freshly ground black pepper
1 tablespoon finely chopped fresh mint
Garnish: Sprigs fresh mint
Few prawns (optional)

Place grated cucumber in a colander, sprinkle with salt, weight down with a saucer and leave for 20 minutes to drain. There is no need to rinse before using unless you have been very heavy handed with the salt. Squeeze dry, place in a bowl, add the cream (if using) and the yoghurt plus the vinegar. Grate over the pepper, add the chopped mint and stir very well. Check seasoning then refrigerate for at least an hour before serving.

When ready to serve, garnish with mint sprigs and the prawns if using.

19

SOMETHING FISHY

I love fish, a good fishmonger's stall is an Aladdin's cave of delights – it's such fun to look and see what unusual catch is being featured today. And a good fishmonger is a fund of preparation advice and recipes, I learn a lot from mine. Fish is quick to cook – so quick there is real danger of its being dry from overcooking – it's versatile and it's healthy. Fish oils have recently been discovered to play a role in regulating cholesterol and fish eaten twice a week can help avoid heart attacks.

Really fresh fish is delicious cooked quite plainly and all its flavour seems to be enhanced by cooking in a microwave. Fillets, cutlets and small whole fish can all be steamed, add a little wine or herbs to the steaming liquid for extra flavour, then serve with a dribble of olive oil or a little butter or just some snipped herbs.

TROUT EN PAPILLOTE

Farmed trout are freely available and very convenient. They come in nice, portion sized fish although they usually need a little imagination to make them really tasty. This basic cooking method, which maximises flavour, is capable of many variations – the ones suggested here are only a beginning. If you are handy with a knife, the trout can be boned out leaving the fillets attached to each other, remove head and tail first. For boned fish reduce cooking time in the oven by a few minutes and in the microwave by 1 minute.

TROUT WITH PRAWNS

Piece of cucumber approx. 7 cm/3 inches long, peeled, deseeded and cut into strips the size of a baby's finger
Salt
50 g/2 oz/¼ cup prawns
1 tablespoon freshly chopped parsley
Freshly ground black pepper
Little melted butter or vegetable oil

2 trout, approx. 225 g/8 oz each, gutted and cleaned
Juice ½ lemon

Salt the cucumber strips lightly and leave in a colander, weighted down with a saucer, to drain for 30 minutes, then blanch in boiling water for 3 minutes. Drain and refresh in cold water, draining again well. Mix with the prawns and parsley, season with a little black pepper. Season lightly inside each fish and stuff with the cucumber and prawn mixture.

Brush two generous sized pieces of tin foil or greaseproof paper with the melted butter or oil, place a fish on each, sprinkle with lemon juice, wrap up loosely but securely, place on a baking tin or dish and cook in a preheated oven at 190°C/375°F/Gas Mark 5 for approximately 25 minutes, or until just cooked.

Serve in the packet accompanied with a green salad or green vegetable and plain potatoes or pasta.

MICROWAVE OVEN: Prepare cucumber and prawn stuffing as above but omit seasoning, stuff fish and place in a gratin dish, arranged head to tail with the bellies towards each other, sprinkle over the lemon juice, cover tightly with cling film and microwave on HIGH for 3 minutes, turning dish halfway through. Leave to rest for 3 minutes before serving.

TROUT WITH SPINACH AND POTATOES

225 g/8 oz frozen chopped spinach OR 450 g/1 lb fresh spinach
12 hazelnuts, roughly chopped
3–4 tablespoons cream or natural yoghurt
Salt and freshly ground black pepper
Grating nutmeg
2 trout approx. 225 g/8 oz each, gutted and cleaned
Little melted butter or olive oil
4–6 new potatoes, scrubbed or scraped, thinly sliced

Defrost frozen spinach or cook fresh, drain well, squeezing out all liquid, and chop. Add the hazelnuts, cream or yoghurt and season to taste. Season belly of fish lightly, stuff with the spinach mixture.

Lightly brush two generous sized pieces of tin foil or greaseproof paper with melted butter or oil, divide potato slices between them, season lightly, add a stuffed trout on each and secure foil loosely round fish, making an airtight seal. Place in preheated oven at 190°C/375°F/Gas Mark 5 for 25–30 minutes, when fish and potatoes should be cooked through. This dish is really a complete meal in itself but a small salad can be served with it.

MICROWAVE OVEN: Prepare trout as above, omitting salt and pepper. Place potato slices in bottom of a suitably sized gratin or other shallow dish. Add 3 tablespoons water. Cover with cling film and microwave on HIGH for 5 minutes. Uncover, add the fish, head to tail and bellies facing each other, cover again and microwave on HIGH for 3 minutes, turning dish halfway through. Allow to stand for 3 minutes before serving.

TROUT WITH MUSHROOMS AND HERBS

1 tablespoon butter or olive oil
100 g/4 oz/2 cups button mushrooms, sliced
Salt and freshly ground black pepper
1 tablespoon chopped fresh herbs (parsley, lemon thyme, tarragon, chives, etc., or a mixture)
2 trout, approx. 225 g/8 oz each, gutted and cleaned

Heat butter or oil, add sliced mushrooms, season, and cook briskly until all juices have been evaporated and mushrooms are tender. Check seasoning, add herbs, use to stuff trout. Wrap in tin foil and cook as above.

MICROWAVE OVEN: Place sliced mushrooms in bowl, add a squeeze of lemon juice if you have it, cover tightly with cling film and microwave on HIGH for 2 minutes. Add herbs, use to stuff fish then cook as for TROUT WITH PRAWNS on page 20.

ACCOMPANIMENTS: A nice salad is really as much as any of the above need as an accompaniment. New potatoes or pasta can accompany the trout stuffed with prawns or mushrooms and herbs.

FILLETS OF TROUT

Fillets of trout can offer many possibilities. Your fishmonger will fillet and skin the trout if you ask but it is quite easy to do yourself, see the BACK TO BASICS section for directions on page 274. The trimmings – do ask the fishmonger for them – can make a quick stock: cover with water, add a dash of wine vinegar or dry vermouth, a slice of onion, a few peppercorns, parsley stalks and a pinch of salt. Bring to the boil, skim, then simmer 20–25 minutes and strain.

If filleting and skinning the trout takes all your energy, you can abandon any more effort and quickly sauté the fillets as in the SALMON WITH HAZELNUT OIL, ORANGE AND CORIANDER in the TONIGHT'S SPECIAL section on page 221, or poach on top of spinach in the microwave, or with a little white wine, stirring a spoonful of cream into the juices before serving. But wrapping in filo pastry as in the following recipe, inspired by a dish eaten in Alistair Little's Soho restaurant, is beautifully simple. You can leave out the potato and lemon thyme mayonnaise if you prefer a lighter dish, it won't alter the timings. Add a little fresh tarragon or chives instead or just use lemon juice. This is the sort of dish you can play around with and invent many variations on.

TROUT IN FILO PASTRY

2 sheets filo pastry
1 large or 2 small trout, filleted and skinned
Little olive oil
Piece of lemon
3 tablespoons good mayonnaise mixed with ½ tablespoon chopped lemon thyme (or good pinch ordinary thyme with little grated lemon)
Approx. 150 g/6 oz/1 generous cup cooked potato sliced 3 mm/⅛ inch thick
Salt and freshly ground black pepper

Take one sheet of filo pastry, keeping the other under cling film or a damp cloth. Fold pastry in half and brush generously with oil. Place trout in centre, placing fillets (if using one fish per portion) head to tail, season lightly and add a good squeeze of lemon juice. Spread thickly with mayonnaise then add a layer of potato slices and season lightly again. Wrap the pastry round neatly. Brush all over with oil and place on oiled baking sheet. Repeat for second packet. Packets can be kept in cool place for several hours if not cooking at once.

When ready to cook, heat oven to 200°C/400°F/Gas Mark 6, bake pastries for 15 minutes until golden brown then serve immediately.

ACCOMPANIMENTS: Green salad or vegetable.

VARIATIONS: Omit potato for a lighter dish. Any of the stuffing suggestions given for the trout at the start of this chapter can also be used with the fillets.

COOK'S TIP: Unused filo pastry can be refrozen for later use.

FISH KEBABS

Kebabs can be cooked either under the grill or on a barbecue, when they make a lighter change from the more usual meat items. The only difficulty in using fish for kebabs is the tendency of the flesh to disintegrate. Choose firm textured varieties – monkfish is ideal, cod works, so do turbot and halibut and all shell fish; cheaper varieties such as coley, pollack and huss will also serve. Marinading helps protect the fragile flesh as well as provide extra flavour. Treat the following recipe as something basic to provide variations on.

350 g/12 oz boned monkfish, cod or other firm fleshed fish, washed, trimmed of skin, cut into 2.5 cm/1 inch cubes

3 tablespoons fruity olive oil

1 tablespoon tarragon wine vinegar

1½ tablespoons freshly chopped mixed herbs (parsley and chives with tarragon or dill or lemon thyme, or any mixture that pleases)

Salt and freshly ground black pepper

Sauce:

1 teaspoon French mustard with green peppercorns

1 teaspoon clear honey

150 ml/5 fl oz/²⁄₃ cup natural yoghurt
2 tablespoons freshly chopped herbs (see mixture on previous page)
Salt and freshly ground black pepper

Place cubed fish in a plastic bag or wide bowl. Mix together the oil, vinegar and herbs with seasoning to taste then pour over the fish, toss well to coat thoroughly and leave in a cool place for several hours, turn from time to time if you remember. Then thread fish on to skewers, brush with the oil left in the bag or bowl and place either under a hot grill or on to a medium hot barbecue until just cooked, turning once. For a grill allow 3 to 4 minutes each side, for a barbecue about 7 to 10 minutes, according to thickness and variety of fish. Don't allow to overcook and become dry, the fish is ready as soon as it becomes opaque. Mix all sauce ingredients together, seasoning to taste, and serve with the fish.

ACCOMPANIMENTS: Serve with rice and mange tout or beans or a green salad. The sauce is not essential but adds a nice touch.

VARIATIONS: Chunks of young courgette, peppers of any colour, button mushrooms, pieces of onion and tomato wedges can be strung on the skewers in between the fish if liked.

KEBABS IN CORIANDER AND ORANGE MARINADE

350 g/12 oz boned monkfish, cod or other firm fleshed fish, trimmed of skin, cut into 2.5 cm/1 inch cubes
3 tablespoons fruity olive oil
1 tablespoon freshly squeezed orange juice
½ teaspoon coriander seeds, crushed
½ tablespoon zest of orange, either grated or removed with a zester in julienne strips
Salt and freshly ground black pepper
6 bay leaves

Mix all together and use to marinade fish as above. String bay leaves on skewers with fish to cook.

Serve with rice and Carrot and Olive Salad:

CARROT AND OLIVE SALAD

3 tablespoons freshly squeezed orange juice
2 tablespoons extra virgin olive oil
1 tablespoon clear honey
Salt and freshly ground black pepper
100 g/4 oz/1 cup grated carrot
12 black olives

Mix together the orange juice, olive oil and honey and season to taste, pour over the grated carrot and toss well. Add the olives and serve.

MONKFISH WITH THYME

This is an incredibly simple recipe that tastes delicious and is best cooked in a microwave. If a microwave isn't available, stir-fry instead, the result will still be very good but it may lack the wonderful freshness of flavour that comes from microwaving. Another alternative would be steaming, which would cut out fat altogether. Sprinkle the fish with the herbs and a little seasoning then steam over simmering water for approximately 10 minutes until just cooked through. Lemon thyme, if it is available, is lighter in flavour and has a softer texture than ordinary thyme but any version of the fresh herb is preferable to the dried. Any firm fleshed fish can be substituted for the monkfish.

350 g/12 oz monkfish, weighed without bone, membrane removed and fish cut into 2.5 cm/1 inch chunks
Juice of a freshly squeezed lemon
½ teaspoon fresh thyme leaves
Salt and freshly ground black pepper
Few thyme leaves to garnish

MICROWAVE OVEN: Place pieces of fish in a suitable sized dish, sprinkle over the lemon juice and thyme leaves, cover tightly with cling film and microwave on HIGH for 1 minute 30 seconds, allow to rest for 2 minutes before serving garnished with sprigs of fresh thyme.

ACCOMPANIMENTS: Green vegetables or carrots or a salad and plainly cooked potatoes or pasta.

VARIATIONS: Omit thyme leaves and instead add a little grated lemon or orange peel. Some diced red pepper can also be added. Plainly cooked monkfish can be garnished with watercress. OR substitute fillets of sole or plaice for the monkfish, leaving the fillets whole but folding them in three skin side inside, or rolling them up.

MOULES MARINIÈRES

Scrubbing mussels can be a tedious business but the amount needed for two should not tax the cook too much and this is a deservedly famous dish. Do use a good wine, the rest of the bottle can accompany the meal. The quantity below should serve two as a main meal. For a starter, divide quantities in half.

2 kg/4 lb/10 cups live mussels, scrubbed
1 medium sized onion, chopped
2–3 sprigs parsley, small sprig thyme
Freshly ground black pepper
25 g/1 oz/2 tablespoons butter
150 ml/5 fl oz/½ cup dry white wine plus same amount of water
5 tablespoons double cream
2 tablespoons lemon juice
2 tablespoons freshly chopped parsley

Scrub mussels and scrape off any encrustations and bits that dangle. Discard any shells that don't close as you work.

Place onion, herbs and a good grinding of black pepper in the base of a wide, thick-bottomed pan. Add the first lot of butter plus the wine and the water. Place the mussels on top, cover and cook over a high heat for a few minutes, giving the pan a good shake every now and then to redistribute the mussels. Take off the lid after 2 minutes and remove any shellfish that have opened and continue cooking until all have cooked. As you remove the mussels, discard half a shell and place other half with its flesh if a warm serving bowl and keep warm (you can also remove the "rubber band" round the flesh if you like). Discard any shellfish that don't open.

When all fish are removed, strain juices through a fine sieve (there will be sand in the liquid) then replace on heat and reduce by a half. Add the

27

double cream, bring to boil, simmer for a moment, then add the lemon juice. Check seasoning and add a little salt if necessary. Add the parsley, pour over the mussels and serve immediately.

ACCOMPANIMENTS: Brown bread and butter. Follow with a green salad.

RED MULLET WITH ORANGE AND HAZELNUT OIL

Red mullet is expensive but very tasty, it has been prized since Roman times, when extraordinarily high prices were reported as being given for fine specimens. In the mid-nineteenth century, Victorians would spend summers in Weymouth in order to eat red mullet and were apparently prepared to offer two guineas a fish. It is mainly available in the summer but there are a few small south-west fishing ports which catch some throughout the year.

The very small red mullet is a Mediterranean delicacy, those caught in English waters tend to weigh between 225 g/8 oz and a kilo/2 lb. Mullet are sometimes known as sea-woodcock because, like the bird, they can be eaten without removing the innards, the liver being considered a delicacy. Small fish are best grilled whole, slashed three times obliquely across the body and served simply. If using a microwave oven, place belly to belly, head to tail, in a suitably sized shallow dish, add 2 tablespoons water, cover tightly with cling film and microwave on HIGH for 2–3 minutes, according to size, then allow to stand for 3 minutes. A rather larger fish can be filleted and the small bones removed from the flesh then used for the following recipe:

1 red mullet approx. 450 g/1 lb, filleted
Freshly squeezed juice 1 orange
Freshly squeezed juice 1 lemon
Zest of ½ orange, either grated or removed with zester

Salt and freshly ground black pepper
1 tablespoon hazelnut oil
1 tablespoon clear honey
1 head chicory
Segments of an orange removed without pith

Use tweezers to remove the small bones sunk in the flesh of each fillet. Place fish in a small shallow pan, sprinkle over the orange and lemon juice plus the zest of the orange, season lightly, cover and poach over low heat until just done, approximately 5 minutes. Remove fish and keep warm. Reduce juices slightly, whisk in hazelnut oil and honey, check seasoning. Arrange fish on serving dish or plates with the chicory and orange segments, pour over the sauce and serve.

ACCOMPANIMENTS: Salad or green vegetable and pasta or new potatoes.

VARIATIONS: Replace citrus juices with 3 tablespoons white wine and 3 tablespoons water, reduce juices slightly after cooking, whisk an egg yolk, pour on boiling juices, whisking hard. Serve immediately with fish and chopped parsley. This sabayon sauce or one made with a whole egg can also be served with any fillets of fish. See FISH FILLETS WITH SABAYON SAUCE below.

MICROWAVE OVEN: Place fillets of fish in suitable size gratin dish or on plate. Sprinkle over orange and lemon juice and orange zest. Cover tightly with cling film, microwave on HIGH for 3 minutes. Pour off juices, leave fish, covered, to rest. Add oil and honey to juices in small jug, return to microwave, microwave uncovered on HIGH for 2 minutes, check seasoning, stir well and serve with fish as above.

FISH FILLETS WITH SABAYON SAUCE

Any fish fillets can be used for this recipe but I am particularly fond of John Dory. A fat flat fish with large black fingermarks either side of its body, left, it's said, by St Peter picking the fish out of the Red Sea, the John Dory flesh is firm and white and delicately flavoured. It has a large proportion of bone to flesh but a good sized fish, say about 600–700 g/1½–1¾ lb in weight, should yield two fillets each large enough to serve one person. Ask the fishmonger to lift each fillet off the carcass and to give you all the trimmings. If you buy ready filleted fish, try to obtain some trimmings to make stock with or buy some stock ready prepared. If nothing else is available, use a light chicken or vegetable stock. Because the stock will be reduced, don't add more than a small pinch of salt.

Fish trimmings (see above), slice onion, bay leaf, parsley stalks, 10 peppercorns, little salt, water to cover, 2 tablespoons wine vinegar (tarragon wine vinegar if available)

---

2 fillets of fish, John Dory, grey mullet, sole, etc., skinned

---

1 egg

Garnish: Little parsley, chervil or tarragon

Place trimmings and other stock ingredients in saucepan, cover and bring gently to the boil, lower heat and simmer for 25 minutes. Then strain stock into a clean saucepan (discard trimmings, etc.), and reduce to 150 ml/5 fl oz/ ⅔ cup.

Place fillets of fish in shallow pan, pour over stock, check seasoning and poach very gently approximately 5 minutes, until fish is just cooked. Remove fish to a serving dish and keep warm.

Place egg in a bowl and beat until pale and very fluffy. Bring stock to a fast boil then, while still beating egg, pour the boiling stock into the bowl. The heat will cook the egg and produce a lightly thickened, foamy sauce. Pour over fillets, garnish with parsley, chervil or tarragon and serve immediately.

ACCOMPANIMENTS: The delicate flavour of this dish needs clean tasting vegetables – beans, peas, carrots, baby corn on the cob are all good – or a green salad. Potatoes are best cooked plainly.

VARIATIONS: The sauce can be made with half white wine and half strongly reduced fish stock. Chopped herbs can be added to the sauce, as can peeled and diced tomato flesh. The herbs can be beaten in with the hot stock but the tomato dice should be stirred in at the end.

COOK'S TIP: If using fillets of sole, fold in half or three for cooking, placing the thinnest ends underneath and skin side inside. Don't cook stock longer than 25 minutes, it can get bitter.

MICROWAVE OVEN: Place fillets in a gratin dish, the thinnest ends in the middle of the dish, or fold in half or three. Pour over 3–4 tablespoons stock, cover tightly with cling film and microwave on HIGH for 1½–2 minutes, according to the size and thickness of the fillets, leave to stand a few minutes while finishing the sauce as above, adding the juices from the dish.

COD STEAKS WITH JULIENNE OF COURGETTES AND CARROT

This is a very simple dish but the combination of clean flavours is excellent. You do, however, need really fresh vegetables and fish for it to taste its best. And, as always, it is essential not to overcook any of the ingredients. If you really don't like garlic, it can be omitted but the flavour is not at all overpowering.

1 tablespoon olive oil
1 clove garlic, crushed
2 cod steaks (175 g/6 oz each)
Salt and freshly ground black pepper
1 medium sized courgette   2 small carrots } both cut in matchstick-sized pieces
Juice of a small lemon
1 tablespoon freshly chopped parsley

Heat the oil in a shallow pan with the crushed clove of garlic, season each cod steak and fry gently for 2 minutes on each side, then lower heat, cover the pan and allow to cook for approximately 5 minutes more, until the fish is just done. Meanwhile, bring a pan of salted water to the boil, add the julienne strips of courgettes and carrot and cook for 2 minutes then drain, cover with a buttered paper and keep warm.

Remove the cooked cod from the pan, place on a serving dish, cover with a buttered paper and keep warm. Remove garlic from pan, drain off any oil remaining and add lemon juice, scraping bottom of pan to deglaze. As soon as juice comes to boil, remove from heat, add chopped parsley, remove buttered paper from fish and pour the parsley and lemon juice over. Add the julienne of vegetables, either on top of each steak or beside, and serve immediately.

ACCOMPANIMENTS: New or creamed potatoes or tagliatelle dressed with olive oil.

VARIATIONS: The julienne strips can be stir-fried if preferred.

COOK'S TIP: To cut the julienne strips, slice a thin piece off the courgette and carrots, then place vegetables cut side against the working surface so that each is completely steady and ready to be cut into more thin slices. Pile several slices on top of each other and slice again along their length into fine strips.

MICROWAVE OVEN: Place cod steaks in gratin dish, dribble over little olive oil, season very lightly, add 2 tablespoons of water, a few slivers garlic and the julienne slices of carrot and courgette on top of the fish, cover tightly with cling film, microwave on HIGH for 3 minutes then leave to stand for 4 minutes.

SKATE WINGS WITH CAPERS

Skate is an old-fashioned fish that is back in favour. The wings are immensely pleasing in shape, architectural with an articulated bone structure that is linked together like a complicated garden fence, no danger of the odd bone getting stuck in the throat with skate. Skate wings are not difficult to find but make sure they have no more than a very slight hint of ammonia. Strongly smelling wings should be rejected. Some experts claim the flavour is stronger and the texture firmer at this stage but I prefer fresher flesh. All ammoniac smell disappears in the cooking. The small wings aren't as good as the larger ones so it's better to buy one wing and divide into two. If you cook double quantities, you can prepare a skate wing mayonnaise for the next day at the same time. The quantities that follow are enough for both dishes, instructions for the mayonnaise dish are given at the end of the recipe. The fish tastes best if a proper *court bouillon* is prepared by simmering the first set of ingredients in sufficient water to cover the fish for about 25 minutes before adding the skate. However, if you haven't the time or the ingredients, just use water, a couple of tablespoons of wine vinegar, salt and some black peppercorns.

For *Court Bouillon*:

Small onion, sliced
Small carrot
Piece of celery
Parsley stalks
Small bay leaf

Salt
Black peppercorns
2 tablespoons wine vinegar
Water to cover fish
1–1¼ kg/2¼–2¾ lb skate wing
1 tablespoon chopped parsley
Squeeze lemon juice
Knob of butter
1 tablespoon capers

To prepare *court bouillon*, place all ingredients in pan (if adding fish to measure quantity of water, remove before heating liquid), bring to boil then simmer gently for 25 minutes. Add fish, bring back to boil, skim, then poach very gently for 15 minutes until cooked, or remove pan completely from heat and leave the residual heat to cook the fish, which will take about 25 minutes. Remove fish from stock, slip off skin and cut the fish into two pieces, cooling one half quickly and refrigerating with a little of the cooking liquid. Cut the other half into two more pieces for serving immediately. You can also, if you like, slip a thin bladed knife between flesh and cartilage bones and lift the flesh off but care is needed if the appearance of the fish is not to be spoilt.

Place the fish in a warm serving dish, or divide between two plates, sprinkle over the parsley and add a squeeze of lemon juice. Keep warm while melting butter in a small pan and cooking until it is a hazelnut brown. Add capers, pour over fish and serve immediately.

ACCOMPANIMENTS: Peas, or carrots sliced obliquely, mashed potatoes.

VARIATIONS: Omit capers OR replace browned butter with freshly squeezed orange juice, a piece of peel can also be added to the cooking liquid. OR add a teaspoon of mustard seed to the cooking water and serve with the following Mustard Sauce.

MUSTARD SAUCE

1 teaspoon Dijon mustard
1 teaspoon clear honey
1 dessertspoon cider vinegar
Salt and freshly ground black pepper
6 tablespoons extra virgin olive oil

Stir together the mustard and honey, add the vinegar and seasonings and mix smoothly; then dribble in the olive oil, beating well to form an emulsion, just as if you were making mayonnaise. Skin the cooked fish and very carefully lift the flesh off the bones in long strips, arranging on individual plates over a little pile of mashed potatoes. Dribble over a little of the sauce and hand rest separately.

MICROWAVE OVEN: Place fish in a suitable dish with 3 tablespoons water mixed with a dash of vinegar. Cover tightly and microwave on HIGH for 4 minutes. Leave to stand for 4 minutes. Then divide in half and finish each half as above.

SKATE MAYONNAISE

For mayonnaise:

Half of 1–1¼ kg/2¼–2¾ lb skate wing cooked as above
5 tablespoons good homemade mayonnaise
½ teaspoon Maille Tarragon French mustard
1 teaspoon anchovy essence
Dash lemon juice
1–2 tablespoons cooking liquid
Garnish: Chopped parsley
Lemon slices

Take reserved piece of cooked skate, remove skin and lift flesh off bones, try and keep it in long strips. Mix together the mayonnaise with the other ingredients, then thin to a coating consistency with the cooking liquid and pour over the skate strips. Sprinkle over the chopped parsley and garnish with lemon slices. Serve with a simple green salad.

CRAB SOUFFLÉ

Dressed crab is one of the nicest of summer treats and still relatively inexpensive. Do make sure the crab is really fresh, which means finding a fishmonger you can trust. Cooked crab still in its shell is cheaper, it's not a difficult business to remove the flesh and a medium sized crab will yield enough meat for a soufflé substantial enough for a main meal for two. To remove meat, twist off the legs, gently crack the leg shells and extract flesh. Twist off and discard the tail flap. Prise the main body out of the shell with a sturdy knife then discard the soft, feathery gills. Use a heavy knife to split the body, crack each half with the flat of the knife and tease out the meat. Scoop out the dark meat from the shell. The shell, scrubbed clean, can be used as a container for the meat, nicely arranged with chopped hard-boiled egg for a dressed crab salad. Or use flesh for following soufflé:

Little melted butter and fine dry breadcrumbs
40 g/1½ oz/3 tablespoons butter
40 g/1½ oz/6 tablespoons flour
1 teaspoon French mustard
Pinch cayenne pepper
225 ml/7½ fl oz/1 cup milk
4 tablespoons dry white wine or sherry
Salt and freshly ground black pepper
3 large egg yolks
Meat from 1 medium sized crab (approx. 175–225 g/6–8 oz/1⅓ cup crab meat)
4 large egg whites

Use melted butter to coat a 1.25 litre/2 pint/5 cup soufflé dish then sprinkle with dried breadcrumbs.

Heat butter, add flour, stir to form a roux and cook gently for a few minutes. Add mustard and cayenne and make a smooth sauce with the milk and the wine or sherry. Season well and remove from heat. Beat yolks then fold into the sauce. Fold in crab meat. Whip egg whites to stiff peak stage, fold one third into crab sauce then briefly rewhisk remaining egg whites and fold in the lightened sauce.

Place into prepared soufflé dish, run edge of thumb round edge of dish to ensure an even rise and bake in a preheated oven at 190°C/375°F/Gas Mark 5 for 20 minutes. To test whether a soufflé is done, hold in oven and gently shake. If it wobbles dangerously, give it another 2–3 minutes. If it just trembles, it's done. Soufflés should be still soft in the middle and should be served by plunging two tablespoons back to back into the centre and pulling apart, then giving some of soft centre and crisp outside to each person. Time soufflés so everything is ready for immediate serving because they will start to sink the moment they are removed from the oven.

Salad or green vegetables are good accompaniments and baby new potatoes cooked in their skins would also be nice.

SMOKED TROUT SOUFFLÉ

Follow previous recipe but replace crab with approximately 175–225 g/6–8 oz/1–1⅓ cup smoked trout, bones and skin removed, flesh flaked. Omit cayenne pepper and use instead one teaspoon anchovy essence and a dash Tabasco sauce.

UPSIDEDOWN FISH PIE

Making fish pie for two is, I think, a bit of a bore – there are so many separate operations. Here is a very simple version that produces the potato and fennel topping on the bottom instead of mashed on top. It uses fennel root. Fennel, with its aniseed flavour is a natural accompaniment to fish and the root mellows in cooking, providing a very delicate partner to the potato. Any left-overs make very good soup.

2–3 tablespoons butter
2 large potatoes, peeled and thinly sliced
1 medium sized fennel root, trimmed and thinly sliced
Handful of chives, chopped
Salt and freshly ground black pepper
Approx. 225 ml/7½ fl oz/1 cup milk
350 g/12 oz fillet fish (cod, whiting, plaice, coley, etc.), skinned

Butter a gratin dish and interleave the slices of potato and fennel and the chives (reserve a little chopped chives for garnishing), season. Add the milk, it should not quite cover the vegetables, and dot with butter to taste. Cover with tin foil and cook in a preheated oven at 190°C/375°F/Gas Mark 5 for approximately 45 minutes, until just cooked (test with the point of a knife). Remove from oven.

Season the fish well. Add the filleted fish on top of the vegetables, butter the tin foil, re-cover and replace in oven for approximately 10 minutes, until fish is just done. Sprinkle over the last of the chopped chives and serve.

ACCOMPANIMENTS: This is almost a meal in itself. Good fresh bread goes well, together with a green salad. Or serve an extra vegetable such as carrots or beans.

VARIATIONS: Chives can be replaced with parsley. The finely sliced white part of one large or two small leeks can be used instead of the fennel. The fish can be covered with a layer of dry breadcrumbs mixed with grated Gruyère or Cheddar cheese and dotted with butter. Omit the tin foil covering for the remainder of cooking.

MICROWAVE OVEN: Interleave the potatoes, fennel and chives (reserving some for garnishing) in a gratin dish (only butter if you want the extra flavour), add milk to not quite cover, cover tightly with cling film and microwave on HIGH for 7 minutes, test for tenderness with the tip of a knife and cook a minute or two longer if required. Uncover, add the fish on top, recover and cook on HIGH for 2 minutes. Sprinkle with reserved chives and serve.

FINGER LICKIN' CHICKEN

Chicken is healthy and versatile and it is possible these days to buy free-range birds tasting something like the treat chicken used to be. It is worth looking out for a good source and stocking up a deep-freeze if your local butcher can't supply them.

Don't worry about having to face a whole cooked bird day after day, with a little knife work, one chicken can yield breasts, legs and wings for three quite different meals (instructions for sectioning a chicken, an unbelievably simple process, are given in the BACK TO BASICS section at the end of this book on page 274).

Use the breasts for a quick sauté or stir-fry or try one of the simple recipes below.

Chicken legs are sensational simply rubbed with a little oil and sea salt and roasted for 40–45 minutes at 190°C/375°F/Gas Mark 5. For something a little more fancy, force some chopped ready-to-eat dried apricots under the skin, wrap in tin foil and cook at the same temperature for 50 minutes (see COTTAGE PACKED CHICKEN on page 46 for a variation on this). For a quick casserole, cook with some vegetables and a little wine and stock or water as follows: brown the legs in a little hot oil, remove and lightly brown the vegetables, pour off any excess fat, replace the legs, add enough hot liquid to come halfway up the legs, bring to the boil, season and place in a preheated oven at 180°C/350°F/Gas Mark 4 for approximately 50 minutes, until cooked. Or bring up to high pressure in a pressure cooker and maintain for 15 minutes.

Chicken wings are great devilled for a snack with a pre-dinner drink. Or add them to the other bits and pieces the carcass will yield and make a risotto, see below for recipe.

Even less-than-the-best chicken is amenable to many different treatments, its tender flesh absorbs flavour nicely and cooks quickly, the only tricky bit is timing that ensures the meat is properly cooked but not dried out.

F CHICKEN BREASTS WITH CRAB AND GINGER PLUS DELICIOUS VARIATIONS

Tender chicken breasts are popular with most people and a sharp knife is all that's required to make a nice pocket that will take a tasty stuffing. Crab is an unusual partner that works well and the fresh ginger adds a nice tang but there is no limit to the variations on this recipe. I am very fond of a stuffing with green peppercorns, spring onions and cream cheese. Mark Gregory of London's Chelsea Hotel suggests dried apricots and Brie or avocado and bacon. Instructions for all these follow the main recipe but try some of your own ideas as well.

2 boneless chicken breasts
Small tin crab meat
½ teaspoon peeled and grated green ginger
Squeeze of lemon
Salt and freshly ground black pepper
Small knob of butter OR 1 tablespoon olive oil
2 tablespoons medium dry sherry
150 ml/5 fl oz/⅔ cup yoghurt mixed with 1 teaspoonful cornflour OR double cream
Garnish: Few sprigs watercress or parsley

Remove the thin white muscle from the underside of the breasts. Insert a thinnish, sharp knife into each chicken breast from the fattest end and open out a deep pocket, being careful not to cut right through the flesh at any point. Mix together the crab meat and grated ginger and season well. Divide in half and use to stuff each breast.

Place butter or oil in a frying pan over a medium heat until hot then add the seasoned breasts and fry gently, turning once, until cooked, about 5–7 minutes each side according to size of breasts. (Test by gently pressing with blunt knife, spatula or finger, cooked meat will not "give" but feel springy – remember stuffing will be very soft.) Remove from pan and keep warm. Pour away any excess fat and deglaze pan by adding sherry and scraping well. Then add the yoghurt (the cornflour will keep it from splitting) or cream and heat through until bubbling, stirring all the time. Check seasoning, pour over breasts, garnish with watercress or parsley.

ACCOMPANIMENTS: Pasta or new potatoes, a simple salad or a green vegetable such as beans, mange tout or peas.

VARIATIONS: Instead of crab and ginger, stuff breasts with one of following:

a) 2 tablespoons cream cheese; the white part of four small spring onions, finely chopped; 1 tablespoon crushed green peppercorns (the soft sort); salt and freshly ground black pepper. Use dry vermouth for sauce instead of sherry, garnish with little chopped chives or green part of spring onion **F**

b) 2 tablespoons soft Brie; 4 ready-to-eat dried apricots, chopped; salt and pepper **F**

c) 2 tablespoons chopped avocado pear; 2 rashers bacon, chopped and gently fried until crisp.

MICROWAVE OVEN: Place yoghurt mixed with cornflour and sherry in a jug, cover tightly and microwave on HIGH for 2–3 minutes until bubbling hot and lightly thickened, or heat cream. Uncover carefully and stir well. Place breasts in dish arranged with thin end of one beside fat end of the other. Pour over sauce, cover tightly with cling film, microwave on HIGH for 3 minutes 30 seconds. Leave to sit for 2 minutes to finish cooking before garnishing with watercress or parsley and serving.

F CHICKEN BREASTS WITH MANGO

A pretty dish that also tastes very good. And the other half of the mango can be used for a fruit salad for tomorrow.

2 chicken breasts, approx. 175 g/6 oz each
Salt and pepper
½ ripe mango
75 ml/2½ fl oz/¼ cup chicken stock
½ teaspoon cornflour mixed with little water
Approx. 1 tablespoon freshly squeezed lemon juice

Remove the thin, white muscle from the breast fillet. Place each breast between two layers of cling film and beat gently with a rolling pin or meat bat to flatten slightly. Season lightly. Remove the skin from the mango and cut the flesh into long slices. Reserve any very odd shaped pieces plus the trimmings round one half of the stone. Place a good slice on each breast and roll up the meat then place in a shallow, lightly greased ovenproof dish with the loose end of the breast underneath. Reserve a couple of nice slices of mango for garnish then add any remaining slices plus the odd bits to the dish, tucking the flesh down between the chicken rolls.

Bring the stock to the boil and pour over the chicken. Cover the dish with tin foil and place in a preheated oven at 190°C/375°F/Gas Mark 5, and cook for 25 minutes. Remove the rolls of chicken and keep warm. Purée the fruit and juices, reheat in a pan, add the slaked cornflour and bring to the boil, stirring all the time, the sauce will thicken very slightly. Check seasoning and sharpen with a little lemon juice to taste.

Cut each chicken roll into three or four pieces and arrange on individual plates or a serving dish with the centre of fruit showing. Pour round some of the sauce, garnish with the reserved two slices of mango, then serve the remaining sauce separately.

ACCOMPANIMENTS: Mange tout peas or French or string beans with new potatoes or pasta.

VARIATIONS: Peaches or apricots can replace mango, prunes are another possibility.

MICROWAVE OVEN: Prepare breasts and mango as above, using a similar dish. Add the cold stock, cover dish tightly with cling film, microwave on HIGH for 3 minutes 30 seconds. Then remove breasts, wrap in tin foil and keep warm. Purée fruit and juices, add the slaked cornflour, stirring in well. Microwave uncovered on HIGH for 2 minutes or until clear and slightly thickened, stirring halfway through cooking. Check flavour and add seasoning and lemon juice as required. Serve as above.

SWEET AND SOUR CHICKEN

It was difficult to know whether to put this dish in this section or in the stir-fry but in the end I decided it belonged here. It is quick, easy and delicious.

2 teaspoons oil
1 large or two small chicken breasts, cut into thin strips
Little more oil
1 clove garlic, peeled and finely chopped
2–3 spring onions, white and pale green parts chopped
1 small or ½ large red or green pepper, stem, core, seeds and white pith removed, flesh cut into thin strips

Sauce:

4 tablespoons chicken stock
1 dessertspoon dry sherry or rice wine
1 teaspoon light soy sauce
1 teaspoon tomato purée
1 dessertspoon cider or Chinese rice vinegar
1 dessertspoon sugar
1 teaspoon cornflour blended with 2 teaspoons water
Salt and freshly ground black pepper

Have the ingredients for the sauce all mixed together.

Heat a wok or large frying pan, add the oil and stir-fry the chicken until the meat becomes opaque, no more than 1–2 minutes. Remove from the pan with a slotted spoon and drain in a colander or on kitchen paper. Clean out pan, add little more oil then the garlic, spring onions and pepper strips to the pan and stir-fry briskly for half a minute. Pour in the sauce ingredients, bring the mixture to the boil, stirring all the time, replace the cooked chicken in the pan, lower the heat and simmer gently for about 4 minutes until chicken thoroughly heated through. Check seasoning and then serve immediately.

ACCOMPANIMENTS: Plain rice.

VARIATIONS: Use turkey escalope instead of chicken, or fresh prawns.

CHICKEN AND ORANGE KEBABS

*Start preparation at least 4–5 hours or day before serving

A recipe with a teasing flavour, a mixture of freshness and spice. It needs time for marinating, four to five hours will do but it tastes better with longer, ideally start the day before cooking.

5 tablespoons natural yoghurt
Grated rind 1 orange
1 teaspoon sherry vinegar (or wine vinegar if sherry unavailable)
½ teaspoon cardamom seeds, measured after removing from papery pods, roughly crushed
Salt and freshly ground black pepper
2 chicken breasts, approx. 175 g/6 oz each, cut into chunks
Flesh of 1 orange removed in segments without pith or membrane (see BACK TO BASICS section at back of book on page 274), or use half slices of orange cut without any pith

Mix together the yoghurt, orange rind, sherry vinegar and crushed cardamom seeds and season to taste. Add the chunks of chicken, turning well to coat, cover and leave in a cool place, or the fridge, for the flavours to permeate and mature for anything from 4 to 24 hours, giving the mixture an odd turn from time to time as is convenient.

Then place chicken on skewers interspersed with the orange segments or the half slices of orange. Place under a hot grill, dribble over marinade and cook for 4–5 minutes, then turn and cook for another 4–5 minutes. Exact time will depend on how large the pieces of chicken are, don't overcook or the meat will become dry and uninteresting.

Serve on the skewers with any remaining marinade poured over. A sprig or two of parsley looks nice.

ACCOMPANIMENTS: A bed of brown rice and a salad or fresh green vegetable such as beans, peas or broccoli.

MICROWAVE OVEN: Place marinaded meat on wooden skewers, interspersed with orange segments or the half slices of orange. Have the meat and fruit pushed well together. Place skewers together on a dish, pour over remaining marinade, cover tightly and microwave on HIGH for 2 minutes 30 seconds. Allow to stand for 2 minutes before serving as above.

BARBECUED KEBABS

Start preparation several hours before serving

Chicken with a rich, barbecue sauce, one that draws heavily on the store cupboard but is very good. Once again, the longer the meat can be left to marinate, the better the flavour.

Sauce:

1 tablespoon corn oil
1½ tablespoons tomato ketchup
1 dessertspoon lemon juice
1 dessertspoon Worcestershire sauce
1 tablespoon mango chutney (cut up any large pieces of fruit)
1 dessertspoon curry sauce
1 teaspoon soft brown sugar
Salt and freshly ground black pepper

2 chicken breasts, approx. 175 g/6 oz each, cut into chunks

Mix together all the barbecue sauce ingredients. Place chicken pieces in a bowl, pour over the sauce and turn to coat all the meat well. Cover bowl with cling film and place in a cool place or the fridge. Leave to absorb the flavours as long as is convenient.

When ready to cook, thread the chicken pieces on skewers then place under a hot grill and cook for about 8–10 minutes, length of time will depend on the size of the chunks but watch to see that it is not overcooked or it can get dry. Turn the skewers and brush with any remaining sauce after 4 minutes.

ACCOMPANIMENTS: Brown rice and a salad.

VARIATIONS: Instead of kebabs, marinade legs or drumsticks and either grill for around 20 minutes, turning and basting frequently, or cook in a preheated oven at 180°C/350°F/Gas Mark 4 for 40 to 50 minutes, according to size of pieces.

MICROWAVE OVEN: Thread marinaded meat on wooden skewers, place skewers together on a dish and pour over remaining marinade, cover tightly and microwave on HIGH for 2 minutes 30 seconds. Allow to stand for 2 minutes before serving as above.

F CHICKEN IN FILO PARCELS

These succulent little parcels take very little time to make and are ideal for using up little bits of chicken left after jointing a whole bird. Or they can be made with a whole chicken breast cut into pieces.

½ teaspoon Maille Dijon mustard
Salt, freshly ground black pepper and pinch sugar
1 dessertspoon wine vinegar
½ tablespoon virgin olive oil
Chopped herbs: few fresh basil leaves or 1 tablespoon snipped chives or ½ tablespoon fresh lemon thyme or 1 tablespoon parsley, chervil and tarragon or just parsley
Approx. 175 g/6 oz boned chicken breast, cut into large dice-sized pieces
2 tomatoes, peeled, deseeded, flesh diced
2–4 sheets of filo pastry
Little olive oil or melted butter

Mix together the mustard, seasonings to taste, vinegar and oil then add the freshly chopped herbs. Add the diced chicken and tomato flesh and toss well.

Lay out two pieces of filo pastry approximately 15 cm/6 inches by 20 cm/8 inches on top of each other (some sheets are about double this size, others nearer it so you will either need one sheet of pastry or two for each packet). Brush top layer with oil or melted butter then turn both layers of pastry over. Add half the chicken and tomato mixture and fold the pastry into a neat parcel around it. Place on a lightly greased baking tray and repeat, making two parcels in all. Bake in a preheated oven at 200°C/400°F/ Gas Mark 6 for 15 minutes.

Serve garnished with a few fresh herbs.

ACCOMPANIMENTS: A green vegetable would be nice, with new potatoes if you feel you need more starch, or a salad.

VARIATIONS: Instead of tomatoes, use 100 g/4 oz/2 cups button mushrooms sautéd quickly in a little butter or oil until any juices have run or been evaporated. There are many other possibilities as well: cucumber, celeriac or fennel, all blanched and drained. Turkey can be used instead of the chicken. Cooked meat can also be used.

COOK'S TIP: Always keep filo pastry wrapped in plastic or tin foil or

45

underneath a damp cloth to prevent it drying out. Unused filo pastry can be refrozen. For another suggestion on using small pieces of uncooked chicken, see HAM KNUCKLE RISOTTO in BUDGET BEATERS section on page 120.

F COTTAGE PACKED CHICKEN

A very different package from the one in the recipe above. Nothing is simpler than this recipe, which has been one of my great standbys for many years. It is exceedingly healthy, full of flavour and dead easy. What more do you want?

100 g/4 oz/½ cup cottage cheese
2–3 tablespoons freshly chopped herbs (parsley, chives, a sprig thyme, 1 mint leaf, tarragon, chervil, etc.)
1 garlic clove (optional), peeled and crushed
Salt and freshly ground black pepper
2 chicken legs, approx. 300 g/10 oz each

Mix the cottage cheese with the chopped herbs, garlic (if using) and seasoning to taste. Using your thumb, ease the chicken skin away from the flesh (quite easy) and then divide the cottage cheese mixture and place half under the skin of each leg, pulling the skin back over the stuffing. Wrap each stuffed leg in a piece of tin foil, making sure the foil is fastened loosely around the leg, leaving room for steam to circulate.

Place packets on a baking tray and cook in a preheated oven at 190°C/375°F/Gas Mark 5 for approximately 50 minutes, a little less for smaller legs, a little longer for larger, until cooked. The foil can be drawn back for the last 10 minutes or so to help brown the skin if liked. To check if the legs are done, insert the point of a sharp knife in the thickest part of the flesh; if the juices that well up are bloodless, the meat is cooked.

The legs can be served still in their packets, nice if you haven't unwrapped them in the oven, then you get a wonderful aroma as the foil is opened. Or they can be arranged on a dish and garnished with a little chopped parsley.

ACCOMPANIMENTS: Rice or new potatoes and a salad or a green vegetable.

VARIATIONS: As with the breast of chicken recipes above, many variations are possible and any of the suggestions for the breast can be used with the leg. Chopped or grated vegetables are another option, blanch briefly before using unless you like them very crunchy.

46

COOK'S TIP: This way of cooking *en papillote* can be used for many other sorts of food: chops, fish cutlets, sliced vegetables, etc. A 2.5 cm/1 inch fish cutlet will take about 25 minutes; a pork chop about 45 minutes, lamb chops or breast of chicken about 25 minutes, all at the above temperature. Adjust your choice of vegetables or flavouring agents, remembering that many will take longer to cook than the meat or fish so don't include onion unless already cooked and slice potato very thinly if using with the shorter cooking items.

MICROWAVE OVEN: Prepare as above then cut round the base of the drumstick, through the skin and tendon, so that it can shrink easily in the cooking. Place in a gratin dish, add 3 tablespoons stock, wine or water and cover tightly with cling film. Microwave at 100% for 9 minutes. Allow to stand for 5 minutes before serving as above.

F CHICKEN LEGS STUFFED WITH HAM

Boning out chicken legs is quite easy and the method is given at the BACK TO BASICS section at the end of the book on page 274. Two legs will take very little time and the result is worth the trouble, succulent flesh with a pocket capable of taking a variety of fillings. There are limitless possibilities for stuffing but a favourite of mine is ham. Don't worry about the garlic cloves, cooked this way the flavour is very subtle.

2 slices ham
2 teaspoons Dijon mustard
2 chicken legs, approx. 300 g/10 oz each, boned out
1 tablespoon olive or arachide/groundnut/ peanut oil
1½ tablespoons tarragon wine vinegar
150 ml/5 fl oz/⅔ cup dry white wine or cider
4 cloves garlic, unpeeled
Salt and freshly ground black pepper
½ teaspoon tomato purée
5 tablespoons cream or natural yoghurt
Garnish: Little freshly chopped parsley

Spread ham slices with a little of the Dijon mustard, roll up and place each inside one of the boned chicken legs. Either sew or tie up meat with string or strong thread or secure with cocktail sticks.

Heat oil in small, heavy based pan or casserole, sauté legs briskly until skin is golden brown then remove. Drain off fat, add the tarragon vinegar and scrape any sediment into the liquid, allowing the vinegar to reduce slightly. Add the wine or cider, the unpeeled cloves of garlic and season to taste. Bring to boil, replace the browned legs, lower heat and simmer very gently until cooked, approximately 50 minutes.

Take out legs, remove string or threads or cocktail sticks, keep the meat warm. Remove fat from surface of juices then boil the liquid until reduced by half. Mix together the remaining mustard, the tomato purée and the cream or yoghurt. Add the reduced juices through a sieve, pressing the cloves of garlic so that they yield their amazingly mild purée. Whisk the sauce well then return it to the cleaned out pan and heat gently until just below boiling point (it will split if you allow it to boil, unless you stabilise the yoghurt with a little cornflour or are using double cream). Check seasoning.

The meat looks pretty with the legs sliced obliquely so that the rosette-shaped ham centre is displayed. The slices can be placed on individual plates or on a serving dish. Or the legs can be left whole. Either way, pour over a little sauce, garnish with chopped parsley and serve remaining sauce separately.

VARIATIONS: Use stuffing as for the STUFFED LEG OF TURKEY in the BUDGET BEATERS section on page 116, or for the STUFFED DUCK'S LEGS in the TONIGHT'S SPECIAL section on page 231. Or use smoked oysters.

MICROWAVE OVEN: Prepare chicken legs as above. Place them in a deep dish, add the tarragon vinegar and liquid, cover dish tightly with cling film and microwave on HIGH for 6 minutes. Remove meat, wrap in tin foil and keep warm. *For sauce:* mix together the remaining mustard, the tomato purée and the cream or yoghurt. Reduce pan juices by a half on the hob (it takes too long in the microwave oven), and finish off as above.

F HONEY BASTED CIIICKEN WITH GRAPES AND ALMONDS

Roasting gives a lovely golden finish to the chicken and a subtly sweet flavour. The crunchy almonds and juicy grapes provide a good contrast in texture. The chicken can be grilled instead, it will take a shorter time but there is a danger of the honey burning; add the basting mixture 10 minutes after the start of grilling and keep a careful eye on the meat.

2 chicken portions, approx. 300 g/10 oz each
1 tablespoon clear honey *1 tablespoon arachide/groundnut/* *peanut oil* *1 tablespoon medium sherry* *½ tablespoon light soy sauce* *Salt and freshly ground black* *pepper*   *all mixed well together*
Small knob butter or dessertspoon olive oil
6 almonds, blanched and split
6 green grapes, halved and depipped

Place chicken portions in small roasting pan or gratin dish, brush with basting mixture, you will not need it all immediately, place in a preheated oven at 180°C/350°F/Gas Mark 4 and cook for approximately 50 minutes, until pink juices no longer well up when the thickest part of the portion is pierced with a sharp knife, basting with the remaining mixture every 10 minutes.

Just before serving, heat the butter or oil in a pan, add the almonds and gently brown. Then add the grapes and toss to heat through.

Sprinkle the toasted almonds and warmed grapes over the chicken and serve.

ACCOMPANIMENTS: Pasta or brown rice with a green salad or a vegetable with a clean, fresh taste, like beans or broccoli.

COOK'S TIP: Almonds can be toasted very quickly and effectively in the microwave oven. Blanch almonds in their skins by pouring boiling water over the nuts, leaving for a few minutes, then slipping the nuts out of the skins. Use a sharp knife to slit almonds in half, place in a single layer on a plate or dish and microwave uncovered, stirring halfway through cooking if the oven has no turntable. 100 g/4 oz/¾ cup freshly blanched almonds will take approximately 6 minutes to toast.

MICROWAVE OVEN: Run a sharp knife round the end of the leg bone, severing the skin and tendon. Coat each piece of chicken thoroughly in the basting mixture and place in a gratin dish with the leg ends towards the middle and alongside each other. Add any remaining mixture to the dish, cover tightly with cling film. Microwave on HIGH for 9 minutes. Pierce film and allow legs to stand for 5 minutes. Meanwhile place almonds on a plate, uncovered, in the oven and microwave on HIGH for 2 minutes. Remove from the oven. Place the prepared grapes in a small dish, cover tightly with cling film, microwave on HIGH for 20 seconds. Uncover the chicken and place in a dish or on individual plates, mix together the almonds and the grapes, sprinkle over and serve as above.

SPICED CHICKEN

I think one of the best ways of adding flavour to chicken is with spices. Now that Madhur Jaffrey and Claudia Roden have introduced us all to the versatility and variety of spices, we can be more adventurous than just reaching out for the curry powder; nor is it necessary to blast the palate with heat to achieve something tasty. The following little clutch of recipes all need time for the spices to permeate the chicken flesh. Which only means a little thinking ahead. Marinade can be prepared at the same time as the previous day's meal, the chicken left in the fridge overnight, then it is all ready to cook without much further fuss the next day. Or prepare in the morning ready for the evening.

F SPICY CHICKEN

*Start preparation several hours or day before serving

This is a deliciously spicy dish that is also very good cold, excellent for a picnic, and the chicken is best marinaded overnight. Freshly crushed spices give a much better flavour than those bought ready ground. A pestle and mortar isn't essential, a quick whizz in a coffee grinder produces an excellent result for minimum effort (and if a little residue perfumes the coffee afterwards, so much the better, but the dust is quite easily wiped away with kitchen paper). Or put the spices in a plastic bag and crush them with a rolling pin. Whatever method you use, don't reduce them to powder, just crush roughly.

2 tablespoons virgin olive oil

½ tablespoon sherry vinegar

½ teaspoon cumin seeds ½ teaspoon cardamom seeds, measured after releasing from their papery pods ½ teaspoon coriander seeds	all crushed together
Small clove garlic, crushed	
1 tablespoon runny honey	
½ teaspoon salt	
2 chicken portions, approx. 300 g/10 oz each	

Mix together all the ingredients except the chicken portions. Put the chicken in a plastic bag and pour over the marinade, rubbing well into the flesh on all sides, easily done by manipulating the plastic, thereby leaving hands clean and not wasting any marinade. Leave in a cool place, or the fridge, for from 3 to 24 hours. Then remove chicken pieces from the bag, place in a pan or ovenproof dish, pour over all the marinade, squeezing any residue out of the plastic bag, and roast in a preheated oven at 180°C/350°F/ Gas Mark 4 for approximately 50 minutes, or until the juices that well up when the thickest part of the thigh is pierced are quite clear. Baste with the marinade every 10 minutes or so.

Skim fat off the top of the juices and serve juices with the meat together with a homemade preserve or jelly if liked.

ACCOMPANIMENTS: Rice or pasta, green salad or a green vegetable.

VARIATIONS: Use one or two poussins, according to size, instead of chicken pieces. Method is exactly the same as is cooking time for two small birds, one larger one may take a few minutes longer.

This recipe is also great for marinading little chicken wings for serving with drinks. I tend to collect these from whole fresh chickens as I section them, popping them into a plastic bag in the deep-freeze. Any number can be marinaded for snacks. Indeed, they can be frozen in the marinade, which helps give a more potent effect. Hot from the oven they vanish in a moment but they are also good cold.

COOK'S TIP: Don't keep spices for longer than six months, they grow stale and lose their potency. Buy small quantities and discard any left after six months.

MICROWAVE OVEN: Marinade chicken as above but before pouring over the marinade mixture, run a sharp knife round the end of the leg bone, severing the skin and tendon. After marinading, place chicken in a gratin dish with the leg ends towards the middle and alongside each other. Pour over all the marinade, and cover tightly with cling film. Microwave on HIGH for 9 minutes. Pierce film and allow legs to stand for 5 minutes. Then serve as above. Cooking and standing time for two small poussins is the same. If using one large poussin, cut it down the backbone and flatten out before marinading by pressing down with the palm of the hand on the breast bone. It will cook better like this, and absorb more marinade. It can then be cut in two along the breastbone before serving.

F SPICY GRILLED CHICKEN

*Start preparation several hours or day before serving

This is a quick recipe, cooked under the grill, with a much more potent result than Spicy Chicken. Again, start preparations well ahead of cooking time, preferably the day before.

2 chicken portions, approx. 300 g/10 oz each or 4–6 drumsticks
1½ teaspoons black peppercorns, crushed
1½ teaspoons chilli powder
1 tablespoon grated onion
1 clove garlic, crushed with ½ teaspoon salt
1 teaspoon muscovado or soft brown sugar
1 tablespoon wine vinegar
1 tablespoon arachide/groundnut or grapeseed oil

With the point of a sharp, small knife, stab each piece of chicken several times. Mix together all the other ingredients. Place chicken in a plastic bag, pour over the marinade and rub well into the meat, manipulating the plastic so your hands don't get messy. Leave in a cool place, or the fridge, for from 5 to 24 hours. Then heat the grill to its hottest point and grill the chicken, a little way from the heat, for about 15 minutes each side, drumsticks will take a slightly shorter time, be careful not to overcook.

ACCOMPANIMENTS: Rice and salad with fruit chutney.

MICROWAVE OVEN: Marinate chicken as above but before pouring over the marinade mixture, run a sharp knife round the end of the leg bone, severing the skin and tendon. After marinading, place chicken in a gratin dish, placing leg ends towards middle and alongside each other. Pour over all the marinade, cover tightly with cling film. Microwave on HIGH for 9 minutes. Pierce film and allow legs to stand for 5 minutes. Then serve as above.

F SPICY CHICKEN WITH AUBERGINE

*Start preparation several hours or day before serving

Another quite different recipe with a lot of zing but not a roof-of-the-mouth blaster. Once again, allow time for marinading, preferably overnight.

5 tablespoons natural yoghurt ½ teaspoon cornflour 1 teaspoon grated fresh ginger root 1 clove garlic, crushed with ½ teaspoon salt 1½ teaspoons ground coriander 1½ teaspoons ground cumin 1½ teaspoons ground turmeric Good pinch ground cinnamon ½ teaspoon cayenne pepper	all blended or processed together

2 chicken pieces, approx. 300 g/10 oz each or a poussin large enough for two, split down the backbone into two halves

1 tablespoon oil

1 medium sized onion, peeled and finely chopped

1 small aubergine, diced, sprinkled with salt, allowed to drain in a colander under a saucer for 30 minutes, rinsed and patted dry

5 tablespoons chicken stock or wine or water

Garnish: Fresh coriander leaves or fresh parsley

Make sure the marinade ingredients are blended or processed into a smooth sauce. Then stab the chicken in several places with the point of a small, sharp knife, place in a plastic bag and cover with the marinade, manipulating the plastic to rub it in well. Put the bag and its contents in a cool place, or the fridge, for several hours or overnight.

When ready to cook, heat oil, add onion and cook gently until soft and transparent but not coloured. Add the drained aubergine and continue cooking for another 10 minutes, until aubergine has absorbed oil and is slightly softened.

Drain off marinade from chicken and add to aubergine and onion mixture with the chicken stock or wine or water. Heat to boiling point, stirring constantly.

Place chicken pieces in small casserole or gratin dish, pour over the vegetable sauce, cover with lid or tin foil, place in preheated oven at

180°C/350°F/Gas Mark 4 and cook for approximately 50 minutes, or until the juices that well up when the thickest part of the thigh is stabbed with the point of a small, sharp knife are quite clear.

If fresh coriander leaves are available, they make a particularly suitable garnish, otherwise a little fresh parsley looks good.

ACCOMPANIMENTS: Brown rice and a side salad.

MICROWAVE OVEN: Marinade chicken as above but before pouring over the marinade mixture, run a sharp knife round the end of the leg bone, severing the skin and tendon. When ready to cook, mix onion and oil in a casserole or gratin dish large enough to hold the chicken easily, cover tightly with cling film, or place in a roasting bag, and microwave on HIGH for 2 minutes. Pierce film, uncover and mix in the prepared aubergine. Re-cover tightly with film, microwave on HIGH for 3 minutes. Remove the chicken from the marinade, scraping it off the flesh. Squeeze out the marinade from the plastic bag and add with the stock to the onion and aubergine, mixing well. Place chicken portions in the sauce in the casserole or gratin dish, leg ends towards the centre and lying alongside each other. Cover tightly and microwave on HIGH for 9 minutes. Allow to stand for 5 minutes. Check that thigh juices are quite clear and then serve as above.

F CHICKEN AND MUSHROOM DRUMSTICKS

An old friend of mine used to consider it an insult to be offered the drumstick from a roast chicken. I could never understand why because I think its flesh is amongst the most succulent of the whole bird. Bought separately, drumsticks are one of the cheaper cuts and cooked in a sauce as in this recipe can provide a really delicious dish. Drumsticks can also be spiced as in any of the above recipes, and are particularly good as tasty snacks for drinks or picnics.

1 tablespoon arachide/groundnut oil and 1 tablespoon butter
4–6 drumsticks
175 g/6 oz/3 cups button mushrooms, trimmed and quartered if large
2 tablespoons flour
150 ml/5 fl oz/⅔ cup chicken stock / 150 ml/5 fl oz/⅔ cup milk } OR all milk

Salt and freshly ground black pepper

1 tablespoon fresh lemon juice

Freshly chopped parsley

Heat the oil and butter and sauté the drumsticks on all sides until golden brown. Remove from the pan, add the mushrooms and sauté briskly until all juices released and evaporated. Add flour and stir well so it absorbs the fat. Lower heat and cook gently, stirring from time to time, 2–3 minutes. Then add the chicken stock gradually, followed by the milk, stirring well to make a smooth sauce, season to taste and add the lemon juice.

Place the drumsticks in a suitable sized casserole or gratin dish, pour the mushroom sauce over and place in a preheated oven at 180°C/350°F/Gas Mark 4 for 40 minutes or until the chicken is cooked.

Sprinkle with chopped parsley and serve.

ACCOMPANIMENTS: Creamed or plain potatoes or pasta with carrots or a green vegetable.

VARIATIONS: A little cream can be added to the sauce if liked. The flavour will be improved by adding a few rehydrated dried mushrooms: place in a jug and pour over about a cup of boiling water and leave for 20–30 minutes. The soaking liquid can be carefully strained (there is usually some grit in it) and used as stock for the sauce as well. A very quick version of this dish can be made by heating a can of concentrated mushroom soup, undiluted, and pouring that over the browned chicken legs and cooking in the oven as above. OR try tomato and basil: liquidise a small tin of peeled tomatoes and their juices, add a tablespoon chopped fresh basil or a teaspoon of dried and pour over the chicken. 10 minutes before the end of cooking, add grated mozzarella or Gruyère or Cheddar cheese. Garnish with whole fresh basil leaves if available.

MICROWAVE OVEN: Omit butter and oil, substitute 1 tablespoon corn-flour for the flour. Make a cut round the end of each of the drumstick bones, severing the skin and tendon, then place in a deepish round or rectangular dish either in a circle with the thick ends outwards, or in a line with thick end next to thin. Add the sliced mushrooms and the stock (or half the milk if using all milk). Cover tightly and microwave on HIGH for 15 minutes. Pierce film, uncover carefully, remove legs and keep warm. Slake the cornflour with 2 tablespoons cold milk. Add the rest of the cold milk and the cornflour mixture to the sauce in the oven, stir well, re-cover tightly and microwave on HIGH for 6 minutes, whisking halfway through. Check drumsticks are properly cooked, if they have given up any pink juices while sitting during the cooking of the sauce, replace in the sauce and cook for another minute. Otherwise replace in sauce and serve as above.

F CHICKEN AND PARSNIP CASSEROLE

Parsnip is an underrated vegetable. It is the most unaggressive of the roots with a sweet flavour and tender texture that beats a sponge for absorbability: butter, cream, oil, stock, it laps them all up, becoming ever more tasty and succulent in the process. Here it is used to add flavour to the chicken, to thicken the sauce and to provide a base for tomorrow's soup.

2 chicken legs, 300 g/10 oz each, or 4–6 drumsticks
1 tablespoon arachide/groundnut oil
1 medium sized onion, peeled and chopped
450 g/1 lb parsnips, peeled, cored and sliced or diced
450 ml/15 fl oz/2 cups chicken stock
Salt and freshly ground black pepper
1 small red pepper, trimmed of core, seeds and white pith, cut into strips and blanched in boiling water 5 minutes, drained and refreshed in cold water
Garnish: Parsley

Heat oil, brown the chicken legs all over, remove, add chopped onion, lower heat and cook gently until soft and transparent. Add the parsnip slices and move around the pan, allowing them to soak up any oil and become coated with the onion. Place the chicken legs in a small casserole dish, add the parsnip and onion. Add the chicken stock to the pan, bring to the boil, season to taste, then pour over the contents of the casserole. Cover and place in a preheated oven at 180°C/350°F/Gas Mark 4 for 40 minutes, or until cooked.

Take out the chicken pieces and keep warm. Liquidise parsnips and stock, check seasoning then reserve two-thirds for soup. Add blanched strips of red pepper to remaining sauce, thin consistency if liked with a little stock, milk or cream, bring back to boil, pour over the chicken legs and serve garnished with a little parsley.

ACCOMPANIMENTS: Boiled or creamed potatoes, sprouts or broccoli.

VARIATIONS: Use white and pale green parts of leeks instead of parsnips, mushrooms are another possibility.

COOK'S TIP: Unless small and very young, I find it is best to quarter parsnips and remove the hard core, otherwise the soft outer part of the vegetable can disintegrate before the centre is cooked through.

MICROWAVE OVEN: Cut round the end of the legs or drumsticks, severing the skin from the bone. Place the onion and oil in a deep dish, cover tightly and microwave on HIGH for 2 minutes. Pierce film, uncover carefully, add the chicken and parsnip plus 350 ml/12 fl oz/1½ cups of the chicken stock, cover tightly and microwave on HIGH for 16 minutes. Pierce film, uncover, remove chicken pieces, wrap in tin foil and leave in warm place while preparing sauce as above, using remaining stock to thin sauce. If any bloody juices have come out of chicken whilst it is standing, microwave chicken in prepared sauce, covered tightly with cling film, for a further 2 minutes.

TOWARDS TOMORROW: For a tasty soup, to the reserved part of the sauce add the contents of a small tin of chopped tomatoes. Reheat gently and finish with a swirl of yoghurt and a sprinkling of parsley before serving.

F POUSSIN CASSEROLE WITH CABBAGE

Poussin are young, spring chickens. Nicely tender, they usually lack the flavour that comes with more mature birds so need a little help. They are sometimes enough for two and sometimes will only serve one. The following recipe works for either one larger bird or two smaller. The cabbage adds great taste and texture, combining with the wine in a way that is really above its station.

1 large or 2 small poussins
1 tablespoon olive oil
Crushed seeds of 6 cardamom pods
1 clove garlic, crushed
Approx. 225 g/8 oz/4 cups shredded green cabbage (Savoy)
150 ml/5 fl oz/⅔ cup dry white wine
3 tablespoons chicken stock or water
Salt and freshly ground black pepper
Garnish: Watercress or parsley

Season the inside of the poussin then brown all over in the oil in an ovenproof casserole dish. Remove. Turn down the heat, add the crushed cardamom seeds and the garlic and stir over the heat for a moment then add the cabbage and stir well to combine the spice and garlic. Add the wine and stock or water, season to taste. Bring to the boil, place the chicken back in the pot on top of the cabbage, cover tightly and cook in a preheated oven at 180°C/350°F/Gas Mark 4 for approximately 40 minutes, until chicken just done. Lay the cabbage in a dish, place the chicken on top, if just the one bird has been cooked, cut it in half, and serve garnished with a little watercress or parsley.

ACCOMPANIMENTS: New potatoes or pasta is the only accompaniment needed.

VARIATIONS: The recipe will also work with chicken quarters, though if they are very big they may need a little extra cooking time.

COOK'S TIP: Crush the seeds either in a mortar or in a bag with a rolling pin.

MICROWAVE OVEN: Halve the poussin, whether you are using one or two. Mix together the cardamom seeds, garlic, cabbage, wine and stock or water, stirring all together well in a large dish. Cover tightly with cling film and microwave on HIGH for 2 minutes. Pierce film with the point of a knife, uncover carefully and place the chicken on top, breast side down. Cover tightly again. Microwave on HIGH for 8 minutes. Leave to stand for 5 minutes then turn chicken right way up and serve as above.

TOWARDS TOMORROW: Double the quantity of cabbage, wine and stock and use half as a soup for the next day with added stock and perhaps a little potato.

CHOPS WITH EVERYTHING

Quick and easy to cook, chops and steaks of all kinds are ideal for two and the possibilities are almost endless.

Chops as well as steak can be peppered: lightly score the flesh with a very sharp knife then rub in crushed peppercorns or coriander seeds before grilling. A good sprinkle with Worcestershire sauce before grilling adds a spicy finish. Or stir-fry slivers of green ginger with shredded spring onion for a zesty finish to a plain grilled chop.

Add some chopped fresh parsley and garlic to a few sliced and sautéd mushrooms for a garnish in the *haute cuisine* class.

LAMB CHOPS WITH CARAMELISED ONIONS (or SHALLOTS)

In this recipe the chops are cooked in the pan. If you wish, they can be grilled and then united with the caramelised baby onions or shallots at the end but they won't absorb any of the flavour whilst cooking. If you have shallots available, they will produce a more subtle result, the method is exactly the same.

2 tablespoons olive oil
1 dozen baby onions or small shallots, peeled
Salt and freshly ground black pepper
2 lamb chump chops (or butterfly chops)

Heat the oil in a small frying pan, add the onions or shallots, shake the pan well to coat them with the oil, then cook uncovered for 10 minutes over a moderate heat, turn the heat down if mixture starts to brown too quickly. Then add a lid slightly askew so that steam can escape and cook for 20 minutes more, stirring from time to time. Uncover pan, raise heat slightly and add the lamb chops, seasoning them well. Brown on both sides then reduce heat slightly and cook until just done, approximately 10 minutes. By this time the onions or shallots should be golden brown and tender.

ACCOMPANIMENTS: Plain potatoes or pasta would go well, together with a small salad or a fresh green vegetable.

VARIATIONS: Substitute steak for the chops. Recipe also works well with pork chops.

BUTTERFLY LAMB CHOPS WITH HERBS

These should not be confused with butterflied leg of lamb, for which the meat is opened out and the bone removed. These chops are cut straight across the saddle, giving a double "eye" of meat, and are shaped rather like a butterfly, hence the name. My butcher calls them space invaders! Whatever the name, the chops are a real treat and the following, very simple, treatment makes the most of them. Don't worry about the amount of herbs used, it seems a lot but the result is tasty rather than overwhelming.

2 double lamb chops
1 tablespoon flour
¼ teaspoon each of dried marjoram, oregano, thyme, basil and tarragon (or ½ teaspoon each of chopped fresh herbs)
Salt and freshly ground black pepper
1 tablespoon vegetable oil
Garnish: 2 wedges lemon, little watercress

Trim excess fat from chops. Mix flour with herbs and seasoning. Heat the oil in a pan that fits the size of the chops. Press each side of the chops into the herb and flour mixture, coating them well, then add to the pan and fry for 8 to 10 minutes each side, until just done. Garnish with watercress and lemon and serve.

ACCOMPANIMENTS: Plain potatoes or pasta, green salad, carrots or beans or peas.

VARIATIONS: The recipe works well with pork chops or with lamb steaks cut from the fillet end of a leg.

COOK'S TIP: Use any remaining watercress in soup. Add roughly chopped leaves to potato and onion soup, simmer for 6 to 7 minutes then serve immediately. If the soup is left, the fresh green of the leaves will turn an unattractive sludge. Blanching the watercress before cooking can help prevent this.

LAMB CHOPS WITH MELON

Melon is a wonderful accompaniment to lamb, its freshness cuts the richness of the meat.

1 tablespoon olive oil
2 lamb chump or butterfly chops, trimmed of excess fat
½ small galia or ogen melon, flesh scooped out in balls, remaining flesh scooped out and finely chopped or processed
Grated rind of a small orange
2 tablespoons freshly squeezed orange juice
Salt and freshly ground black pepper
Garnish: 1 tablespoon freshly chopped parsley

Heat oil in small frying pan, season and seal chops on both sides. Drain fat from pan, add the chopped or processed melon, the orange rind and juice, season lightly, reduce heat, cover and simmer gently for 20 to 30 minutes until chops are cooked. Add the melon balls and allow to heat through, then arrange on a heated plate or serving dish and garnish with the parsley.

ACCOMPANIMENTS: Creamed potatoes are very nice with this dish and rice is good. Plainly cooked broccoli goes well, so do beans.

TOWARDS TOMORROW: Use the other half of the melon cut into chunks and mixed with flaked smoked mackerel to make a salad. The combination of the melon flavour with the smoked fish is quite sensational. OR make a quick fruit salad with a little additional fruit; if it's the raspberry season, they make a particularly good combination with melon.

LAMB CHOPS WITH GRAINY MUSTARD

2 chump chops OR 4–6 cutlets OR loin stripped from bone and fat, etc.
Salt and freshly ground black pepper
2 tablespoons light olive oil
1 shallot or 2 spring onions (white part only), finely chopped
2 tablespoons white wine or water
1 clove garlic
1 tablespoon Maille à l'Ancienne grainy French mustard (or similar)
1 tablespoon chopped fresh herbs (parsley, chives, chervil, etc., whatever is available to choice)

Trim the chops of excess fat. Heat the oil, season the chops then fry them for about 4 minutes on each side, a little longer if you prefer the meat well done. Or cook the loin as in LOIN OF LAMB WITH ROSEMARY AND ONION SAUCE in the POT POURRI section on page 80. Then transfer meat to a warm dish and keep warm.

Add the chopped shallot or spring onion to the pan (if loin has been roasted, place the roasting pan over the hob or scrape the sediment into a small pan) and soften over a gentle heat. Then add two tablespoons of white wine or water to the pan and bring to the boil, scraping the bottom of the pan well to dislodge all sediment. Allow liquid to reduce by half then squeeze in the garlic through a garlic press and add the mustard, stirring in well. Check seasoning, add the herbs, spread the sauce over the surface of the meat (if using loin, have it cut into *médaillons* as in the LOIN OF LAMB recipe mentioned above) and serve.

ACCOMPANIMENTS: A green salad and gratin of potatoes would be lovely with this dish.

COOK'S TIP: No need to peel garlic cloves before squeezing through a press.

CHEESY LAMB CUTLETS

This is a very simple recipe but very tasty. The cutlets are also good cold, a nice choice for a picnic.

4–6 lamb cutlets
1 egg, beaten

Salt and freshly ground black pepper
2 tablespoons dry breadcrumbs
2 tablespoons grated cheese, Parmesan or tasty Cheddar or a mixture
1 tablespoon light oil

Season the beaten egg, mix together the breadcrumbs and the cheese. Then dip the cutlets first in the egg and then in the breadcrumb and cheese mixture, pressing well to make it adhere to the cutlets. Heat the oil in a small frying pan and add the cutlets, browning on both sides then lowering the heat a little and cooking the chops for about 4 minutes on each side.

ACCOMPANIMENTS: Plain vegetables with a few new potatoes are best, a green salad is very good and watercress goes well.

VARIATIONS: Add a little chopped sage to the beaten egg. Instead of lamb chops, use little beaten escalopes of pork tenderloin, they will only need to be browned on each side, see PORK WITH ORANGE AND LEMON on page 68.

MUSTARDY PORK CHOPS

The following recipe could hardly be more simple or more delicious. The basting mixture is just as good on lamb chops and gammon steaks.

2 large pork chops trimmed of excess fat
1 heaped teaspoon Dijon mustard
1 teaspoon good vegetable oil
Dash Worcestershire sauce
1 heaped tablespoon redcurrant jelly
Salt and freshly ground black pepper

Heat grill. Mix together all ingredients except the first then spread half on chops. Place under hot grill for 5 minutes. Turn, spread other side with remaining sauce, grill another 5 minutes then reduce heat and continue grilling until chops cooked, about 5 to 10 more minutes depending on thickness.

ACCOMPANIMENTS: Baked or new potatoes plus a salad or green vegetable.

VARIATIONS: Use the basting sauce with lamb chops or gammon steaks.

MICROWAVE OVEN: This just about works in the microwave. The result is very different from grilling but just as attractive, worth while for the delicious sauce as the meat cooks. Place chops in shallow dish with wide ends facing outwards. Spread with half sauce. Cover with cling film. Microwave on HIGH for 1½ minutes. Turn chops over, reposition slightly, spread over remaining sauce, re-cover and microwave on HIGH for further 2 minutes. Cover with foil and leave to sit for 5 minutes for cooking to finish before serving.

PORK CHOPS À LA HONGROISE

À la Hongroise, or in the Hungarian manner, always means with paprika. Although there is a hot paprika, most of that available in the UK is the mild variety. A little extra spice for this recipe is added with a dash of Tabasco, a useful store cupboard sauce hot with chilli peppers. The sauce looks very pretty with the diced red pepper and it is nicely piquant. If you prefer, the yoghurt can be replaced with soured cream.

2 pork chops
2½ teaspoons paprika powder
6 tablespoons thick yoghurt, preferably low fat
½ teaspoon cornflour
2–3 dashes Tabasco sauce
Salt and freshly ground black pepper
½ small red pepper, seeds, stem and inside membrane removed, flesh cut into small dice, blanched in boiling water for 2 minutes, drained, refreshed in cold water and drained again
1 tablespoon freshly chopped parsley
Grated rind ½ orange

Trim chops of excess fat. Score flesh lightly with the point of a sharp knife then sprinkle both sides of the chops with 1 teaspoon of the paprika, rubbing it into the meat. Grill each side for 5 minutes.

Meanwhile, mix the yoghurt with the cornflour, the other 1½ teaspoons of paprika, the dashes of Tabasco (adjusting quantity to your taste, it is very hot), a little salt and pepper, then bring to the boil, stirring constantly. When sauce has thickened, add the diced red pepper and heat through. Stir in the chopped parsley and grated orange rind, check seasoning, spoon over the cooked chops and serve immediately.

ACCOMPANIMENTS: Plain boiled potatoes or pasta dressed in olive oil plus a green vegetable such as cabbage or beans. Or a green salad.

COOK'S TIP: Any bought sauce can be used in the same way for cooking pork chops in the microwave. The result will not be as good as with freshly made sauce but if you can find one you like, it makes for a very quickly prepared dish.

MICROWAVE OVEN: Mix together the yoghurt, cornflour, 1½ teaspoons paprika, the dashes of Tabasco (adjusting quantity to taste, it is very hot) and the grated orange rind, microwave on HIGH for 3 minutes, stirring halfway through, until thickened and bubbling. Add the diced and blanched red pepper and the chopped parsley. Place chops, prepared as above, in a suitable sized shallow dish, with the bones facing outwards. Cover chops with the sauce, cover tightly with cling film and microwave on HIGH for 4–5 minutes, according to size of chops. Allow to stand for 5 minutes, then serve.

TOWARDS TOMORROW: Use the remaining half of the red pepper with a few *petits pois* and some soaked raisins with rice to make a pilaff.

PORK CHOPS SWEET AND SOUR

A very simple, very tasty way of cooking pork chops. A recipe that works in the microwave as well as in the conventional oven.

2 loin pork chops
1 tablespoon mango chutney, any pieces of fruit well chopped
1 teaspoon Worcestershire sauce
Dash Tabasco (hot red pepper) sauce
½ teaspoon Maille Bordeaux (lightly spiced) mustard (if unavailable use Dijon)
1 teaspoon wine vinegar
1 teaspoon light brown muscovado sugar
Salt and freshly ground black pepper

Trim chops of excess fat and place in a shallow, ovenproof dish. Mix together all other ingredients and spread over top of chops. Place in preheated oven at 160°C/325°F/Gas Mark 3 for 25 minutes, or until cooked.

ACCOMPANIMENTS: Rice, creamed potatoes or pasta; courgettes or parsnips or a green salad.

MICROWAVE OVEN: Place trimmed chops in a shallow dish with bones facing outwards and thick end next to thin. Mix together all other ingredients and spread over chops. Cover tightly with cling film. Microwave on HIGH for 6 minutes, leave to stand for 5 minutes before serving.

CURRIED PORK CHOPS

I know ready mixed curry powder is not as effective as making your own mixture but when dealing with such small quantities, it is very practical.

2 pork chops
2 teaspoons good curry powder
150 ml/5 fl oz/⅔ cup yoghurt
1 clove garlic
2 slices onion
Small knob of peeled fresh ginger, roughly chopped
Salt and freshly ground black pepper
1 tablespoon light vegetable oil
Garnish: Freshly chopped parsley or coriander leaves
Accompaniments: Roasted almonds, a sliced banana, chutney

Sprinkle half the curry powder over both sides of each pork chop and season with salt and pepper, rubbing all the seasonings well into the meat. Place the yoghurt, garlic, onion, ginger and a little salt and pepper into a blender or processor and process until reduced to a paste.

Heat the oil in a small pan, brown the pork chops on both sides. Remove the chops, lower heat, add remaining half of curry powder, cook 1–2 minutes then add the yoghurt paste and return chops to pan, turning the meat so that it gets well coated. Simmer, uncovered, for 10–15 minutes, according to thickness of chops (the yoghurt will separate but do not worry, this is part of the cooking process). Serve garnished with the fresh herbs and accompanied by the almonds, banana and chutney.

ACCOMPANIMENTS: Rice, which can be cooked with turmeric or mixed with a little diced red or green pepper, some *petits pois* and soaked raisins to make a pilaff.

COOK'S TIP: Make sure you buy a good brand of curry powder, suiting its strength to your taste, keep the tin tightly stoppered and use within six months of opening. If any is left after this time, discard, it will soon start tasting tired and dusty.

MICROWAVE OVEN: Try to use curry paste rather than powder, the paste has been prepared and does not need the frying process. Spread half over chops and place them in a suitable sized gratin dish, bones facing outwards. Add the other half of the curry paste to the yoghurt sauce, processed as above. Coat the chops with the sauce. Cover tightly with cling film, microwave on HIGH for 4 minutes 30 seconds then allow to stand for 5 minutes before serving.

PORK WITH CARROTS AND GINGER

*Start 30 minutes–2 hours before serving
Another recipe using the little escalopes of pork tenderloin prepared as above. It is low fat and so very healthy. It also tastes deliciously fresh.

1 pork tenderloin, 300–350 g/10–12 oz
Juice of 1 small lemon
100 g/4 oz/1 cup grated carrot
Grated rind of ½ small orange
Juice of 1 small orange
½ tablespoon finely chopped peeled fresh ginger root
1 tablespoon light olive oil
Salt and freshly ground black pepper
3 tablespoons chicken stock OR white wine OR cider
75 ml/2½ fl oz/5 tablespoons low-fat yoghurt mixed with ½ teaspoon cornflour
½ tablespoon freshly chopped mint

Strip the tenderloin of any fat and the silvery membrane. Cut obliquely into slices about 2 cm/¾ inch thick then beat out into small escalopes between two layers of cling film. Sprinkle the escalopes with the lemon juice and leave for at least 30 minutes and up to 2 hours.

Place the grated carrot, grated orange peel, the orange juice and the chopped ginger in a non-stick pan and cook gently, stirring, for 2–3 minutes, until lightly cooked. Place in a shallow serving dish and keep warm.

Brush the base of a non-stick or heavy based frying pan with the oil and heat. Drain the escalopes, reserving the lemon juice, pat dry, season and fry for 1–2 minutes each side until browned. Arrange on the carrot and keep warm. Add any lemon juice from the drained meat to the pan, scraping the bottom well to dislodge any sediment, and reduce to half. Mix together the stock, white wine or cider with the yoghurt and cornflour. Pour into the frying pan and bring to the boil, stirring all the time. Simmer for 2–3 minutes, check seasoning, add the chopped mint and spoon over the meat.

ACCOMPANIMENTS: Pasta or new potatoes and a green salad.

MICROWAVE OVEN: Mix together the grated carrot, grated orange peel, the orange juice and the chopped ginger, place in the bottom of a shallow dish. Drain the pork from the lemon juice and lay the meat on top of the carrot mixture, overlapping the slices. Add a tablespoon of the drained lemon juice to the stock or wine and mix with the yoghurt and cornflour, season lightly. Place in a jug, cover tightly with cling film and microwave on HIGH for 2 minutes, uncover, stir and pour over the pork, making sure it covers all the meat. Cover dish tightly with cling film and microwave on HIGH for 3 minutes 30 seconds. Leave to stand for 4 minutes then uncover, sprinkle with the chopped mint and serve.

PORK WITH ORANGE AND LEMON

*Start preparation a day ahead

A tenderloin of pork usually weighs about 350 g/12 oz and is ideal for two people. It is expensive but there is no waste. For those with small appetites, butchers will cut to size. I like to trim the meat of any bits of fat and silvery skin then cut it obliquely across into little *médaillons* which can then be beaten out between layers of cling film into small escalopes which cook in no time and are beautifully tender. They can be used in a wide range of dishes. This one adds extra flavour with a marinade.

1 tenderloin of pork (350 g/12 oz), prepared as above

Marinade:

Juice 1 orange and ½ lemon

Small piece peel without pith of orange and lemon

68

1 clove garlic, crushed
1 tablespoon olive oil
Sprig lemon thyme
Little salt and freshly ground black pepper

2 tablespoons olive oil
1 tomato, peeled, deseeded, the flesh diced
Garnish: Few leaves of lemon thyme

Mix together all ingredients for the marinade. Place the little escalopes of pork in a plastic bag, pour in the well-mixed marinade, arrange the bag in a dish so that the meat is covered with the marinade and leave in a cool place overnight.

When ready to cook, drain the meat, reserving the marinade, then pat completely dry with kitchen paper. Heat the two tablespoons of oil in a pan and fry the escalopes briskly on each side until golden brown, removing as cooked to a serving dish and keeping warm. Discard any oil left in the pan, remove the orange and lemon peel then add the marinade to the pan, scraping up all sediment from the bottom and letting the sauce bubble up and reduce slightly. Remove garlic and the piece of thyme, check seasoning, add the prepared tomato dice, allow to heat through then pour over meat. Garnish with the leaves of lemon thyme and serve immediately.

ACCOMPANIMENTS: Rice or pasta, watercress salad or a green vegetable.

VARIATIONS: Instead of pork, lamb cutlets can be marinated in the same way, then cooked a little longer, or grilled. When cooking in the microwave, follow the method for pork.

MICROWAVE OVEN: Marinade the meat as above, drain, place meat in overlapping slices in a gratin dish. Pour over the marinade, add the diced tomato, cover tightly with cling film and microwave on HIGH for 3 minutes. Allow to stand for 5 minutes to finish cooking then remove the pieces of citrus peel and the garlic, garnish with the fresh leaves of lemon thyme and serve immediately.

FILLET OF PORK WITH CARAMELISED APPLES

Pigs love rootling around orchards and pork goes extremely well with apples, the richness of the meat contrasting nicely with the slight acidity of the fruit. This is particularly noticeable if you can manage to get hold of organic pork, now becoming more easily available. This is another recipe using the tenderloin of pork but here the meat is left in little *médaillons* instead of being beaten into small escalopes.

1 pork tenderloin, 300–350 g/10–12 oz
½ teaspoon cornflour
150 ml/5 fl oz/⅔ cup natural yoghurt
Small knob of butter
1 tablespoon light vegetable oil
Salt and freshly ground black pepper
1 crisp eating apple, cored and sliced
2 tablespoons light brown sugar

Trim the tenderloin of any fat and silvery membrane, then cut the meat obliquely into slices about 2 cm/¾ inch thick. Mix together the cornflour and yoghurt, bring to the boil in a sauté or fireproof pan large enough to hold the meat in one layer and simmer for 2–3 minutes, stirring. Remove from the heat. Heat the butter and oil in a frying pan. Brown the pork slices on both sides, season then place in the stabilised yoghurt, cover and simmer very gently for 8–10 minutes.

Using the same fat and pan in which the pork was browned, briskly fry the apple rings, sprinkling with half the sugar as the apples are added. After 2 minutes, turn the apples and sprinkle with the remaining sugar. Fry until apples are lightly caramelised then arrange on top or at the side of the cooked pork.

ACCOMPANIMENTS: New potatoes or pasta, green beans, broccoli, spinach or a salad.

PORK WITH PRUNES AND CHICORY

There is a famous French dish with pork cooked with prunes and cream – very rich and very delicious. This recipe tastes equally good but is low fat and so much healthier. It contrasts the richness of the pork and prunes with chicory, whose characteristic slight bitterness is mellowed through the cooking.

1 pork tenderloin, 300–350 g/10–12 oz
100 g/4 oz/1 cup ready-to-eat prunes, pitted
2 small heads of chicory, thick stalk trimmed out, heads cut in 2 cm/¾ inch slices
225 ml/7½ fl oz/1 cup dry cider
Salt and freshly ground black pepper
Garnish: 1 tablespoon freshly chopped parsley

Trim tenderloin of any fat and silvery membrane, cut obliquely across in 2 cm/¾ inch thick slices, place in small casserole dish, add prunes. Blanch the chicory in boiling water for 1 minute, drain immediately and refresh under cold water. Place in the dish with the pork and prunes, add seasoning.

Bring cider to the boil, pour over the contents of the casserole, cover with lid or tin foil and place in preheated oven at 160°C/325°F/Gas Mark 3 for about 35 minutes, until meat is just cooked. Pour off juices and keep meat warm. Boil juices to reduce by half. Divide meat, prunes and chicory between two plates, pour over reduced sauce, garnish with the chopped parsley and serve.

ACCOMPANIMENTS: Rice or pasta, peas or beans or a green salad.

VARIATIONS: Omit chicory and replace cider with cream.

MICROWAVE OVEN: Place the chicory in a bowl with 2 tablespoons water, cover with cling film and microwave on HIGH for 1 minute. Drain, refresh under cold water, drain again. Place in deep dish with meat and prunes. Reduce cider to half by boiling, season, pour over contents of dish, cover tightly with cling film, microwave on HIGH for 4 minutes. Leave to stand for 5 minutes before serving garnished with chopped parsley.

GAMMON STEAK WITH SPICED APRICOTS

Most butchers sell slices of gammon steak. These are quickly cooked and can be served in a number of ways. My favourite is with spiced apricots and this is a quick and easy version.

2 gammon steaks (soaked overnight if recommended by butcher)
6 dried apricots, soaked in boiling water for a couple of hours
2.5 cm/1 inch piece of cinnamon stick
3 cloves
6 allspice berries
1 bay leaf
1 tablespoon demerara sugar
1 dessertspoon wine vinegar
1 tablespoon butter
Freshly ground black pepper
½ teaspoon cornflour, slaked with a little cold water

Measure apricot water, you should have 300 ml/10 fl oz/generous cup, make it up with more water if necessary (quantity is same whether 6 or 12 apricots are being cooked – see TOWARDS TOMORROW below). Place with fruit and spices in a saucepan, bring to boil and simmer gently for 20 to 30 minutes until tender. Add sugar and stir to melt, bring to boil and simmer for a couple of minutes. If cooking double quantity, remove half the fruit at this stage and reserve. Add the vinegar.

Pat ham dry if it has been soaking. Heat butter in a sauté pan till foaming, add gammon slices and brown on both sides. Discard spices and add the spiced apricots and their juices to the pan. Bring to boil, lower heat, cover and simmer very gently for 10 minutes, turning meat halfway through.

ACCOMPANIMENTS: Boiled or creamed potatoes, green vegetable or a green salad.

VARIATIONS: Tinned apricots can be used, add to the ham with the spices without prior cooking. Pineapple, without the spices, is an alternative fruit that goes well with the gammon, use tinned fruit, juices can be thickened after cooking with a tablespoon cornflour slaked with 2 tablespoons water.

MICROWAVE OVEN: Use to cook apricots: place dried fruit, without soaking, with water and spices, in a deep bowl (allowing half as much again

72

water for double the quantity of fruit), cover tightly with cling film and microwave on HIGH for 10 minutes, stirring or shaking fruit lightly halfway through cooking.

TOWARDS TOMORROW: Do double the amount of apricots needed for the recipe and use the other half for an APRICOT CLAFOUTIS (custard), see SWEET TALK section on page 206, for tomorrow; or they can be served with cold meats.

PEPPERED STEAKS

A good steak is such a treat it hardly needs anything to improve it but I have a weakness for peppered steaks.

2 rump steaks
Crushed black or green peppercorns
Salt

With a sharp knife, lightly score the steak on either side then rub in the crushed peppercorns (the green peppercorns can either be the dried variety or the soft sort preserved in brine). Have the grill heated to its highest, lightly brush steaks with oil or melted butter then grill for a few minutes either side according to how well you like your steaks done.

COOK'S TIP: To judge how well meat is done, gently press surface with a spatula or finger. The more give there is, the bloodier the meat. The less give, the more it is cooked. If you acquire the habit of always checking like this as you cook, you will soon know exactly what the inside of any piece of meat looks like at any stage of its cooking simply by pressing it.

73

POT POURRI

This section is a catch-all for recipes that don't fit anywhere else! Many are the sort of dishes that may not always be thought of when cooking for two but can work very well, sometimes maximising preparation and providing two different meals.

RACK OF LAMB WITH HERBS

A roast for two is not usually an economic proposition, an exception is a rack of lamb, which provides just the right quantity of meat. The rack should have the upper part of the bones well trimmed and cleaned, the butcher can do most of the work, and be chined, the spine severed from the ribs so that this can be cut off after cooking, allowing the chops to be separated. However, I usually leave the ribs untrimmed, it doesn't look so good but you get the maximum amount of meat and crispy fat.

1 fat clove garlic
1 rack of lamb (6–7 chops)
1 tablespoon olive oil
2 tablespoons mixed chopped fresh herbs or 1 tablespoon dried
Salt and freshly ground pepper
4 tablespoons medium dry white wine
1 tablespoon redcurrant jelly

Skin the garlic and cut into slivers then insert between the chine bone and meat. Using a sharp knife, score the skin and fat of the lamb in a diamond pattern. Rub in the oil then sprinkle over the herbs, pressing well in, and season. Place in preheated oven at 200°C/400°F/Gas Mark 6 and roast, basting every 15 minutes, for 45 minutes, a little longer if you prefer well-done meat. Remove the meat from the pan and keep warm. Pour off fat from pan juices, place roasting tin on the hob on a medium heat, deglaze with the wine, scraping up all the sediment and incorporating it into the wine and juices, add the redcurrant jelly and stir well to melt and meld together. Check seasoning and strain into small jug, adding any juices that have seeped out from the meat while it has been standing.

ACCOMPANIMENTS: Creamed or new potatoes. Courgettes or carrots go particularly well but almost any vegetable would be good, or a small salad.

VARIATIONS: Use the MUSTARDY PORK CHOPS coating (see page 63) instead of the herbs, or a spicy seasoning made from: 10 cardamom seeds (the contents of around 3 pods), pinch cumin seeds, 2 allspice berries, 6 white peppercorns, 1 dried bay leaf, all ground together.

MICROWAVE OVEN: I really cannot pretend that the result in a microwave is a match for oven roasting but, done this way, it is acceptable. Preheat a browning dish for 5 minutes on HIGH. Add oil, then place lamb skin side down. Microwave, uncovered, for 2 minutes on HIGH, let stand for 2 minutes then turn over and microwave again for 3–5 minutes according to how well done you like your meat. Remove joint, cover and keep warm (it should stand for at least 5 minutes before being carved). Meanwhile skim off fat from pan juices, add wine and redcurrant jelly, stir in well, microwave on HIGH for 3 minutes, stirring halfway through. Strain sauce into small jug, adding juices from meat, and serve.

FRUITY SHOULDER OF LAMB

A half shoulder of about 1½ kg/3 lb should yield enough meat for two meals for two people. The following recipe is for a spicy-fruity roast. The left-overs are then perfect for the LAMB AND AUBERGINE GRATIN that follows.

1 half shoulder of lamb, approx. 1½ kg/3 lb
100 g/4 oz/½ cup ready-to-eat dried apricots, sliced
2–3 tablespoons olive oil
Salt
1 teaspoon whole black peppercorns   ⎫ *2 teaspoons cumin seeds*   ⎬ *roughly crushed together* *1 teaspoon coriander seeds*   ⎭
300 ml/10 fl oz/generous cup light stock OR a mixture of wine and stock or water
2 tablespoons natural yoghurt or cream

Lightly score the fat on top of the joint in a criss-cross pattern, then wiggle the blade of a sharp knife between the lamb flesh and shoulder blade, opening up a pocket into which you can stuff some of the sliced apricots. Push them into the joint as deeply as you can. Then press the meat together again. Rub over with oil and brush the surface of the roasting tin as well. Sit the joint on the remaining slices of apricot. Rub the crushed spices into the scored skin of the lamb, dribble over a little more oil, then place in a preheated oven at 190°C/375°F/Gas Mark 5 and roast, basting every 20 minutes, for 1 hour 20 minutes, when the meat should be very faintly pink, or a little shorter or longer time according to how you like your lamb. Remove meat from pan and keep warm.

Skim off fat from the pan juices then add the liquid and scrape the bottom of the tin well to deglaze. The cold liquid should precipitate any remaining fat to the surface so it can also be skimmed off. Then tip the contents of the pan, including the apricots cooked underneath the meat, into a processor or push through a sieve. Place processed or sieved sauce in a small saucepan and heat gently to boiling point, stirring well. Check seasoning, stir in a couple of tablespoons of natural yoghurt or cream, being careful not to let the sauce come back to the boil, and serve with the meat.

ACCOMPANIMENTS: Rice and a green vegetable or salad.

VARIATIONS: Omit spices or fruit and spices. Traditional gravy can be made by mixing two tablespoons of the fat with two tablespoons of flour, stirring over a gentle heat for a few minutes, then making a smooth sauce with meat or vegetable stock, adding a little at a time. Adjust seasoning when consistency is right.

TOWARDS TOMORROW: When the remainder of the joint is cold, cut off the meat and use for the following recipe:

LAMB AND AUBERGINE GRATIN	
	1 tablespoon olive oil
	1 small onion, peeled and finely chopped
	1 clove garlic, finely chopped
	Small tin peeled tomatoes, flesh chopped, juices reserved
	Good pinch cinnamon
	100–175 g/4–6 oz/1–1½ cups cooked lamb, finely chopped or minced
	Salt and freshly ground black pepper
	1 aubergine, sliced then blanched in salted boiling water for 3 minutes, drained and refreshed in cold water, drained again on kitchen paper
	150 ml/5 fl oz/⅔ cup natural yoghurt 1 egg yolk } *blended together and seasoned*

---

2 tablespoons grated cheese, Parmesan, Cheddar or other hard cheese

---

Heat the oil and gently cook the onion and garlic until soft and transparent. Add the chopped tomato flesh and the cinnamon and stir well before adding the lamb and mixing in, add some of the tomato juices to achieve a somewhat sloppy consistency. Season to taste.

Lightly oil a small soufflé dish then arrange half the aubergine slices in the bottom. Add the lamb mixture and arrange the remaining aubergine slices on top then cover with the mixture of yoghurt and egg. Finally, sprinkle over the grated cheese. Place in a preheated oven at 180°C/350°F/Gas Mark 4 for 40 minutes.

VARIATIONS: Substitute any other left-over meat for the lamb. Plainly cooked meat can have a few raisins added with the tomatoes for a sweet note. Any lamb still remaining from the joint can go to make a SPANISH TORTILLA, see TIME FOR A SNACK section on page 254.

COOK'S TIP: Blanching aubergine is an alternative to sautéing in oil. It provides the necessary precooking without adding additional oil to the dish and can be used in other recipes which use aubergine.

MICROWAVE OVEN: Use to cook the onion; place with the oil in a small dish, cover tightly with cling film and microwave on HIGH for 2 minutes. Mix in the tomatoes and cinnamon then the meat and assemble the dish as above, adding 1 teaspoon cornflour to the mixture of egg yolk and yoghurt, to prevent it curdling. When ready to eat, cover the dish tightly with cling film and microwave on HIGH for approximately 13 minutes (exact timing will depend on amount of meat in the dish) or until the whole dish is bubbling hot. Leave to sit for 4 minutes for the temperature to equalise before serving.

LOIN OF LAMB WITH HONEY AND GINGER

*Start preparation several hours or day before serving
A marvellously tasty recipe that benefits from several hours marinading, making it excellent for preparing at the same time as another meal, then leaving it in the fridge in its plastic bag until the next day, when it is all ready to cook. Or prepare in the morning to cook in the evening, perhaps when you come in from work or a trip out. The actual cooking takes very little time. As with the previous recipe, ask the butcher to strip out the nugget of meat

from the skin and bones, leaving a totally lean piece of meat, plus two little strips that can be used for a stir-fry, see the recipe for SPICY STIR-FRIED LAMB WITH MANGO in the WOK'S UP section on page 102. Make sure you take the bones and trimmings home as well, it will serve as the basis for an excellent stock to make soup and sauce.

Marinade:

2 tablespoons virgin olive oil
½ tablespoon tarragon wine vinegar
1 small crushed clove of garlic
1 tablespoon clear honey
1 cm/½ inch piece peeled green ginger, very finely sliced
½ teaspoon black cumin seeds, lightly fried in a dry pan for 1–2 minutes
Salt and freshly ground black pepper
1 loin of lamb, the nugget of meat stripped of fat and bones
A little Dijon mustard

Mix together all the marinade ingredients. Place the nugget of lamb in a large plastic bag, pour over the marinade and rub well into the lamb, this can be done by manipulating the plastic over the meat or by hand if you prefer. Place bag with its contents in a bowl so that the meat is kept in contact with the marinade. Leave for 6 to 24 hours in a cool place or fridge, turning the bag occasionally.

When ready to cook, place the loin in a small roasting pan and roast in a preheated oven at 200°C/400°F/Gas Mark 6, basting with the marinade halfway through cooking, for 15 minutes, or a little longer if you don't like very pink lamb. Leave the meat in a warm place to sit for a few minutes whilst you strain off the juices from the pan and remove any fat. Then stir in about a quarter of a teaspoonful of Dijon mustard and reheat, whisking briskly. Check seasoning. Slice the meat obliquely across into six small *médaillons* and serve with the juices from the pan.

ACCOMPANIMENTS: Pasta, rice or new potatoes with a side salad or a fresh green vegetable such as green beans or mange tout.

VARIATIONS: Instead of the loin, a best end of neck can be stripped out in the same way but it will not yield as much flesh. Another alternative is the shoulder fillet that some butchers sell separately and is much the cheapest option. The same marinade can be used for lamb steaks or chops or even kebabs.

COOK'S TIP: It is useful to have a small quantity of ready prepared black cumin seeds on hand, they are very tasty and useful with all sorts of spicy mixtures. Keep in a small spice jar.

MICROWAVE OVEN: As long as you like your lamb a little pink, this dish will microwave fairly satisfactorily and the honey in the marinade will help brown the meat. Keep the lamb in its marinade bag, turning it to make sure all the meat is well covered with the marinade. Place it in the microwave with the ends of the bag tucked underneath the meat. Microwave on HIGH for 3 minutes, giving the bag a half turn (unless the oven has a turntable) halfway through. Pour off the juices and leave the lamb in its bag covered with a cloth to stand for 5 minutes. Skim any fat off the juices, add about a quarter of a teaspoonful of Dijon mustard to the juices, stir well, check the seasoning. Microwave on HIGH for 1 minute then slice the meat as above and serve with the sauce.

TOWARDS TOMORROW: Use the bones and trimmings from the loin to make a tasty broth with chopped onion, a little barley, some diced potato and carrot, celery if you have it, salt and black pepper and a bouquet garni. Rescue the bits of meat at the end of cooking, discarding the fat and bones but replacing the meat for a hearty soup. 20 minutes in a pressure cooker should produce a well-flavoured broth, or use the microwave as in following recipe.

LOIN OF LAMB WITH ROSEMARY AND ONION SAUCE

The sauce for this dish has a wonderful flavour that perfectly complements the lamb. A loin boned out and stripped of all fat and membrane is perfect for two people, the meat sweet and lean. Use the fat eye for this dish and cut the remaining strips of meat into thin shreds and stir-fry for another dish (see TOWARDS TO-MORROW). The bones and trimmings can be used to make a good stock. Half will provide the basis for the excellent sauce and the other half can be used to make soup or a sauce for some other meal.

Sauce:

1 tablespoon light oil
Loin trimmings
Few mushrooms
2 slices onion
1 clove garlic, crushed
1 sprig fresh thyme
1 sprig fresh rosemary (or ½ teaspoon dried)
1 loin of lamb, boned and stripped of all fat and tissue
Salt and freshly ground black pepper
1 tablespoon light oil
2 sprigs fresh rosemary or ½ teaspoon dried
1 tablespoon light oil
1 medium sized Spanish or other sweet onion, peeled and finely chopped
2 tablespoons dry sherry
1 tablespoon sherry vinegar
Dash fresh lemon juice
Garnish: Fresh rosemary sprigs

Start off by making the stock: heat the oil in the bottom of a pressure cooker and brown the lamb trimmings. Then add the mushrooms and onion slices and brown for a couple of minutes. Add the remaining ingredients and

80

cook at high pressure for 20 minutes. Reduce pressure, strain stock, skim off all fat, refrigerate half for another dish and place other half in a saucepan and boil until reduced by half. There should be about 100 ml/3–4 fl oz/½ cup left.

Season loin well. Heat oil in a small roasting pan on the hob and brown lamb on all sides. Slip the rosemary sprigs underneath the meat (or scatter the dried rosemary on top) and place in a preheated oven at 190°C/375°F/ Gas Mark 5 and roast for 15 minutes. This will produce meat that is nicely pink. If you like lamb well done, increase the roasting time slightly. Then turn off the oven and leave meat to rest for at least 5 minutes.

Meanwhile, heat the remaining tablespoon of oil and sauté the chopped onion over a medium heat until it is tender and starting to brown. Add the sherry and sherry vinegar and continue cooking gently until all the liquid has evaporated, about 10 minutes. Add the reduced stock, check seasoning, add a squeeze of lemon juice to sharpen the flavour, process then sieve to achieve a completely smooth sauce.

Slice the lamb into small *médaillons*, discarding rosemary, strain any juices into the sauce. Swirl some of the sauce in the bottom of a serving dish or on two plates, arrange the meat on top, then pour over the remaining sauce, garnish with fresh rosemary sprigs and serve.

ACCOMPANIMENTS: New or creamed potatoes or haricot beans; cabbage, carrots or carrots cooked with cucumber, both cut into batons.

VARIATIONS: Instead of onion, add thin julienne strips of carrot and celery to the reduced stock and cook for 1 minute, OR sliced mushrooms can be sautéd in a little arachide/groundnut/peanut oil then added to the reduced stock.

COOK'S TIP: When reducing a liquid, look at the amount in the pan before starting and get a mental picture of what the reduced amount should look like. Check when you think the right point has been arrived at by measuring. If by any chance you have overshot the mark, add some water to bring the liquid up to the right quantity again.

MICROWAVE OVEN: Stock can be cooked in a microwave: add all ingredients to a generous sized bowl (3 litres/4–5 pints), cover tightly with cling film, microwave on HIGH for 15 minutes. Reduce half of the stock by half in a saucepan on the hob. To cook meat: brush a film of oil over loin of lamb, place on a plate or shallow dish with rosemary sprigs slipped underneath the lamb (or sprinkle dried rosemary on top of the meat). Add 2 tablespoons of stock, cover tightly with cling film and cook on HIGH for 2 minutes. Uncover carefully, wrap meat in tin foil and leave to sit in a warm place for at least 8 minutes while preparing sauce. For sauce: place onion and oil in bowl, cover tightly with cling film and microwave on HIGH for 6 minutes. Add sherry and sherry vinegar, cook uncovered on HIGH for another 6 minutes, when liquid should have almost evaporated. Add reduced stock, stir well, check seasoning, add a squeeze of lemon to sharpen flavour. Process and sieve to achieve a smooth sauce, adding the juices produced from the loin while it has been standing. Serve as above.

TOWARDS TOMORROW: Use the other little strips of meat for a stir-fry, cutting them into small shreds and frying as for SPICY STIR-FRIED LAMB WITH MANGO in the WOK'S UP section on page 102, using a generous amount of slim batons of carrot, celery and green pepper instead of mango and stir-frying just long enough to achieve tenderness. Use the other half of stock for a soup or sauce.

YOGHURT AND HERB LAMB KEBABS

*Start preparation several hours or day before serving

Kebabs cook very quickly. The recipe needs time to marinate but is ideal for preparing in the morning and cooking in the evening, neither operation takes long. The yoghurt and herbs give the lamb an attractively fresh tang. Use either shoulder fillet, which is cheapest if you can find it, or top of leg cut.

350–450 g/12 oz–1 lb boned lean lamb, cut into chunks
5 tablespoons natural yoghurt
1 tablespoon chopped fresh herbs: marjoram, basil, thyme, tarragon, etc.
½ tablespoon chopped fresh parsley
1 small clove garlic, crushed (optional)
½ tablespoon freshly squeezed lemon juice
Salt, freshly ground black pepper

Mix together the yoghurt with the herbs, garlic, lemon juice and seasoning. Add the lamb and stir well to coat the meat with the marinade. Leave in the fridge for 5–8 hours, stirring occasionally if convenient, then thread the meat on skewers.

Heat the grill on maximum, place the kebabs underneath and grill for 3 minutes on each side, or a little longer if you don't like lamb too pink but don't let the meat become dry through overcooking. Serve immediately.

ACCOMPANIMENTS: Rice and a salad.

VARIATIONS: Young courgettes cut in thick slices can be interspersed with the meat. With the above quantity of meat, you will not need another vegetable, or you can cut the amount of meat and serve a salad as well.

COOK'S TIP: It is not necessary to have all the above herbs but make sure the stronger varieties such as thyme, sage and mint do not predominate.

F QUICK CASSOULET

The following dish does not pretend to be a traditional French cassoulet, which calls for long, slow cooking, but it does give a hint of the richness of the original.

1 tablespoon arachide/groundnut/peanut oil
1 medium sized onion, peeled and finely chopped
1 fat clove garlic, peeled and chopped
1 thick slice belly of pork, cut in chunks
2 lamb cutlets, meat removed from bone and halved
225 g/8 oz garlic sausage, preferably uncooked, cut in chunks
1 tin haricot or cannellini beans (or 1 cup cooked beans)
Salt and freshly ground black pepper
2 teaspoons tomato purée
450 ml/15 fl oz/2 cups stock or water
1 bay leaf
8 tablespoons fresh white breadcrumbs

Heat the oil in a heat-proof casserole dish and cook onion and garlic gently until transparent. Push to the side of the pan, raise heat and brown meats. Add the beans, season well, add the tomato purée, the stock or water and the bay leaf. Bring to the boil, add the breadcrumbs on top of the casserole and place in a preheated oven at 180°C/350°F/Gas Mark 4 for 50 minutes.

ACCOMPANIMENTS: A green salad is nice but not strictly necessary, this being one of those dishes that is a complete meal in itself.

VARIATIONS: Any kind of boneless lamb can be used as long as it is fairly lean. Don't use lean pork instead of the belly, though, the dish needs some fat with the beans.

PRESSURE COOKER: Proceed as above for oven cooking, softening onion and browning meat in bottom of pressure cooker. Add remaining ingredients except breadcrumbs, add lid, bring up to HIGH pressure and maintain for 15 minutes. Cool rapidly, place cassoulet in suitable sized fireproof dish, scatter over breadcrumbs, dribble over a little oil and brown under a hot grill for a few minutes before serving.

MICROWAVE OVEN: Not as good as cooking in the oven but acceptable. Place onion, garlic and oil in bottom of deep dish, cover tightly and microwave on HIGH for 2 minutes. Add all remaining ingredients, sprinkling breadcrumbs on top, omitting seasoning, cover tightly and microwave on HIGH for 7 minutes. Allow to sit for 5 minutes before serving.

TOWARDS TOMORROW: This is a hearty dish and if appetites are small there may well be some left over. In which case turn it into soup by chopping all the meat up small and adding additional liquid and a garnish of chopped parsley.

F PIGEONS IN MUSTARD SAUCE

Pigeons are single portion birds. Plump and slightly gamey, they are healthily lean. So you can afford to cook them with cream, which makes a really succulent dish. The mustard adds a nice tang. With this dish using the microwave makes a spectacular saving in time and still produces a very good result.

2 pigeons
A little butter, softened
1 tablespoon arachide/groundnut/peanut oil
Salt and freshly ground black pepper
5 tablespoons double cream
1 tablespoon Maille Poivre Vert French mustard

Loosen the skin from the breast meat of each bird and work a little butter underneath, about a walnut-sized piece for each bird, then draw the skin back over the flesh.

Heat the oil in a heavy based pan with a lid deep enough to take the birds, add a knob of butter then brown the birds all over. Season well. Stir together the cream and the mustard and pour over the birds. Lower the heat until the cream just simmers, cover with the lid and cook very gently for about 1½ hours, or until the birds are tender, turning them from time to time. Then serve with the creamy juices.

ACCOMPANIMENTS: Creamed or boiled potatoes, cabbage or other hearty vegetable, very simply cooked. A redcurrant or cranberry jelly goes well.

VARIATIONS: The recipe can also be used for poussin or spring chicken, but cooking time will be reduced to about 50 minutes. If preferred, the dish can be cooked in the oven at 180°C/350°F/Gas Mark 4 but I find it easier to keep turning the birds when they are on top of the stove.

MICROWAVE OVEN: Prepare the pigeon in the same way, omit the seasoning. Place the birds in a dish that will hold them nicely. Mix together the cream and mustard, pour over, cover dish tightly with cling film and microwave on HIGH for 7 minutes. Leave birds to sit for 4 minutes then serve.

F PORK AND APPLE OLIVES

A rather different use for pork tenderloin than the recipes included in the CHOPS WITH EVERYTHING section. This recipe originates from Denmark, which has built an entire industry round the pig and has a particular love of pork combined with apple. There the recipe would be made with double cream, here healthier yoghurt has been substituted. The olives of the title refer to the shape of the pork rolls.

1 pork tenderloin, approx. 225–350 g/8–12 oz
Salt and freshly ground black pepper
Little creamed horseradish sauce
2 small Cox's orange pippin apples, peeled, cored, coarsely grated and tossed with juice of ½ lemon and 1 tablespoon freshly chopped parsley
1 tablespoon arachide/groundnut/peanut oil
5 tablespoons dry cider or white wine
5 tablespoons Greek-style natural yoghurt, mixed with 1 teaspoon cornflour
Garnish: Parsley

Trim any fat and membrane from the pork tenderloin, cut it very obliquely into 6 thick slices, place each between two sheets of cling film and hammer out into escalopes; a rolling pin or milk bottle will do if you haven't a meat bat or the side of a heavy cleaver to hand. Season each escalope and spread very lightly with a little horseradish sauce. Divide the grated apple between each escalope and roll them up. Secure each roll with a cocktail stick or tie with thread.

Heat the oil and brown the rolls on all sides. Discard excess oil then add the cider, bring to the boil then lower heat and cook very gently, at no more than a simmer, for 10 minutes, when the meat should be cooked. Remove the rolls and keep warm. Reduce the cooking juices slightly, then add gradually to the yoghurt mixed with cornflour. Return sauce to the pan, bring to the boil, stirring constantly, and cook until slightly thickened. Check seasoning, pour over olives and serve garnished with the parsley.

ACCOMPANIMENTS: Creamed potatoes or pasta with a green vegetable.

VARIATIONS: Half the apple can be replaced with three stoned and chopped ready-to-eat prunes. Instead of yoghurt, double or single cream can be used. With double cream, omit the cornflour and reduce sauce to a nice coating consistency.

MICROWAVE OVEN: Reduce cider to 2½ tablespoons, mix with yoghurt and cornflour, cover tightly and microwave on HIGH for 3 minutes, until thickened, whisk well. Place prepared rolls in a deep dish, pour over sauce, cover tightly and microwave on HIGH for 3 minutes. Allow to rest for 5 minutes then serve:

F BEEF CASSEROLE WITH TWIN TOPPINGS

The bore about making casseroles for two is facing the same dish next day, for making just enough for one meal is neither economic nor very successful. However, different toppings at the end of cooking can transform a basic dish, rather like accessories that can dramatise a little black dress in different ways. Here is a good example.

1 kg/2 lb shin of beef, trimmed and cut into chunks
1 medium sized onion, finely sliced
150 ml/5 fl oz/generous ½ cup robust red wine
150 ml/5 fl oz/generous ½ cup stock or water
1 clove garlic, crushed
Handful parsley and few sprigs thyme and a bay leaf, all tied together
Salt and freshly ground black pepper

First Topping:

1 dessertspoon arachide/groundnut/peanut oil
Few walnuts, cut in large pieces
1–2 stalks celery, sliced diagonally
Peel ½ orange, pared thinly without pith, finely sliced, brought to boil in cold water, simmered 2 minutes, drained and refreshed

Second Topping:

1 tablespoon arachide/groundnut/peanut oil
2 slices smoked back bacon, cut in strips
Few mushrooms, sliced
Few sprigs parsley finely chopped with 1 small clove peeled garlic

Mix together beef and onion and place in a suitably sized casserole dish.

Bring wine and water to boil, pour over meat and onions, add crushed garlic and bunch of herbs, pushing down well into meat, season well. Bring back to boil over heat then place in preheated oven at 140°C/275°F/Gas Mark 1 for 2½ hours. Then remove half, cool quickly and refrigerate for tomorrow. Allow other half to cook for further 30 minutes.

For the first topping, heat oil, add walnuts and celery and sauté gently to warm through. Add orange peel, tossing well. Place on top of casserole and serve.

ACCOMPANIMENTS: Creamed potatoes and a green vegetable.

COOK'S TIP: Shin of beef is one of the cheapest cuts and looks horribly gristly uncooked. However with long, slow cooking, those dire-looking pieces soften and dissolve into wonderfully tender meat and tasty gravy. But the cooking does have to be long and slow. If you want a speedier dish, use braising steak; soften the onion first then cook the casserole for 1½–2 hours. Just cook walnuts sufficiently long to heat them through, they can turn bitter if cooked too long.

PRESSURE COOKER: Prepare casserole as for oven cooking, place in pressure cooker, add lid and bring to HIGH pressure. Cook, maintaining pressure, for 20 minutes. Then proceed as for oven cooking. To reheat, bring to pressure and maintain for 2 minutes.

MICROWAVE OVEN: Don't try microwave cooking this dish with shin but it can be quite successful with good chuck or braising steak. Place the oil and onion in a dish first, cover and microwave on HIGH for 3 minutes. Then add the beef and other ingredients, stir well, cover tightly and microwave on HIGH for 7 minutes. Leave to sit for 5 minutes, stir well, re-cover and microwave on HIGH for 5 minutes. Remove half of casserole, cool and refrigerate. Toss together walnuts, celery and orange peel, add to top of remaining half of casserole, re-cover and microwave again on HIGH for 1 minute. Serve.

TOMORROW: Place second half of casserole in suitable sized dish. Cover tightly, microwave on 80%/REHEAT for 10 minutes or until bubbling hot. Remove from oven. Place the bacon strips on a plate, cover with kitchen paper and microwave on HIGH for 1 minute. Remove. Place sliced mushrooms in a bowl and microwave on HIGH, uncovered, for 2 minutes. Mix together with the bacon, add to top of casserole, sprinkle over the freshly chopped parsley and garlic mixture and serve.

TOWARDS TOMORROW: Reheat second half of casserole in preheated oven at 160°C/325°F/Gas Mark 3 for approximately 40 minutes, until bubbling hot. For second topping, heat oil, gently fry bacon strips and remove. Add mushrooms and sauté until all juices evaporated and mushrooms tender. Add the cooked bacon and heat through. Place on top of casserole, add the freshly chopped parsley and garlic mixture and serve with baked potatoes and a green vegetable or salad.

F BRAISED OXTAIL

Oxtail is a dish that takes a long time to cook and advocating it for two is perhaps a bit extravagant. But it tastes delicious, one tail provides a good meal for two and probably enough left over to make a soup for the next day, cooking can be spread over two days, the actual preparation doesn't take long and if you have a pressure cooker, neither need the cooking. So I think it's well worth the effort.

1 oxtail, jointed
Salt and freshly ground black pepper
Bouquet garni (bay leaf, sprigs of thyme and parsley and celery stalk if available, all tied together)
2 medium sized onions, sliced
2 carrots, scraped, trimmed and sliced
1 leek, cleaned, white and pale green parts thickly sliced

---
1 tablespoon redcurrant jelly
---
1 tablespoon flour blended with 1 tablespoon softened butter (optional)

Garnish: Chopped parsley

Place oxtail pieces in a generous sized saucepan, cover with cold water, season well and add the bouquet garni. Bring to the boil, skim off the scum that rises, lower heat, cover and simmer very gently for 2 hours. Then remove the oxtail and strain the stock. After stock has cooled, remove fat. At this point the oxtail can be replaced in the stock and the dish refrigerated until the next day.

To finish cooking: if oxtail has been replaced in stock, remove and place with the sliced onion, carrot and leek in a casserole dish, packing in neatly. Use just enough stock to cover ingredients, reserving remainder, check seasoning and add more if necessary, then bring to boil, cover and place in preheated oven at 160°C/325°F/Gas Mark 3 for 2½ hours.

At the end of cooking, if you wish to thicken the sauce, strain it off the meat and vegetables into a saucepan, add the redcurrant jelly then the flour blended with the butter (*beurre manié*) in little bits and stir in over a gentle heat until the sauce has thickened, check seasoning then pour back over the oxtail and its vegetables, sprinkle with parsley and serve. If you prefer not to thicken, juices can be reduced, then add the redcurrant jelly, stir to melt then pour back over the meat and vegetables, check seasoning, sprinkle with parsley and serve.

ACCOMPANIMENTS: Creamed potatoes and cabbage or sprouts.

VARIATIONS: Whole, button onions can be used instead of the sliced onions.

COOK'S TIPS: 1) To peel button onions, blanch in boiling water for 2–3 minutes then trim off tops and brown outer leaves but leave part of root attached so the onions stay whole. 2) When using a *beurre manié*, either stop cooking as soon as the liquid is thickened or continue simmering for 10–15 minutes, otherwise there is a danger the sauce will taste floury.

PRESSURE COOKER: Place meat in base of cooker, add sufficient water to come halfway up large pieces of meat, add seasoning and bouquet garni, place on lid, bring up to HIGH pressure and maintain for 30 minutes. Then reduce pressure, strain off stock and skim off fat (stock and meat can be refrigerated until next day as above if liked). Add the vegetables to the meat in the base of the cooker, pour over the degreased stock, replace lid, bring up to HIGH pressure and maintain for 35 minutes. Finish off as above.

TOWARDS TOMORROW: For soup: remove remains of oxtail meat from any left-over bones and reserve, process gravy and vegetables, add sufficient of the reserved stock to make soup a good consistency, reheat, add left-over meat and continue simmering until heated right through. Serve with little cream or natural yoghurt on top and sprinkled with freshly chopped parsley. A few sautéd sliced mushrooms can also be added if liked.

F CHILLI CON CARNE AND SAUCE BOLOGNESE

Here the same basic mince mixture is used for two quite different dishes: Chilli Con Carne for today and Sauce Bolognese for tomorrow. The quantities given below are enough for both dishes. It is really not economical to cook mince in smaller quantities.

1 tablespoon arachide/groundnut/peanut oil
1 large onion, finely chopped
450 g/1 lb best minced beef
1 medium sized carrot, finely chopped
2 celery stalks, finely chopped
1 bay leaf
Salt and freshly ground black pepper
450 ml/15 fl oz/2 cups stock or water

For Chilli:

½ tablespoon arachide/groundnut/peanut oil
1–1½ level teaspoons chilli powder OR 3–6 chilli peppers (according to strength), deseeded and finely chopped
½ green pepper, deseeded and finely chopped
2 teaspoons tomato purée
1 small tin red kidney beans, rinsed

For Bolognese Sauce:

150 ml/5 fl oz/⅔ cup dry white wine
1 tablespoon arachide/groundnut/peanut oil
3 rashers streaky bacon, diced
50 g/2 oz/1 cup mushrooms, chopped
1 tablespoon freshly chopped parsley

For the basic mince: heat oil in a heavy based pan, add chopped onion and cook gently until transparent. Scrape onions to side of pan, raise heat, add the beef and cook, stirring continually, until well browned. Add the chopped carrot and celery and cook, still stirring, for 4–5 minutes. Add the bay leaf, the seasoning, the stock or water, bring to boil then lower heat and, uncovered, simmer very slowly for 1½ hours or until really tender. Then divide into two portions, cool one rapidly and refrigerate, keep the other hot.

For Chilli: In a small pan heat the oil and gently fry the chilli powder or chopped peppers for 2–3 minutes. Add the green pepper and continue frying 2–3 minutes more, until well softened. Add the tomato purée and the kidney beans and tip the whole thing into the hot half of the cooked mince. Cook gently for 5–10 minutes for the mince to absorb the additional flavours then serve.

For Bolognese Sauce: Add the white wine to the second prepared half of the mince and heat gently until bubbling hot. In another pan heat the oil, add the diced bacon and fry until cooked. Raise the heat slightly, add the chopped mushrooms and cook rapidly until tender. Add all to the mince and stir in well. Add the chopped parsley, check seasoning and serve with spaghetti and freshly grated Parmesan cheese.

ACCOMPANIMENTS: For the Chilli Con Carni, a green salad. Baked potatoes go well but are not traditional and pitta bread is brilliant. Nothing is needed with the Spaghetti Bolognese.

VARIATIONS: The Bolognese Sauce can be used to make lasagne, layering with precooked lasagne pasta and topping with a cheese sauce. Or for stuffing pancakes.

COOK'S TIP: Taking the seeds out of chilli peppers removes the hottest part. After touching chilli pepper seeds, wash hands very well in lots of cold water before touching lips or eyes or they will sting very badly. To judge how much of the pepper to add to a dish, taste a very tiny bit. Dried red peppers can be used but need pre-soaking in boiling water for about 20 minutes beforehand as they will not be cooked very long.

PRESSURE COOKER: Prepare as above in the base of the pressure cooker. Cut amount of stock or water by a half, add with the seasonings, fix on the lid and bring up pressure to HIGH and maintain for 15 minutes, then reduce pressure and proceed as above.

MICROWAVE OVEN: Use to cook onion: place chopped onion and oil in a bowl, cover tightly and microwave on HIGH for 3 minutes. Also use to reheat. Each half of the above, covered tightly with cling film, will take 6 minutes on 80%/REHEAT.

BURGERS

Homemade burgers are a very different proposition from the butcher's version. Lean meat and good flavourings produce a burger that rates as a real meal rather than a quick snack. The very best burgers are made from freshly chopped or minced rump steak. You may think that a poor end for rump steak but the result is truly delicious, a real burger. Braising steak also produces a reasonable result if not quite so succulent.

---

350 g/12 oz freshly chopped or minced good quality beef, see above

---

Salt and freshly ground black pepper

---

1 medium sized onion, finely chopped or grated

Mix all ingredients together, pat into two rounds, or four if you prefer little burgers, and place under a grill heated to its hottest. If the burgers are very fat, lower heat, or, after searing top and bottom, take burgers a little further away from the heat source. Length of cooking time will depend on size of burgers. Judge by pressing gently with a finger or spatula, they should still "give" a little when they are ready.

ACCOMPANIMENTS: A toasted hamburger bun and a green salad, or just serve with the salad.

VARIATIONS: As additional flavourings, one of the following can be added to the above mixture: 50 g/2 oz/4 tablespoons grated tasty Cheddar; good dash Worcestershire sauce and a small dash Tabasco sauce; 1 tablespoon freshly chopped mixed herbs; 1 stalk finely chopped celery. Crushed garlic can be added to any of the burgers if liked.

COOK'S TIP: The action of mincing meat squeezes out some of the juices, which is why the best meat for burgers is chopped with a heavy, very sharp knife. A processor is next best but can leave "strings", particularly if the meat hasn't been carefully trimmed before processing. Ready prepared burgers have a high proportion of fat to meat, giving a very distinctive "feel" in the mouth as well as flavour. It is possible some people may not like the low-fat burger made with quality meat at first. Remember that to be juicy, burgers like these require undercooking, make sure they have a bit of "give" when pressed.

WOK'S UP –
STIR-FRY MEDLEY

No cooking is quicker than the Chinese technique of stir-frying. Originally developed to cope with a chronic shortage of fuel, the food is chopped and sliced thinly and evenly then tossed in a wok, developed to provide the maximum area of hot metal for rapid cooking. For small quantities, however, a large frying pan can serve as well. As for the preparation, a food processor can chop ingredients in a twinkling but slicing by hand can be very soothing and the finished result is usually more satisfactory.

Any tender meat can be stir-fried, with or without vegetables. So can fish but choose one with a firm flesh such as monkfish or scampi, the flakier varieties tend to disintegrate in the cooking. A *mélange* of vegetables can be very satisfactory either as an accompaniment to a grill or on their own. Devise your own mixture, start the cooking with those ingredients that will take longest and use a sauce from one of the following recipes, adding it in a clear space in the middle of the pan so it will come to the boil and thicken quickly, then stir in the other ingredients.

Remember to heat the pan well. Meat and fish are often cooked first, removed, then added to the other ingredients at the end of cooking.

This is one branch of cookery in which the microwave cannot compete, it won't save time nor will the result be as satisfactory.

STIR-FRIED MONKFISH WITH MANGE TOUT

*Start recipe 30 minutes before cooking
Only the fish is stir-fried in this recipe, the mange tout peas are cooked very quickly in boiling water then added to the fish at the end of cooking. Marinading the fish before cooking improves the flavour. Choose a really firm fleshed fish for this dish otherwise it will disintegrate in the cooking.

350 g/12 oz firm fleshed fish such as monkfish, halibut, perch, etc., any skin and membrane removed, flesh cut into smallish pieces

Marinade:

Small piece fresh ginger root, peeled and finely chopped *Good pinch salt, freshly grated black pepper* *1 teaspoon rice wine or dry sherry* *1 teaspoon light soy sauce*	*all mixed together*

100 g/4 oz mange tout peas, stringed

1 tablespoon arachide/groundnut/peanut oil

½ teaspoon cornflour *3 tablespoons fish stock or water* *1 tablespoon oyster sauce OR* *½ tablespoon anchovy sauce* *½ teaspoon light soy sauce*	*all mixed together*

Place the fish in a bowl, mix together the marinade ingredients, pour over and toss well to coat all the pieces. Leave in a cool place for 15–30 minutes.

When ready to cook, bring a generous sized pan of salted water to the boil, add the mange tout, bring the water back to the boil and allow the peas to cook for no more than 1 minute, draining immediately and refreshing in cold water. If the peas are very tender (perhaps picked from the garden), they may need nothing more than being brought to the boil.

Heat the oil in a wok or large frying pan, drain the fish, reserving the marinade, and add. Stir-fry for just long enough for the fish to lose its transparent look and become opaque. Add the remains of the marinade to the sauce mixture, push the fish to the side of the pan, add the sauce to the middle and bring to the boil, constantly stirring, until it becomes clear and slightly thickened. Stir in the fish, add the mange tout and turn all together to mix. Serve immediately.

ACCOMPANIMENTS: Pasta butterfly shapes go well with this dish, so will rice. No other vegetable is necessary.

VARIATIONS: Beans or broccoli can be used instead of the mange tout peas. Scallops, scampi or huss can replace the monkfish.

COOK'S TIP: The peas have a string running down the pod, easily removed by snapping off the end of the stalk with the fingers and pulling off the attached string. Repeat with the pointed bit at the other end if necessary.

STIR-FRIED PRAWNS IN TOMATO

This recipe is best with uncooked prawns but if you can't get hold of these – they are sometimes hard to find – it also works with cooked prawns.

1 tablespoon arachide/groundnut/peanut oil
2 teaspoons finely chopped green ginger root
3–4 spring onions, white and green parts separated, both cut into 2.5 cm/1 inch lengths and split into halves or quarters according to thickness
450 g/1 lb uncooked prawns in the shell, peeled and deveined (see below) OR 225 g/8 oz peeled prawns
Salt
Small tin peeled tomatoes, flesh sliced
1 teaspoon chilli sauce
1 teaspoon light soy sauce
Pinch sugar
½ teaspoon sesame oil
½ teaspoon potato flour or cornflour dissolved in 1 tablespoon water

Heat the oil, add the green ginger and the white parts of the spring onions and stir for a moment or two, then add the uncooked prawns and season with salt. Stir-fry until the prawns lose their transparency and become opaque, then remove from pan. Add the tomatoes, the chilli and soy sauce and the sugar and cook, stirring constantly, until the tomatoes are well flavoured and slightly reduced to a good consistency. Add the sesame oil and the slaked potato or cornflour (stir well before adding), bring back to boil, stirring, until the sauce is slightly thickened. Add the green parts of the spring onions and the prawns. Cook, stirring constantly, until the prawns are heated through. Serve immediately.

ACCOMPANIMENTS: Rice and a salad.

VARIATIONS: Scampi can be used instead of prawns. Additional vegetables can be added such as mange tout peas, beans, etc. Blanch these before adding, as for the STIR-FRIED MONKFISH WITH MANGE TOUT on page 94.

COOK'S TIP: The large uncooked king prawns, best for this dish, have a fine digestive cord running down the back which should be removed before cooking. That and peeling the prawns are quite easy: twist off the head (if it's still on), pull off the tail, then remove the rest of the shell. Take a sharp knife, make a shallow incision along the back of the fish beside the cord and tweak it out. If a recipe calls for "butterflied" prawns, make the incision deeper so that when the fish is cooked, the flesh opens out on either side of the cut. See note on sesame oil in STIR-FRIED PORK WITH WATERCRESS on page 98.

STIR-FRIED BEEF WITH MUSHROOMS AND LEEKS

A gutsy dish full of flavour. Make sure the mushrooms are really button and very fresh or their juices will discolour the dish.

2 tablespoons good vegetable oil
225 g/8 oz steak, fillet, rump or entrecôte, cut into small strips across the grain
175 g/6 oz/3 cups button mushrooms, sliced
225 g/8 oz leeks (1 big or 2 small leeks), white and pale green parts trimmed, sliced and carefully cleaned

Sauce:

2 tablespoons medium sherry *2 tablespoons water or light stock* *½ tablespoon light soy sauce* *Dash Worcestershire sauce* *Salt and freshly ground black pepper* *½ teaspoon cornflour*	*all mixed together*

Garnish: Little freshly chopped parsley

Heat one tablespoon oil in wok or large frying pan. Add the beef and stir-fry until browned all over. Remove from pan and keep warm. Add remaining tablespoon oil and stir-fry mushrooms briskly until any juices released and evaporated, then add drained leeks. Stir-fry until leeks slightly softened but still crisp. Replace beef and stir together with vegetables. Push food to sides of pan, give sauce a good stir and pour into centre. Heat, stirring, until boiling and slightly thickened, stir together with beef, mushrooms and leeks. Check seasoning and serve sprinkled with the chopped parsley.

ACCOMPANIMENTS: Rice, preferably brown.

VARIATIONS: This recipe works equally well with chicken or turkey.

STIR-FRIED PORK WITH WATERCRESS

The peppery watercress in this dish adds an invigorating note without being over-powerful.

½ tablespoon sesame oil, ½ tablespoon arachide/groundnut/peanut oil
1 small clove garlic, peeled and chopped
1 pork tenderloin, approx. 225 g/8 oz, cut across the grain into strips
1 bunch watercress, tough stalks removed, well washed

½ teaspoon Dijon mustard 1 tablespoon demerara sugar 1 teaspoon light soy sauce 1 tablespoon sherry sauce or medium sherry 1 tablespoon water A dash Tabasco Little salt Freshly ground black pepper 1 teaspoon cornflour	all mixed together

Heat oil in a wok or large frying pan, add the garlic and the strips of pork and stir-fry until well browned. Remove from the pan and keep warm. Add watercress and stir-fry until just wilting, push to the sides of the pan, add the sauce in the middle and heat, stirring, until bubbling and slightly thickened. Add the cooked pork and toss in the sauce, mixing with the watercress. Serve immediately.

ACCOMPANIMENTS: Rice or noodles plus thin batons of cucumber tossed in a teaspoon of rice wine then mixed with seasoned yoghurt. If preparing this beforehand, sprinkle the cucumber batons with salt, place in a colander weighted with a saucer and leave to drain for 20 minutes, then proceed as above.

VARIATIONS: The watercress can be replaced with thinly sliced leek, cook until just tender. Chicken or turkey can be used instead of the pork.

COOK'S TIP: Sherry sauce is sherry marinated with chilli peppers, giving it a bite. Make your own by stuffing a small bottle with chilli peppers stabbed in several places with a pin (the tiny ones are hottest, buy at ethnic grocers), pouring over medium sherry, screwing on the lid and leaving for several weeks. You can make chilli-flavoured oil the same way. There are two kinds of sesame oil, the toasted variety is much stronger than the paler ordinary oil. Choose whichever you prefer.

STIR-FRIED PORK WITH BACON AND CELERIAC

A very untraditional stir-fry dish but the combination of pork with the smoky bacon and cleanly earthy flavour of celeriac is excellent. Yoghurt with a dash of balsamic vinegar provides the sauce.

1 tablespoon arachide/groundnut/peanut oil
225 g/8 oz lean pork cut into small strips across the grain of the meat
100 g/4 oz smoked bacon, cut into strips
100 g/4 oz/1½ cups celeriac trimmed and cut into matchstick pieces
6 tablespoons natural yoghurt mixed with 1 teaspoon cornflour and 1 teaspoon balsamic vinegar
Salt and freshly ground black pepper
Garnish: Freshly chopped parsley

Heat the oil in a wok or large frying pan. Add the pork and stir-fry rapidly until the meat is browned and opaque. Remove from pan and keep warm. Add the bacon and the celeriac and cook until the vegetable is tender. Push to the sides, add the yoghurt and cornflour and vinegar mixture, bring to the boil, stirring constantly. When lightly thickened, add the pork and stir in with the other ingredients, season to taste and serve immediately garnished with a little chopped parsley.

ACCOMPANIMENTS: Rice or noodles or new potatoes, green salad.

VARIATIONS: Chicken or turkey can replace the pork. Sherry or wine vinegar can be used instead of the balsamic, though wine in particular will not add the same richness of flavour. NB: Sherry vinegar is made from sherry and is rather richer than wine vinegar. Balsamic vinegar is made from wine vinegar that has been slowly matured and aged and is incredibly mellow and rich in flavour. It tastes the least acidic of any of the vinegars and a little is wonderful used to deglaze pans after frying meat, adding to various dressings or as an extra tone to sauces.

COOK'S TIP: Celeriac is a knobbly vegetable that can be difficult to peel. Cut into thick slices then trim off the outside.

TOWARDS TOMORROW: Cut remaining celeriac in thick slices, cook in boiling salted water, drain again then keep until next day. Coat in egg and breadcrumbs then fry to make fritters.

STIR-FRIED CHICKEN WITH VEGETABLES, GINGER AND SPRING ONIONS

A good example of how a generous helping of vegetables can stretch a small amount of meat to make a colourful dish with plenty of zing.

1 tablespoon arachide/groundnut/peanut oil
1 small chicken breast (approx. 175 g/6 oz), skinned, cut into thin strips across the grain of the meat
Walnut-sized piece of green ginger, peeled and shredded
2 small or 1 large courgette, cut into matchstick pieces
½ red pepper, finely sliced
2 stalks celery, cut into matchstick pieces
Few green beans, cut on slant into two or three pieces
Salt and freshly ground black pepper

Sauce:

1 tablespoon chicken stock or water mixed with 1 teaspoon cornflour
1 tablespoon light soy sauce
Pinch caster sugar
1 teaspoon Worcestershire sauce
1 tablespoon white and pale green part of spring onion, chopped
1 teaspoon wine vinegar

} *all mixed together*

Mix together all ingredients for the sauce. Heat half the oil in a wok or large frying pan then stir-fry chicken for 1 minute, until the flesh has turned white. Remove from pan and keep warm. Wipe out pan with kitchen paper, add remaining oil then the vegetables. Season and stir-fry for about 2 minutes until they are almost cooked but still have a certain amount of crunch. Push to the sides of the pan, add the sauce and bring to boil, stirring all the time. As soon as it has become clear and lightly thickened, add the cooked chicken and stir together with the sauce and other ingredients, season to taste. Serve immediately.

ACCOMPANIMENTS: Rice. Or the dish can be eaten as a complete meal.

VARIATIONS: Turkey or pork can replace the chicken.

TOWARDS TOMORROW: Use any remaining vegetables, red pepper, celery, etc., to make a salad for the next day.

STIR-FRIED CHICKEN WITH BROCCOLI AND ALMONDS

The combination of the broccoli with the chicken works extremely well and the almonds add a final triumphant touch of texture and flavour.

2 tablespoons arachide/groundnut/peanut oil
175 g/6 oz breast of chicken (1 small breast), without skin, finely shredded
Approx. 225 g/8 oz (1 bunch) broccoli, cut into small florets with a little of the stalk attached, blanched in boiling water for 2 minutes, drained, refreshed in cold water and drained again
Salt and freshly ground black pepper
3 spring onions, finely chopped   *1 tablespoon light soy sauce*   *2 tablespoons rice wine or dry sherry*   *1 tablespoon chicken stock or water* — *all mixed together*
2 tablespoons flaked almonds, toasted

Heat 1 tablespoon of the oil in a wok or large frying pan, stir-fry the chicken until the flesh whitens and becomes opaque. Remove from the pan. Wipe out the pan, heat the remaining tablespoon of oil, add the broccoli, season and stir-fry briskly until warmed through. Add the spring onion mixture and stir well to coat all the vegetables. Add the cooked chicken and continue to stir-fry for a minute or two to reheat. Serve immediately topped with the flaked and toasted almonds.

ACCOMPANIMENTS: Brown rice or noodles.

VARIATIONS: Pork or turkey can replace the chicken.

COOK'S TIP: The easiest way to toast almonds is in a medium to low oven, perhaps while cooking something else. Under the grill or in a frying pan is much quicker but the nuts can very quickly colour too much. They can also be browned in a microwave, see page 49.

SPICY STIR-FRIED LAMB WITH MANGO

This is a succulent dish, originally from the south of China.

175–225 g/6–8 oz fillet of lamb, trimmed, cut into thin strips

Marinade:

Pinch salt, little freshly ground black pepper

Pinch sugar

½ teaspoon light soy sauce

½ teaspoon dark soy sauce

½ teaspoon rice wine or medium dry sherry

1 teaspoon potato flour

1 tablespoon water

Sauce:

½ teaspoon potato flour
1 teaspoon Worcestershire sauce
½ teaspoon light soy sauce } *all mixed together*
1 tablespoon rice wine or medium dry sherry
1 tablespoon water

2 tablespoons arachide/groundnut/peanut oil

1 clove garlic, peeled and finely sliced

4 spring onions, white and pale green parts cut into slivers same length as the mango strips

½ mango, peeled and cut into strips

Small knob of green root ginger, peeled and shredded

Place meat in a bowl, mix together the marinade ingredients and pour over, stirring well to coat. Leave in a cool place for 30 minutes. Have all the sauce ingredients mixed together.

Heat 1 tablespoon of the oil in a wok or large frying pan, add the lamb, stir-fry until browned, remove from pan and keep warm. Wipe out the pan, heat the remaining oil, add the garlic, allow it to colour, add the spring onions, the mango and the root ginger. Stir-fry for 1 minute, then push to the side of the pan, add the sauce to the centre, heat, stirring, until clear and slightly thickened. Add the cooked lamb, stir to coat with sauce and mix with other ingredients then serve immediately.

ACCOMPANIMENTS: Tagliatelle tossed in a little sesame oil and either a salad or a plainly cooked green vegetable.

VARIATIONS: The lamb can be replaced with beef.

COOK'S TIP: Mango has a flattish stone and the flesh follows its outline, it is therefore possible to see where to slice through so that a "cheek" of mango flesh is lifted off the stone. Another way is to remove the flesh off in segments, cutting down to the stone each time. Make sure the fruit isn't too ripe for this recipe, it should be firm.

TOWARDS TOMORROW: Turn the other half of the mango into a fruit salad for tomorrow with segments of orange and a few grapes.

SPICY CELERY, PEPPERS AND TOFU STIR-FRY

A vegetarian stir-fry that provides a complete meal. It is delicious also served with cold or simply grilled meats, when the tofu can be omitted.

1 tablespoon arachide/groundnut/peanut oil
1 clove garlic, peeled and finely chopped
Small piece green root ginger, peeled and finely chopped
3 stalks celery / *½ medium sized red pepper* / *½ medium sized green pepper* — *all cut into thin strips*
Salt and freshly ground black pepper
4–6 spring onions, dark green leaves and root ends trimmed off, onions split into strips same length as peppers and celery
2 teaspoons light soy sauce / *1 tablespoon rice wine or dry sherry* / *½ teaspoon chilli sauce* — *mixed together*
100 g/4 oz/¾ cup tofu, cut into large dice
Garnish: A few toasted almonds

Heat oil in a wok or large frying pan, add garlic and ginger, the celery and peppers, season and stir-fry for 1 minute. Add spring onions and stir-fry another minute, by which time the vegetables should be tender but still slightly crisp. Add the spicy mixture and toss the vegetables, making sure they are well coated. Finally add the tofu and stir gently for a brief period to mix and heat through. Serve immediately garnished with the toasted almonds.

ACCOMPANIMENTS: Can be served with rice and a salad for a more substantial meal.

VARIATIONS: Substitute Greek feta cheese for the tofu.

COOK'S TIP: Tofu is made from bean curd and looks rather like a white cheese. It is full of protein. Tofu has very little flavour but is excellent at absorbing the taste of whatever it is mixed with.

TOWARDS TOMORROW: Use the remainder of the celery head for BRAISED CELERY IN CIDER in the VEGETABLES section on page 164. The rest of the peppers can be cut into wide strips and served with AIOLI (see MAYONNAISE in the SAUCY IDEAS section on page 191) with drinks or as a starter or snack.

MUSHROOMS WITH GREEN BEANS AND WATER-CHESTNUTS

Another good vegetarian dish that can also accompany plainly grilled meat. Oyster mushrooms are best for this dish, their meaty texture stir-fries beautifully and the flavour melds well with that of the beans. Shiitake also have lots of flavour and texture and the brown cap mushrooms, often available organically grown, are another good choice, full of flavour and firm textured. Use fresh water-chestnuts if you can find them, if not, the tinned will do very well.

1 tablespoon arachide/groundnut/peanut oil

350 g/12 oz/6 cups mushrooms, oyster preferably, thickly sliced

Salt and freshly ground black pepper

175 g/6 oz thin green beans, topped and tailed, blanched in boiling water for 2 minutes, drained, refreshed in cold water and drained again

100 g/4 oz water-chestnuts (drained weight if using tinned), peeled if fresh, drained and rinsed if tinned, thinly sliced

3–4 spring onions, white and pale green parts finely chopped 1 tablespoon light soy sauce 3 tablespoons water Good pinch of sugar 1 teaspoon seasame oil	all mixed together

Heat the tablespoon of arachide oil in a large frying pan, add the mushrooms, season lightly and stir-fry until any moisture released and evaporated and mushrooms tender. Add the water-chestnuts if using fresh. Stir-fry for 2–3 minutes, add the drained beans and continue cooking for 1–2 minutes until vegetables hot and tender but still crunchy. If using tinned water-chestnuts add now, then the spring onion mixture. Toss well to coat all the vegetables, check that beans and water-chestnuts are cooked to your taste and serve.

ACCOMPANIMENTS: Angel hair pasta tossed in sesame oil.

VARIATIONS: Mange tout peas can be used instead of the beans.

COOK'S TIP: Mushrooms do not need peeling nor should they be washed, they are very absorbent and can become soggy. If necessary, wipe with a damp kitchen towel. See note on sesame oil in COOK'S TIP in STIR-FRIED PORK WITH WATERCRESS recipe on page 99.

There are also stir-fry recipes using liver and kidney in the IT'S NOT AWFUL section.

BUDGET BEATERS

Some dishes that stretch strained household budgets without calling for great effort. The results are pretty tasty though.

F PORK WITH HARICOT BEANS

Belly of pork is a nice cheap cut of meat. In this recipe the richness of the meat is nicely offset by the floury beans, and juniper and allspice berries add extra flavour. This is a dish capable of many variations, some suggestions follow the recipe, plus ideas for using the rest of the beans if you cook double quantities.

100 g/4 oz/⅔ cup haricot beans, soaked overnight and cooked in fresh water with seasoning and herbs until nearly tender
1 tablespoon light vegetable oil
450 g/1 lb lean belly of pork, rind and bones removed, meat cubed
1 medium sized onion, chopped
1 clove garlic, crushed
450 ml/15 fl oz/2 cups bean stock
6 juniper berries and 5 allspice berries, crushed
1 bay leaf
Salt and freshly ground black pepper
2 stalks celery, trimmed and sliced obliquely
100 g/4 oz/2 cups button mushrooms, quartered if large
Garnish: Chopped parsley

Drain beans, reserving stock. Heat oil in an ovenproof casserole and brown pork on all sides then remove. Add onions and garlic to pot and cook gently until transparent. Replace meat, add beans. Bring stock to boil and add to casserole with seasonings. Cover casserole and place in preheated oven at 150°C/300°F/Gas Mark 2 for 60 minutes. Add the celery and mushrooms and cook for another 20 minutes. Sprinkle with chopped parsley and serve.

ACCOMPANIMENTS: The casserole is almost a meal in itself; according to appetites you could add baked potatoes, cooked in the oven at the same time, or pasta; a green salad or an additional vegetable such as green beans or thinly sliced cabbage.

VARIATIONS: Substitute 225 g/8 oz Jerusalem artichokes for the celery and mushrooms, or a small aubergine, cut into large dice, with a small tin of tomatoes made up with stock to quantity of liquid, omit juniper berries and allspice, add good pinch of cinnamon with onions and garlic.

COOK'S TIP: A tin of haricot or flageolet beans can be used instead of the freshly cooked variety but add halfway through cooking otherwise they may disintegrate. If using tinned beans, don't use the liquid from the tin, it will contain a lot of starch, substitute water for the stock.

PRESSURE COOKER: This dish is ideal for the pressure cooker. Prepare in base of cooker as above to point of placing in oven, add celery and mushrooms, add cooker lid, bring to HIGH pressure and maintain for 20 minutes. Cool and serve as above.

MICROWAVE OVEN: If the belly of pork is particularly lean, the dish can be quite successfully microwaved but it will lack the melting succulence given by slow cooking in a conventional oven. Start with the onion and garlic, stirred with the oil, cover tightly with cling film, microwave on HIGH for 3 minutes. Then add the meat, seasonings and half amount of stock or water, preheated, re-cover as before and microwave on HIGH for 6 minutes. Leave to stand for 5 minutes then add beans (cooked on conventional stove) and other vegetables, re-cover tightly and microwave on HIGH for another 6 minutes. Prick cling film, leave dish to stand for 5 minutes, garnish with parsley and serve.

TOWARDS TOMORROW: Cook twice or three times the amount of beans required and use surplus for BEAN AND TOMATO SOUP (see MOTHER HUBBARD section on page 265) or for QUICK CASSOULET (see POT POURRI section on page 83). Or toss while hot in good French dressing then add chopped fresh herbs when cold for a salad to serve with cold meats.

F PORK SWEET AND SOUR

*Start preparation 1 hour or more ahead of recipe

This is not a recipe for battered pork, I have an ingrained dislike of deep frying, too smelly, too fattening, too dangerous, but it captures some of the subtle balance of flavours of the classic Chinese dish.

350–450 g/12 oz–1 lb lean belly of pork, trimmed of skin, bones and excess fat and cut into cubes
½ teaspoon salt
1 tablespoon light soy sauce
1 tablespoon cider vinegar or Chinese rice vinegar
1 tablespoon dry sherry or rice wine
2 tablespoons arachide/groundnut/peanut oil
1 medium sized onion, peeled and finely chopped
½ green pepper, seeds and pith removed, cut into strips
½ red pepper, seeds and pith removed, cut into strips
300 ml/10 fl oz/generous cup light stock or water
1 tablespoon brown sugar
1 orange, segments removed without pith or membrane
2 teaspoons cornflour, mixed with a little cold water
Garnish: Chopped parsley

Prepare the pork. Mix together the salt, soy sauce, vinegar and dry sherry or rice wine in a bowl, add the pork and toss well. Leave to marinate anything from 20 minutes to 1 hour. Then drain, reserving the marinade.

Heat the oil and brown the pork on all sides, removing as soon as browned. Lower the heat and cook the onion until transparent. Add the strips of green and red peppers and the stock or water and bring to the boil, scraping the bottom of the pan well. As soon as the mixture is boiling, add the pork, turn down the heat, cover tightly and cook gently, either on top of the stove or in a preheated oven at 160°C/325°F/Gas Mark 3 for 1 hour or until pork is cooked and tender. Remove from oven, stir in the brown sugar and add the orange segments. Take a couple of tablespoons of the hot liquid to mix with the cornflour then add that to the contents of the dish and stir well over heat until mixture returns to the boil and the sauce thickens slightly and becomes transparent. Garnish with chopped parsley to serve or with blanched strands of orange peel.

ACCOMPANIMENTS: Plain boiled or steamed rice is all that is necessary plus perhaps a green vegetable or salad.

MICROWAVE OVEN: Marinate the pork as above. Mix oil with chopped onion, place in a large dish, cover tightly with cling film and microwave on HIGH for 2 minutes. Pierce film, uncover, add the pork, marinade, red and green peppers, half the amount of stock or water, preheated, and mix well. Cover tightly again with cling film and microwave on HIGH for 7–8 minutes (according to amount of meat). Leave to stand for 5 minutes. Pierce film, uncover, add sugar, stir, add orange segments. Take a couple of spoons of the hot liquid and add to the slaked cornflour. Pour in rest of liquid from casserole, stir well, then microwave on HIGH for 2 minutes until sauce has slightly thickened and is transparent. Pour back over meat, stir well and serve garnished with chopped parsley or blanched strands of orange peel.

TOWARDS TOMORROW: Use the other halves of the red and green peppers for a salad or in SPICY CELERY, PEPPERS AND TOFU STIR-FRY in the WOK'S UP section on page 103.

F PORK WITH RED CABBAGE AND JUNIPER

Red cabbage has a great deal more class than green. It is a meaty, full of flavour vegetable and a small specimen will go a long way. Most greengrocers will cut them in half but they keep well, are great shredded in salads and it is always worth cooking double quantities and using the second half for tomorrow, or even the day after. The juniper berries add a subtle, clean flavour that goes well with the depth of the cabbage and the richness of the pork. In this dish the pork can be bought already cut into slices, this way it comes boned and skinned and you can easily see the proportion of lean to fat.

25 g/1 oz/2 tablespoons butter
350 g/12 oz/5 cups red cabbage, trimmed and finely sliced
8 juniper berries, crushed
Salt and freshly ground black pepper
2 tablespoons wine vinegar or freshly squeezed lemon juice
2 tablespoons demerara sugar
450 g/1 lb (approx. 6 slices) lean belly of pork, sliced and trimmed of skin and bone
1 teaspoon French Dijon mustard / *3 tablespoons redcurrant jelly, preferably homemade* } *stirred together*

Heat the butter, add the finely sliced red cabbage and the crushed juniper berries and stir over a brisk heat for a couple of minutes, then add the seasoning and the vinegar or lemon juice, lower the heat, cover the pan and cook gently until nearly tender, approximately 1 hour. Then stir in the sugar, check seasoning and lay the red cabbage in a shallow ovenproof dish that will take the slices of pork in one layer. Add the pork on top, each slice seasoned and spread with the mixture of mustard and redcurrant jelly. Cover with tin foil and place in a preheated oven at 160°C/325°F/Gas Mark 3 for 45 minutes. Then remove the tin foil and give the dish another 10 minutes or so to brown on top and serve.

ACCOMPANIMENTS: Baked potatoes make this a very substantial meal, creamed go very well. No other vegetable is needed but a salad afterwards would be very refreshing.

MICROWAVE OVEN: Not as tender and succulent a result as the slower method of cooking but acceptable if you are in a hurry. Omit butter. Place prepared cabbage, juniper berries and vinegar or lemon juice plus 3 tablespoons water in a shallow dish. Omit the seasoning. Cover tightly and microwave on HIGH for 15 minutes. Pierce film, uncover, stir in the sugar. Place pork slices on top, spread with the mustard and redcurrant jelly. Cover tightly again and microwave on HIGH for 6 minutes. Leave to stand for 5 minutes. Serve as above.

CRISPY ROAST PORK

Again that useful cut, the belly, here with the skin cooked to golden crispness, the meat succulent. A bit of a cheat, really, because the skin is cooked separately from the meat and the meat is braised, not roasted, which means it is beautifully tender and full of flavour, giving a very satisfactory dish at a bargain price. It tastes so good cold that I make no apologies for the fact that the joint will actually serve four people.

1 kg/2 lb belly pork, boned, skin removed, bones and skin reserved
Little arachide/groundnut/peanut oil
Salt
1 small onion, peeled and chopped
300 ml/10 fl oz/1 cup light stock OR mixture water and wine OR water
3 tablespoons light soy sauce
Freshly ground black pepper

Make sure the butcher has scored the skin, rub it with oil, sprinkle with salt and place, with the skin side up, on a baking tray, place in a preheated oven at 200°C/400°F/Gas Mark 6.

Heat 1 tablespoon of oil in a fireproof dish, brown the meat on all sides then remove. Lower the heat, add the onion and cook, stirring, until transparent. Add the liquids, season well, bring to the boil, add the pork and the reserved bones, tucking them down beside the meat, bring the liquid back to a simmer, cover the dish and place in the oven underneath the roasting skin, lowering the temperature to 160°C/325°F/Gas Mark 3. Cook for 1½–2 hours, until the meat is cooked and tender. Halfway through the cooking time, pour off the fat that will have been released by the skin. By the time the meat is cooked, the skin should be crackling crisp and golden.

When the meat is ready, discard the bones and strain off all the juices, allow them to stand for a few moments then remove the fat from the surface. Either reduce slightly or thicken: have a teaspoonful of cornflour mixed with a little cold water, add some of the hot liquid then pour it all into a saucepan and heat to boiling point, stirring constantly, until the sauce is slightly thickened and transparent. Cut the crackling into pieces and serve on top of the sliced meat, hand the sauce separately.

ACCOMPANIMENTS: Plain boiled or steamed rice, green vegetables.

VARIATIONS: For a more Eastern flavour, add some slices of green ginger and a teaspoon of five spice powder to the braising liquid, OR add a few stoned prunes and a sliced dessert apple to the meat, fold the flesh over the fruit and tie with string before browning. This gives a particularly good cold dish.

COOK'S TIP: The crackling will crisp up after it is removed from the oven so don't despair if it doesn't feel quite right at the end of the cooking time.

TOWARDS TOMORROW: With the cold pork serve a homemade jelly, or a good commercial brand. Baked soufflé potatoes (see page 253) would be nice, these could be cooked and prepared at the same time as the pork then given their final baking the next day. A simple green salad or vegetable is the only other accompaniment needed.

F LAMB'S NECK WITH CIDER AND CELERIAC

I don't find breast of lamb nearly as useful as belly of pork, it tends to be much fattier. I like to use it to make Scotch broth, for which it is excellent. But scrag end of neck of lamb (if the other cut is known as "best end of neck", I have often thought I should ask for "worst end" instead of scrag), is another matter. The only drawback to this cut is that it has more bone than meat but that is easily dealt with by starting with a goodly serving for each person. Use the following method and vary the flavouring ingredients, there are many possibilities and some suggestions follow the recipe. The cider and celeriac here add clean, sweet flavours that contrast well with the richness of the lamb. It's one of those dishes ideal for winter months, meaty and satisfying. A pressure cooker can help save time and energy.

1 tablespoon arachide/groundnut/peanut oil
Approx. 750 g/1¾ lb scrag end of neck of lamb
Salt and freshly ground pepper
450 ml/15 fl oz/2 cups cider (such as Taunton's Autumn Gold or Exhibition)
225 g/8 oz/1½ cups celeriac, peeled and sliced or cut into chunks, see below for PRESSURE COOKER
Garnish: Freshly chopped parsley

Heat the oil and brown pieces of lamb on all sides. Place in a casserole dish and season. Bring cider to the boil and pour over. Arrange slices of celeriac over the top, season again, cover and place in a preheated oven at 160°C/325°F/Gas Mark 3 for 1½ to 2 hours. Garnish with the freshly chopped parsley before serving.

ACCOMPANIMENTS: Plain or mashed potatoes or pasta noodles would go well plus a small fresh salad or green vegetable or a puréed vegetable such as carrot or swede. Grilled or stuffed tomatoes are another good partner.

VARIATIONS: Stock or water, or a mixture of water and wine, can be used instead of the cider. Potatoes can be substituted for the celeriac. Sliced dried apricots can be added, or chopped herbs, try lemon thyme or winter savory. Most of the root vegetables go well: Jerusalem artichokes, carrots, turnips, etc. Flageolet or haricot beans also go well and can provide extra protein, canned ones are expensive but save on time and energy, add halfway through cooking.

PRESSURE COOKER: Have celeriac cut into cubes, place browned meat in bottom of cooker with the celeriac, season, add the hot cider, cover, bring heat up to highest pressure and cook for 25 minutes.

MICROWAVE OVEN: Not quite as successful as the other methods but acceptable. Place slices of neck round the edge of a deep dish, add the celeriac, cubed, in the centre. Add the cider, cover tightly with cling film and microwave on HIGH for 12 minutes. If liked, sauce can be thickened by slaking 1 tablespoon cornflour in a little cold water, adding 2 tablespoons of the hot cooking liquid then stirring in the remaining juices from the dish. Microwave on HIGH for 2–3 minutes by which time the juices should be slightly thickened. Pour over the meat, garnish with the parsley and serve.

POTATO AND BACON ENDS GRATIN

Butchers often offer bits of ends of bacon or misshapes at bargain prices. There are various ways of using them, all delicious. Apart from quiches, they can be used in a risotto (like the HAM KNUCKLE RISOTTO on page 120), in rissoles, served in a white sauce, used as part of a SPANISH TORTILLA (see TIME FOR A SNACK section on page 254), and I am sure you can think of more ways yourself. One of my favourites is the following gratin. Have the pieces of bacon neatly sliced rather than in the chunks they are so often sold in.

175 g/6 oz/1 cup bacon ends or misshapes, sliced
350 g/12 oz/2 cups potatoes, peeled and sliced
Salt and freshly ground black pepper
150 ml/5 fl oz/⅔ cup milk or milk and cream
Grated cheese, Gruyère or Cheddar OR little butter

Lightly fry the bacon pieces. Grease a gratin dish, place half the potato slices in the bottom, season lightly, bearing in mind the saltiness of the bacon, add the bacon pieces, arrange the remaining potato slices nicely on top and season again. Heat the milk or milk and cream and pour over. Sprinkle over the grated cheese or dot with flakes of butter, cover with tin foil and place in a preheated oven at 180°C/350°F/Gas Mark 4 for approximately 1 hour and 20 minutes, taking off the foil for the last 15 minutes or so, or until the potatoes are cooked through and nicely golden on top.

ACCOMPANIMENTS: A green salad is best but any other vegetable can provide additional interest and vitamins.

VARIATIONS: Add some sliced and sautéd onions, or slices of peeled and deseeded tomatoes. Add herbs, lemon thyme goes particularly well.

MICROWAVE OVEN: Prepare gratin dish as above, reducing the amount of milk by a third and adding it cold, then cover tightly with cling film instead of foil. Microwave on HIGH for 10 minutes, or until potato is cooked through (test with the point of a sharp knife through the cling film, then patch the slit if continuing cooking).

POTATO AND ANCHOVY MOULD

Potatoes are full of good things and taste good too. Here they are combined with anchovy for a hot dish with a better pedigree than potato cakes but just as simple.

350 g/12 oz/2 cups potatoes
3 tablespoons butter
1 whole egg and 1 egg yolk, lightly beaten
2 tablespoons grated cheese, Cheddar, Parmesan or similar
1 tin anchovy fillets, drained of oil and soaked for 20 minutes in a little milk then drained again and chopped
1 clove garlic, crushed
Little salt
Freshly ground black pepper
1 dessertspoon fine dry breadcrumbs

Boil the potatoes in their skins, then peel them and either push the flesh through a potato ricer or sieve it. Add 2 tablespoons of the butter, the beaten eggs, the grated cheese, chopped anchovy and garlic, season and mix together very well.

Use the remaining butter to grease a 600 ml/1 pint/2½ cup soufflé or other fireproof dish and coat with the dry breadcrumbs. Add the potato mixture, place in a preheated oven and cook at 200°C/400°F/Gas Mark 6 for approximately 50 minutes, until risen, golden brown and firm to touch. Turn out on to a warm plate to serve.

ACCOMPANIMENTS: A tomato sauce (see SAUCY IDEAS section on page 183) or natural yoghurt plus a salad.

VARIATIONS: Instead of using the chopped anchovy, flavour the cheesy potato mix with chopped fresh herbs or a little chopped onion cooked with oil or butter until transparent and golden. Or use chopped spring onion, no need to cook before adding to the potato mixture.

COOK'S TIP: Do not try to use a processor for mashing potatoes, it overworks the starch, usually producing a gluey mess.

MICROWAVE OVEN: Prepare potato mould as above. After placing mixture in dish microwave, uncovered, on HIGH for 6 minutes.

TOWARDS TOMORROW: Prepare double quantity of potato, divide sieved potato in half, using one half for above dish then make MASHED POTATO by adding butter, seasoning and hot milk to other half, placing in greased fireproof dish and making a decorative pattern on the top with a fork. To reheat, add a little milk to top of mashed potato, or dot with butter, and place in a preheated oven at 190°C/375°F/Gas Mark 5 for 30 minutes. If liked, an egg yolk can be added to the mashed mixture, the white whipped stiffly and folded in. SOUP: Or use the potato as a base for a thick soup, adding chopped or puréed vegetables as available and milk or milk and stock to thin to required degree. Season with salt, freshly ground black pepper and chopped herbs.

STUFFED LEG OF TURKEY

*Allow 2–3 hours for soaking apricots before start of preparation

Now that escalopes of turkey breast have become so popular, butchers have to dispose of the rest of the bird and often have drumsticks of turkey to sell (usually frozen) at what seem to me incredibly low prices. I am surprised at the modest price because the meat is delicious, nicely tender and capable of being used in a number of ways. And usually one turkey drumstick is just the right size for two people. You can, of course, quite simply roast it, and very nice it is too. But there are much more exciting ways of dealing with it. The meat can be taken off the bone and used for a casserole, see page 119, or the leg boned out – not a difficult operation – and stuffed. One advantage of taking the meat off the bone, whether in chunks or boned out, is that you can get rid of the tendons, those nasty, inedible crosses between bone and muscle that run down the lower part of the leg.

TO BONE OUT LEG: Grasp the joint end in one hand and use a small, sharp knife to make scraping cuts down the bone, easing the meat away. As you go, turn the meat back on itself, rather like taking a child's arm out of its sleeve. Finally, pull the meat away from the last bit of bone so it is only connected by the skin and ends of the sinews. Trimming off the sinews is usually easiest with a pair of scissors but a knife can also be used. Then cut through the skin, detaching the meat from the bone. Season then turn the meat back inside the skin. It is now ready for stuffing.

4 dried apricots, chopped and soaked for 2–3 hours in juice of 1 orange
100 g/4 oz/½ cup bacon ends, finely chopped or minced
2 tablespoons chopped parsley
Grated rind 1 orange
1 boned-out turkey drumstick (see above)
1 tablespoon Maille Moutarde au Poivre Vert
1 tablespoon arachide/groundnut/peanut oil
1 tablespoon tarragon vinegar
225 ml/7½ fl oz/1 cup light stock or water
Salt and freshly ground black pepper
150 ml/5 fl oz/⅔ cup natural yoghurt mixed well with 1 teaspoon cornflour

Mix the chopped and soaked dried apricots together with the chopped or minced bacon ends, including any unabsorbed orange juice, the chopped parsley and grated rind of orange. Season well with freshly ground black pepper. Spread the inside of the turkey leg with the green pepper mustard and stuff with the apricot and bacon mixture. Fasten the end of the leg by sewing or tying up with fine string or strong thread or by closing with a cocktail stick.

Heat the oil in a small saucepan or casserole in which the leg fits nicely and brown the meat on all sides. Drain off excess fat, deglaze with the tablespoon of tarragon vinegar, cover the pan, lower the heat and cook very gently for 5 minutes. Then uncover, add the stock or water, season with a little salt, bring to boiling point, lower heat again, cover and cook very gently for 1 hour, or until leg tender and cooked through. Remove meat and keep warm. Add the yoghurt and cornflour mixture to pan, stirring into the juices and gradually bringing to the boil, stirring constantly. The sauce will thicken slightly. Check seasoning and strain if liked.

To serve: remove any string or fastening, slice the leg obliquely, revealing the stuffing, and arrange the slices on a serving dish. Pour over a little of the sauce and serve the remainder separately.

ACCOMPANIMENTS: Plain potatoes or rice with carrots, leeks or beans.

VARIATIONS: Instead of the apricots and bacon, stuff leg with prunes, stones removed and replaced with fillets of anchovy. OR a slice of ham spread with the mustard and rolled up. OR a stuffing of breadcrumbs or rice mixed with chopped onions cooked in a little butter or oil with mushrooms or peppers and chopped fresh herbs. OR anything else that takes your fancy.

COOK'S TIP: Leg is slightly easier to bone out if you cut down its length before easing off the bone. It will, though, leave you with a bit more sewing to do after stuffing.

PRESSURE COOKER: Proceed as above, using base of cooker to brown. After cooking the leg with the tarragon vinegar for 5 minutes, add the stock or water, cover with lid, bring up to HIGH pressure and cook for 10 minutes. Reduce pressure, remove meat and finish sauce as above.

MICROWAVE OVEN: Bone out and stuff leg as above. Place in a deep dish, a soufflé one is ideal, with the tarragon vinegar, cover tightly with cling film and microwave on HIGH for 3 minutes. Uncover, add half quantity stock or water, re-cover tightly and microwave on HIGH for 6 minutes. Remove meat, wrap in tin foil and leave in warm place while cooking sauce. Add the yoghurt and cornflour mixture to the juices, stirring well, re-cover tightly and microwave on HIGH for 3 minutes, when it should be thickened, check seasoning and cook a little longer if necessary. Serve meat as above.

F TURKEY CASEROLE

Once you have removed the meat from the leg and detached the sinews, the turkey can be made into this very tasty casserole. Chicken can also be used instead of turkey.

1 tablespoon arachide/groundnut/peanut oil
1 small onion, peeled and chopped
3 stalks celery, trimmed and sliced
1 small tin peeled tomatoes, roughly chopped
1 teaspoon fresh thyme leaves, or ½ teaspoon dried
Salt and freshly ground black pepper
1 large turkey drumstick, meat removed (see previous recipe) and cut into nice sized chunks
Garnish: Chopped leaves of celery

Heat oil, add onion and cook gently until transparent. Add the celery, the chopped tomatoes, with their juices, and the thyme and cook for several minutes, stirring, until tomato has slightly reduced. Season carefully, add the chunks of turkey, bring back to the boil, lower heat and cook very gently on top of stove or in preheated oven at 180°C/350°F/Gas Mark 4 for 45 minutes.

To serve: garnish with a few chopped leaves of celery.

ACCOMPANIMENTS: Mashed potatoes or rice or pasta plus a green vegetable or salad.

VARIATIONS: Any vegetables can be used, according to availability and choice. Stock can replace the tinned tomatoes, or a mixture of wine with stock or water. Sliced potatoes can cover the top of the casserole, watch that they are properly cooked.

PRESSURE COOKER: Proceed as above, using base of cooker for cooking onion. After adding remaining ingredients, cover with lid, bring up to HIGH pressure and cook for 10 minutes. Reduce pressure and serve with vegetables.

MICROWAVE OVEN: Place chopped onion in a deep dish or jug. Add the oil, cover tightly and microwave on HIGH for 2 minutes 30 seconds. Add remaining ingredients, stir well, and microwave uncovered on HIGH for 5 minutes, then leave to stand for 5 minutes before serving as above.

HAM KNUCKLE RISOTTO

Butchers often have the knuckle end of ham to sell. If it's uncooked, it can be poached to produce both wonderful stock and enough meat on the bone to be served hot with a parsley sauce. The stock can then be used for soup with lentils or split peas, add potatoes as well if it is very salty. Sometimes the knuckles are already cooked and yield a serviceable quantity of ham pieces. Again, these can be reheated in a parsley sauce, layered with potatoes for a gratin, as for POTATO AND BACON ENDS GRATIN on page 114, tossed with new potatoes, chopped chives and a French dressing for a salad, etc. Or they can be used for a quick risotto-type dish as follows:

3 tablespoons butter, preferably unsalted
1 small onion, peeled and finely chopped
150 g/5 oz/⅔ cup short-grain white rice, preferably Arborio
A little over 600 ml/1 pint/2½ cups hot chicken stock or water
Freshly ground black pepper
1 bay leaf
Meat from 1 knuckle ham, cooked or uncooked, diced
100 g/4 oz/2 cups shiitake or button mushrooms, sliced
Juice 1 lemon
Approx. 4–6 tablespoons grated cheese, preferably Parmesan but Cheddar or other hard cheese will do
2 tablespoons freshly chopped parsley

Heat 2 tablespoons of butter and cook onion gently until soft. Add the rice and stir well to mix thoroughly, then cook for 1–2 minutes until the rice looks slightly transparent. Add the stock or water and season with pepper (the ham should add sufficient saltiness). Add the bay leaf, a third of the hot stock or water, the meat if it's uncooked and the mushrooms and bring to the boil, stirring constantly. Cover, remove from the heat and leave for 20 minutes, by which time the stock should be absorbed and the rice half cooked. (I owe this tip to Anna del Conte, our best Italian cookery writer.) Now return to the heat, add the ham if it's cooked and a little hot stock and cook gently, uncovered, stirring from time to time and adding more hot stock when necessary until the rice is cooked, about another 10 minutes or so, by which time you should have used just about 600 ml/1 pint/2½ cups liquid. If you like a looser consistency to your risotto, add a little more of the remaining hot stock. Check seasoning, remove the bay leaf, add the lemon juice. Remove from the heat, add the remaining butter and a good table-spoon of grated cheese, replace the lid and leave for 2 minutes for the butter and cheese to melt, then give the risotto a good beat with a wooden spoon to develop the traditional creamy texture. Finally stir in the chopped parsley and serve with more grated cheese.

ACCOMPANIMENTS: This dish can form a meal in itself or be served with a salad or green vegetable according to taste and appetite.

VARIATIONS: The variations on this risotto are endless, if not Italian: add tomatoes, olives, carrots, celery, etc., different herbs. Use bacon ends. Add left-over chicken or turkey instead of the ham. The risotto is an excellent way of using the odd bits of chicken left after sectioning a whole chicken, or use a breast of chicken, diced or thinly sliced. OR omit any meat and increase the mushrooms, adding several dried (after reconstituting) for extra flavour, and use a vegetable stock to make an excellent vegetarian dish, the soaking water from the mushrooms will do very well. If you omit the mushrooms as well, you are left with a classic risotto *bianco* that will go excellently with cold meats or can be eaten on its own.

COOK'S TIP: The flavour of this dish depends in large part on the stock used. Best of all is a really good chicken stock. Stock cubes will be too salty, so may the stock from the knuckle of ham. Lots of fresh herbs can help compensate for the lack of a good stock. This is one recipe where the rice should not be washed before cooking, the starch helps provide the risotto's typical creamy quality.

MICROWAVE OVEN: The microwave doesn't offer a great saving in time but the risotto needs less attention than it does if cooked over the stove, which releases time for other things. Place 2 tablespoons butter in a deep bowl, microwave on HIGH, uncovered, for 1 minute. Add the chopped onions, stir to coat and microwave, uncovered, on HIGH for 3 minutes. Add rice and stir to coat. Microwave, uncovered, on HIGH for 3 minutes. Stir in the ham, the sliced mushrooms, add the bay leaf and 600 ml/1 pint/2½ cups hot stock and microwave, uncovered, on HIGH for 8 minutes. Stir well and microwave again, uncovered, on HIGH for another 8 minutes. Then remove from oven and stand, uncovered, for 5 minutes while risotto finishes absorbing stock. Add further stock to loosen consistency if liked and check seasoning, adding salt and pepper if necessary, then add the last tablespoon butter and a tablespoon grated cheese, cover for a couple of minutes then give the risotto a good beat with a wooden spoon to develop the traditional creamy texture. Finally stir in the chopped parsley and serve with more grated cheese.

HERRING COBBLER

Fish is not the budget choice it used to be but there are still bargains to be had on the fishmonger's counter. Here herring fillets are combined with an oatmeal scone topping for a dish that provides energy against winter cold.

4 fillets of herring
1 tablespoon arachide/groundnut/peanut oil
medium sized onion, peeled and thinly sliced
Salt and freshly ground black pepper
2 tablespoons freshly chopped herbs including thyme, preferably lemon thyme
3 tablespoons dry cider

For Cobbler Topping:

50 g/2 oz/5 tablespoons high extraction rate flour such as Jordan's Country Cookbook
Pinch salt
½ teaspoon bicarbonate soda
1 teaspoon cream of tartar
50 g/2 oz/5 tablespoons medium oatmeal
25 g/1 oz/2 tablespoons butter
Approx. 6 tablespoons cold milk

Cut each herring fillet in three. Heat the oil and gently soften the onion without colouring. Layer the herring and the onion in a lightly oiled small gratin dish, seasoning and sprinkling with the herbs. Add the cider.

To make the cobbler topping: sift the flour with the salt and raising agents, mix in the oatmeal and rub in the butter. Mix with sufficient cold milk to make a soft dough. Place on a floured working surface and pat out to thickness of a medium-sized finger then use a pastry cutter or glass to cut into rounds. Arrange these on top of the herring and onion mixture, using the left-overs to make a suitable sized shape for the middle, brush with milk and bake immediately in a preheated oven at 220°C/425°F/Gas Mark 7 for 10 minutes, then lower heat to 180°C/350°F/Gas Mark 4 for a further 20 minutes.

ACCOMPANIMENTS: Green vegetable or salad.

TOWARDS TOMORROW: Double up on the scone mixture, divide into two before adding milk. To the reserved half, add 3 tablespoons plain flour, a tablespoon of sugar and a few raisins if liked, then keep in a plastic bag or small box in the fridge until scones for tea seem a good idea. The mixture will keep for 6–8 weeks. To use, mix to a soft dough with cold milk and cook on floured baking sheets in a preheated oven at 220°C/425°F/Gas Mark 7 for 10 minutes, or until risen and golden brown. Serve with butter or clotted cream and jam.

MACKEREL WITH APPLE

Like all oily fish, mackerel are extremely good for you and the fresher the mackerel, the better it tastes. This dish is particularly good in autumn, when apples are plentiful and crisp. Try to use the apple juice made from naturally pressed fruit, not from concentrate; it's more expensive but the flavour really is better.

300 ml/10 fl oz/generous cup apple juice
2 mackerel
A few fresh sage leaves
1 crisp eating apple, Cox's, Laxton's, Granny Smith or similar
Salt and freshly ground black pepper

Heat apple juice. Clean fish and remove heads if they are still on. Place a couple of sage leaves in the bottom of a gratin dish that will hold the fish nicely and place them on top. Core the apple and cut into thick segments. Slip these, skin side up, around the fish. When the apple juice is at boiling point, pour over the fish, it shouldn't quite cover it, season with salt and pepper and add another couple of sage leaves. Cover the dish with foil, place in a preheated oven at 190°C/375°F/Gas Mark 5 for approximately 20 minutes, or until the fish are just cooked (use the point of a sharp knife to ease the flesh away from the bone, if it clings, give the fish another few minutes but be careful not to overcook). Remove the tin foil before serving garnished with a sprig of fresh sage.

ACCOMPANIMENTS: Pasta or mashed potatoes with cabbage, sprouts or green beans.

VARIATIONS: Mackerel can be cooked the classical French way in half white wine and half water, omitting the apple and sage, when they taste very good cold. Or slash the side of each fish two or three times and grill, excellent with a gooseberry sauce.

MICROWAVE OVEN: Cut apple juice by half. Do not heat before pouring round fish and apple prepared as above. Cover dish tightly with cling film and microwave on HIGH for 4 minutes, allow to rest for 3 minutes before serving.

HUSS CASSEROLE

Huss is used here for a simple casserole that plays up the sweetness of the flesh.

350 g/12 oz huss, central bone removed and fish cut into 2.5 cm/1 inch pieces
A small head of fennel, trimmed and sliced, blanched in boiling water for 5 minutes, drained and refreshed in cold water
4 dried pears, thinly sliced
150 ml/5 fl oz/⅔ cup fish stock or blanching water from fennel
½ teaspoon anchovy essence
Salt and freshly ground black pepper

Place fish, blanched fennel and sliced pears in a small casserole dish. Mix the fish stock or blanched vegetable water with anchovy essence, season, bring to boil then pour over contents of casserole, cover and place in preheated oven at 190°C/375°F/Gas Mark 5 for 25 minutes, until just cooked. Garnish with fennel fronds before serving, there are usually a few peeking out of the stalk.

ACCOMPANIMENTS: Creamed potatoes and carrots or sprouts.

VARIATIONS: Substitute 4–5 sticks of celery for the fennel. Prepare and use in the same way.

MICROWAVE OVEN: Prepare as above but omit the heating of stock or blanching water. Cover dish tightly with cling film and microwave on HIGH for 4 minutes.

QUICHES

A small quiche is very easy and quick to make, usually inexpensive, and the possibilities for fillings are endless. Just remember that only the pastry and the custard will get cooked in the oven, anything else has to be edible just as it is, so have other ingredients precooked.

MUSHROOM AND PARSLEY QUICHE

Half quantity basic shortcrust pastry (see recipe in BACK TO BASICS section on page 274)
1 tablespoon arachide/groundnut/peanut oil
225 g/8 oz/4 cups mushrooms, sliced
1 clove garlic, chopped
1 medium sized egg, lightly beaten
125 ml/4 fl oz/½ cup milk or single cream
2 tablespoons parsley
Salt and freshly ground black pepper

Use pastry to line a 18 cm/7 inch flan tin, or two individual flan tins, and bake blind at 190°C/375°F/Gas Mark 5 for 20 minutes if you have time as this will give a crisper finish. Heat the oil and sauté mushrooms with the chopped garlic until tender and juices have been evaporated. Place in flan. Add milk or cream to egg and mix thoroughly. Add the chopped parsley, season to taste and pour over the mushrooms in the flan. Bake in preheated oven at 190°C/375°F/Gas Mark 5 for approximately 30 minutes, until custard is set (test by slipping the point of a sharp knife into the centre, it should emerge clean) and golden on top. The flan is best eaten warm.

ACCOMPANIMENTS: A green salad would be delicious but any vegetable makes a good accompaniment.

VARIATIONS: 1) Use 2–3 leeks, cleaned well, sliced and cooked in water then drained and refreshed in cold water. Squeeze all liquid out with hands then arrange in bottom of flan. Add custard made as above with 1 medium sized egg and 125 ml/4 fl oz/½ cup milk or single cream, seasoned to taste. Finish with 2–3 tablespoons grated cheese, Cheddar or Caerphilly, and bake as above. 2) Slice and cook a small onion in a little oil, add some chopped bacon and a few mushrooms, arrange in flan and pour over custard as above. Grated cheese can also be added. 3) Use some smoked salmon off-cuts, grate a little nutmeg over the custard and add some chopped parsley.

COOK'S TIP: If you haven't time to bake the flan case before filling, pop a baking sheet into the oven when you put it on. Placing the flan straight on to the hot sheet will help prevent a soggy pastry bottom.

TOWARDS TOMORROW: Make a different quiche with the other half of the pastry or use for a fruit pie or tart.

IT'S NOT AWFUL (OFFAL)

I try hard to be tolerant of people who say they can't eat offal but it is difficult when I find it all so delicious! When you are cooking for two it is easy to check if the other likes it as well, as the numbers being fed go up so does the likelihood of someone saying "no". It's a bonus that most offal is cheap, the exception being calf's liver, which, if you can find it, is so good it's worth its premium price. And check around, some butchers charge much less than others.

Both liver and kidneys cook very quickly, especially when sliced thinly, ideal for instant meals. Rice and pasta can provide accompaniments that are very simple to cook and a small green salad or a few green beans can provide a fuss free accompaniment.

KIDNEYS IN MUSTARD AND ORANGE SAUCE

This is one of my favourite recipes, ideal to make in small quantities.

2 tablespoons oil or 25 g/1 oz butter
6–8 lamb's kidneys or 4–6 pig's kidneys, membrane removed, kidneys halved and cores removed, pig's kidneys cut in half again
1 small onion, chopped
2 tablespoons medium sherry
Salt and freshly ground black pepper
5 tablespoons double cream OR yoghurt mixed with ½ teaspoon cornflour
Grated rind ½ orange mixed with dessertspoon grainy mustard
Garnish: Segments from 1 orange released from all pith and membrane

Heat half the oil or butter and brown the kidneys on both sides. Remove from pan and place in colander over a plate. Add more oil or butter if necessary and soften onion. Add sherry, bring to boil, season and add the cream or yoghurt and mustard mixture, stirring to incorporate all into a smooth sauce. Add the kidneys and their juices and simmer very gently for about 5 minutes. Kidneys should still give slightly when pressed. Check seasoning, garnish with orange segments and serve immediately.

ACCOMPANIMENTS: Pasta – tagliatelle or spirals – and a green salad.

VARIATIONS: Use lamb's liver cut into strips but simmer in sauce only long enough to warm liver through.

CHINESE LIVER AND KIDNEY

This is a simple but quite elegant dish with a subtle flavour.

225 g/8 oz lamb's liver
4 lamb's kidneys
1 tablespoon rice wine or dry sherry
1 tablespoon soy sauce
½ tablespoon grapeseed or arachide/ groundnut/peanut oil
1 clove garlic crushed with little salt
6–8 spring onions, trimmed down to white and light green parts and split in half lengthways
100 g/4 oz/2 cups very fresh mushrooms, sliced (oyster would be best if available)
100 g/4 oz fine beans, trimmed, blanched in boiling water for 1 minute, drained, refreshed in cold water and drained again
Salt and freshly ground black pepper
Garnish: Chopped parsley

Trim liver and kidneys, removing all membranes, and cut into thin strips. Mix together the sherry and soy sauce, pour over the liver and kidneys, toss well then leave to marinate for 20 minutes. Drain the meat, reserving the marinade.

Heat the oil in a wok or frying pan, add the meat and garlic and stir-fry for 2 minutes. Remove to a colander sitting on a plate in a warm place.

Clean out your pan, add a little more oil then the mushrooms, season and stir-fry until tender. Add the beans, stir to mix and heat through. Remove from pan and keep warm. Add the marinade and the juices that have drained out of the meat, then the cooked meat and stir-fry for 1 minute to heat through. Check the seasoning then place meat on a dish or two plates, surround with the mushroom and bean mixture, garnish with parsley and serve immediately.

ACCOMPANIMENTS: Pasta or rice. A salad would go well but is not necessary.

VARIATIONS: If you have fresh runner beans in the garden, or dwarf French beans, they can be substituted for the fine beans.

COOK'S TIP: Make sure the mushrooms are really fresh and pale or they will exude dark juices that could spoil the look of the dish.

LIVER STIR-FRY WITH GARLIC AND GINGER

A quick dish that has a lot of flavour.

1 tablespoon arachide/groundnut/peanut oil
1 clove garlic, sliced into thin slivers
1.25 cm/½ inch piece of peeled root ginger, cut into fine slivers
350 g/12 oz lamb's liver, trimmed of membrane and cut into strips
Salt and freshly ground black pepper

Heat oil gently, add the garlic and stir-fry for a moment or two, then add the slivers of ginger and continue stir-frying over the gentle heat for a couple of minutes. Raise heat slightly, add the strips of liver and stir-fry for about 1 minute until they are browned on all sides but still tender. Season to taste then serve immediately.

ACCOMPANIMENTS: Rice and a green salad.

COOK'S TIP: The garlic should not be allowed to brown or it may become bitter. Don't overcook the liver as it will become hard and unpleasant, it should still be slightly pink in the middle.

LIVER STIR-FRY WITH LEMON AND HERBS

This is the most simple of recipes but the result is very fresh and appealing. If you can obtain calf's liver, the result is even better but it is good with lamb's liver as well.

Knob butter or tablespoon olive oil
350 g/12 oz calf's liver or lamb's liver, trimmed of all membrane and cut into thin strips
1 tablespoon freshly squeezed lemon juice
1 tablespoon freshly chopped parsley
Salt and freshly ground black pepper

Heat butter or oil, add the liver strips and stir-fry for 1 minute until the liver is lightly browned all over. Remove to a warm dish, deglaze the pan with the lemon juice then add the chopped parsley and season to taste, replace the meat in the pan, toss together briefly then serve immediately.

ACCOMPANIMENTS: Rice and a tomato salad or green vegetable.

LIVER SAUTÉ WITH MUSHROOM, BACON AND HERBS

Another variation on stir-fried liver, the combination goes together very well.

4 rashers streaky bacon, cut into strips
About 1 tablespoon olive oil
100 g/4 oz/2 cups fresh mushrooms, sliced
225 g/8 oz lamb's liver, cut into thin strips
2 tablespoons freshly squeezed lemon juice
1 tablespoon freshly chopped herbs (parsley, marjoram, savory and thyme, or similar)
Salt and freshly ground black pepper

Sauté the bacon in a frying pan, remove and keep warm. Heat a tablespoon of oil in the pan and sauté the mushrooms until all moisture has been evaporated and mushrooms are tender. Add these to the bacon. If necessary, add a little more oil to the pan then stir-fry the liver until just browned all over then add to the bacon and mushrooms. Deglaze the pan with the lemon juice, add the chopped herbs, season to taste (with the herbs you may not want to add much, if any, salt and pepper), add the bacon, mushrooms and liver, stir together briefly then serve immediately.

ACCOMPANIMENTS: Brown rice. A green vegetable can also be added if liked but is not really necessary.

VARIATIONS: The mixture of herbs can be anything that is available or attracts but go easy on the strongly flavoured herbs such as thyme, sage and mint.

LIVER WITH ONION JAM

Liver and onions are natural partners. For this dish the onion has been allowed to cook down to a sweet jam, making the most of its natural sugar. The jam goes very well also with pork dishes.

50 g/2 oz/4 tablespoons butter
225 g/8 oz onion (1 large onion), peeled and sliced very thinly
Salt
2 tablespoons sherry or balsamic vinegar
1 tablespoon demerara sugar
350 g/12 oz calf's or lamb's liver, trimmed of any membrane and cut into flattish slices
Freshly ground black pepper
Garnish: Chopped parsley

Melt two-thirds of the butter in a heavy based pan, add the thinly sliced onion and a little salt and cook gently for some 30 minutes until soft and golden. Add the vinegar and sugar, raise the heat a little and cook until nicely brown and "jammy", about 5–10 minutes. Keep warm whilst cooking the liver.

Heat the remaining butter in a clean frying pan; as soon as it is foaming, add the liver and cook for a minute or two on each side, according to the thickness of the slices. The liver should be well browned but still give when pressed lightly. Season to taste, garnish with parsley and serve immediately with the onion jam.

ACCOMPANIMENTS: Mashed potatoes and a green vegetable.

VARIATIONS: Whole, peeled shallots or baby onions can be prepared in the same way as the sliced onion and are equally good.

COOK'S TIP: To slice the onion, peel it leaving the root in place. Cut the onion in half through the root, then place the cut side flat on a chopping board and use a sharp knife to slice finely, keeping the flat of the blade against the knuckles of the hand holding the onion, moving the hand back gradually so the slices are automatically measured.

MICROWAVE OVEN: Only cook the onion in the microwave, the liver is best sautéd over conventional heat as above. Place sliced onion in dish with ⅔ of the butter, cover tightly with cling film and microwave on HIGH for 8 minutes. Mix together the vinegar and sugar well, stir into the onion, cover tightly again with cling film and microwave on HIGH for 6 minutes, stirring halfway through, until caramelised. Remove from oven.

TOWARDS TOMORROW: Make double the amount of onion jam or caramelised shallots/baby onions and keep half to serve with simply grilled pork chops or cold roast pork.

LAMBS' HEARTS STUFFED WITH APPLE AND APRICOT

Hearts have much to recommend them, taste and economy being two great advantages, but they do require a certain amount of preparation, this is quite quickly done when only two are required. They also need slow cooking, for which a pressure cooker is ideal. The bonus with hearts is that they come with a ready made pocket for stuffing, a definite challenge to the creative cook. Try the following two recipes then get going on some ideas of your own.

2 lambs' hearts

Stuffing:

4 ready-to-eat apricots, chopped

1 small apple, cored and chopped

2 tablespoons brown breadcrumbs

1 tablespoon freshly chopped parsley

2 tablespoons dry cider

Salt and freshly ground black pepper

Approx. 225 ml/7½ fl oz/1 cup dry cider

2 tablespoons yoghurt or cream

Garnish: Chopped parsley

To prepare the hearts, shave off the fat lying on the outside of the hearts and trim out the tubes and gristle from the open ends. Then mix together the stuffing ingredients, seasoning to taste, and push into the heart cavities.

Lay the stuffed hearts in a small, deep dish, heat sufficient cider to cover them to boiling point and pour over, cover the dish and place in a preheated oven at 150°C/300°F/Gas Mark 2 for approximately 2 hours, until really tender, testing with the point of a sharp knife. Some of the stuffing will escape into the cooking liquid. Remove the cooked hearts and place in a suitable serving dish. Keep them warm.

Sieve the liquid with its odd bits of debris, check seasoning, reheat if necessary and reduce if liked. Then pour over the hearts, swirl over the yoghurt or cream, garnish with the chopped parsley and serve.

ACCOMPANIMENTS: Creamed or new potatoes and a simple vegetable.

VARIATIONS: Try a different stuffing, such as chopped celery, a little cooked rice and freshly chopped lemon thyme or chervil. For cooking liquid, use a small tin of liquidised canned tomatoes with a dash of Worcestershire sauce.

PRESSURE COOKER: Prepare as above, place stuffed hearts with cider in bottom of cooker, cover, bring to HIGH pressure, cook for 20 minutes then reduce pressure quickly and finish as above.

TOWARDS TOMORROW: 1) Make a little more than double the stuffing and use the remainder to stuff green peppers, blanching the peppers in boiling water for 3–4 minutes before stuffing. They will then require about 40 minutes cooking at 180°C/350°F/Gas Mark 4. Toasted pine nuts can be added for a little difference. 2) Use the oven to make one of the casserole dishes (see BUDGET BEATERS section) at the same time, then reheat tomorrow either in the oven at 180°C/350°F/Gas Mark 4 for 30–40 minutes, or the microwave on REHEAT or 80% for 15 minutes or until bubbling hot.

LAMBS' TONGUES PIQUANT

A whole ox tongue is too much for two people to work their way through but little lambs' tongues are perfect for small quantities. Again, like hearts, they require a few minutes preparation but are well worth the trouble. The following recipe is particularly tasty.

2–4 lambs' tongues, depending on size
1 medium sized onion, peeled and trimmed
1 carrot, scrubbed and trimmed
1 bay leaf
6 allspice berries
6 black peppercorns
Salt
2 tablespoons olive oil

1 large onion, peeled and finely sliced
2 tablespoons flour
225 ml/7½ fl oz/1 cup of the tongue cooking liquid
2 tablespoons red wine vinegar
2 teaspoons demerara sugar
1 tablespoon sultanas
Little freshly squeezed lemon juice
Freshly ground black pepper
Garnish: 1 dessertspoon toasted flaked almonds

To prepare and cook lambs' tongues: soak the tongues for several hours then place in fresh cold water and bring to the boil. Drain immediately. Heat enough water to cover tongues with the onion, carrot, bay leaf, allspice berries and peppercorns and a little salt. When at boiling point add the parboiled tongues, lower the heat to simmering point and cook very gently until really tender, about 1 hour. If using tongues immediately, skin and pick out the little bones and gristle. If using later, they can cool in the liquid but remove skin and bones whilst warm, it will be easier than when they are cold.

For piquant sauce: heat the oil, add the sliced onion and cook gently until soft and golden. Stir in the flour, cook for a moment or two then make a lump-free sauce by gradually stirring in the tongue stock.

In a separate pan heat the vinegar with the sugar then, stirring constantly, allow it to boil until the mixture is syrupy. Add to the sauce, stirring in well. Add the sultanas, season with lemon juice, salt and pepper, the sauce should be nicely piquant.

To serve, slit each lamb's tongue in half lengthways, place in a warm dish and pour over the sauce. If the tongues are not already hot, cover the dish with tin foil or a lid and warm through in a preheated oven at 180°C/350°F/Gas Mark 4 for 25 minutes. Before serving, garnish with the toasted almonds.

ACCOMPANIMENTS: Creamed potatoes or pasta with a side salad or a simple, crisp vegetable, such as beans or mange tout.

VARIATIONS: Prepare a mushroom and onion sauce with 1 large onion, finely chopped, cooked gently in 25 g/1 oz/2 tablespoons butter, then add 175 g/6 oz/3 cups sliced mushrooms and continue cooking until moisture evaporated and mushrooms tender. Add 2 tablespoons sweet vermouth and season with salt and freshly ground black pepper. Pour over the tongues sliced lengthways, sprinkle with 2 tablespoons grated Parmesan and reheat in a preheated oven at 180°C/350°F/Gas Mark 4 for 25 minutes.

PRESSURE COOKER: Use to cook tongues. Prepare and parboil as above. Place with liquid and flavourings in cooker, bring to HIGH pressure and cook for 15 minutes then remove from heat. Continue recipe as above.

MICROWAVE OVEN: Cooking the tongues in the microwave is not recommended but the onions can be microwaved, with the oil or butter (melt it first), covered for 4 minutes on HIGH. If making the piquant sauce in the microwave, substitute cornflour for the flour in the recipe. Lambs' Tongues Piquant can be successfully reheated in the microwave: cover tightly with cling film and microwave on REHEAT or 80% for 12 minutes or until bubbling hot.

TOWARDS TOMORROW: Cook double quantity tongues and use other half for the following recipe: TONGUE EN CROÛTE.

TONGUE EN CROÛTE

The softness of the tongue flesh contrasts nicely with the crisp pastry in this recipe.

1 small knob of butter
1 small onion, peeled, trimmed and finely chopped
Few button mushrooms, quartered
2–4 lambs' tongues, cooked as above, approx. 225 g/8 oz, diced
1 hard-boiled egg, peeled and diced
Salt and freshly ground black pepper
1 dessertspoon freshly chopped parsley
2 tablespoons sweet vermouth
Small packet puff pastry
Little milk or beaten egg for glazing pastry

Melt the butter and gently cook the onion until soft and golden. Add the mushrooms, increase the heat a little and cook until any mushroom liquid has been absorbed and mushrooms are tender. Mix with the diced tongues and hard-boiled egg. Season to taste, add the chopped parsley and the vermouth.

Roll out the pastry and make either one large or two small packets with the tongue mixture, damping the edges of the pastry and sealing well. Cut steam hole in top, decorate if liked with trimmings. Brush with milk or egg glaze, chill for at least 30 minutes. Cook in preheated oven at 220°C/425°F/ Gas Mark 7 for 25 to 30 minutes until well risen and golden.

ACCOMPANIMENTS: Leeks or a puréed vegetable such as carrots or spinach would go well. Potatoes are optional. Salad would be excellent.

VARIATIONS: Instead of puff pastry, use a double layer of filo brushed with melted butter or oil. Turn the oven down a little after about ten minutes, when the packets are nicely golden, so the pastry doesn't overbrown.

COOK'S TIP: Use any left-over pieces of puff pastry to make cheese straws: Pile up trimmings neatly on top of each other, roll out in rectangle to a thickness of a 10p piece, brush with egg mixed with a dash of Worcestershire sauce and a pinch of cayenne pepper, sprinkle with grated cheese, either Cheddar or Parmesan or a mixture, fold pastry in two, roll out again slightly, repeat egg brushing and sprinkling with grated cheese, pressing into pastry slightly. Cut into straws or triangles, chill for at least 30 minutes, bake at 220°C/425°F/Gas Mark 7 for approximately 10 minutes, until risen and golden. Serve whilst warm. NB: If these pastry nibbles are frozen uncooked, they can be popped into the oven straight from the freezer and provided freshly baked within 10 to 15 minutes. Very useful!

OX KIDNEY IN WINE WITH BACON

*Start recipe 2 hours before serving
This recipe is adapted from one in Elizabeth David's *French Provincial Cooking*, the surprisingly short cooking time produces a very succulent dish. Soaking the ox kidneys before preparing the dish softens their strong flavour.

225 g/8 oz ox kidneys, soaked in water for 2 hours
2 tablespoons butter
4 rashers smoked bacon, cut into strips
50 g/2 oz/1 cup button mushrooms, sliced
Salt and freshly ground black pepper
2 tablespoons brandy, warmed
6 tablespoons good red wine
6 tablespoons chicken or beef stock
4 tablespoons double cream

Drain the kidneys, trim out any membrane then cut the kidneys into slices about 1.25 cm/½ inch thick. Heat the butter until it is foaming, add the kidney and bacon and stir-fry for a moment or two. Then add the mushrooms and season. Pour over the warmed brandy, light and allow the spirit to burn itself out, shaking the pan until it does. Add the wine, bring to the boil, then add the stock.

Pour everything into a small casserole dish, cover and cook in a preheated oven at 150°C/300°F/Gas Mark 2 for approximately 35–40 minutes, until kidney is tender.

Then bring the cream to the boil in a small frying pan, pour in the kidney sauce, stir well and reduce over a high heat to a good consistency. Check seasoning and pour back over the kidneys, bacon and mushrooms.

ACCOMPANIMENTS: Croûtons fried in butter or olive oil, rice or creamed potatoes, a side salad or a fresh green vegetable.

COOK'S TIP: Keep back a glass of red wine when you are drinking a nice bottle, tip it into a small empty tonic or similar bottle that will hold it without much air, stopper tightly and it should keep well for several days, ready to be used for a dish such as this.

NO MEAT NO FISH

Vegetable meals can be completely satisfying and easier on the budget than fish or meat and there are many good reasons for lessening our dependence on animal protein. Their one drawback is the time required for preparation but when there are only two to be catered for, this is not a great problem and chopping and slicing can be very relaxing.

BAKED COURGETTE WITH PINE NUT AND RAISIN STUFFING

Many vegetables can be successfully stuffed and courgettes are perfect to use. Choose slightly larger courgettes than you would normally like to use for sautéing or steaming, they produce a robust and tasty dish. The stuffing will serve for other vegetables as well.

2 largish courgettes
1 tablespoon olive oil
1 smallish onion, peeled and finely chopped
Approx. 100 g/4 oz/1 cup cooked brown rice (if cooking from raw, use half that quantity)
2 tomatoes, peeled, deseeded and flesh chopped
Salt and freshly ground black pepper
2 tablespoons raisins, soaked in little white wine or vegetable stock
2 tablespoons pine nuts, sautéd until golden in little arachide/groundnut/peanut oil
Chopped basil, preferably fresh
150 ml/5 fl oz/⅔ cup white wine or stock or water

Drop the whole courgettes in boiling water and blanch for 5–10 minutes, according to size. This helps cut down cooking time in the oven. Immediately after blanching, drain and refresh in cold water and pat dry with kitchen paper. Halve and carefully scoop out flesh from middle, leaving a good casing. Chop the flesh, removing some of the seed part if you like, and reserve.

Heat the oil and gently cook the onion until transparent and golden. Add the chopped courgette flesh, plus dried basil if fresh isn't available, raise

137

heat and cook about 5 minutes until tender. Add the brown rice, tomato, seasoning, raisins and pine nuts and stir all well together. Check seasoning and add chopped fresh basil. Pile into the courgette shells.

Place the stuffed courgettes in an ovenproof dish, pour the wine, stock or water around, cover the whole dish with tin foil and bake in preheated oven at 190°C/375°F/Gas Mark 5 for approximately 40 minutes until cooked through.

ACCOMPANIMENTS: Really good bread and perhaps a salad. Noodles would also go well.

VARIATIONS: The tomatoes can be omitted or a teaspoon of tomato purée used instead, which produces a stronger effect. Breadcrumbs can replace the rice. Grated or diced cheese (Cheddar, Gruyère or feta) or tofu, etc., can also be added. Fresh but not dried parsley or thyme and oregano can be substituted for the basil. Stuffing can also be used for peppers (increase amount of rice slightly to compensate for loss of courgette flesh) and large tomatoes (omit the blanching, leave on skins and sieve the inside of the tomatoes into the onion and rice mixture. Cut the baking time to approximately 20 minutes).

MICROWAVE OVEN: Blanch courgettes as above. Mix together onion and oil, cover tightly and microwave on HIGH for 2 minutes. Add the chopped courgette flesh from the middle of the vegetables, cover and microwave on HIGH for 2 minutes. Mix together all ingredients except the wine, stock or water, and pile into the courgette shells. Arrange shells in a circle round a dish or plate, add 3 tablespoons of white wine, stock or water in the middle, cover tightly with cling film and microwave on HIGH for 7 minutes.

STUFFED CHAYOTE

A rather different type of stuffed vegetable and slightly unusual is the chayote, one of a whole army of gourds that offer tender flesh of subtle flavour and repay careful handling. The chayote is, I think, one of the nicest gourds. Also known as chocho and christophene, it is a native of Central America, pale green and almost heart-shaped and comes either smooth skinned or ridged, with crisper flesh than that of most gourds. The following recipe is for stuffing as a main dish but it can also provide a good accompaniment to plainly cooked meat, a grilled chop perhaps, or sliced cold meat. Chayotes can also be sliced and briefly, very briefly, boiled or

138

sautéd, then dressed in butter, oil or a sauce. The flat seed is also edible, usually treated as a cook's perk.

2 chayote
1 tablespoon olive oil
1 medium sized onion, peeled and finely chopped
2 tomatoes, peeled, deseeded and flesh chopped
1 dessertspoon freshly chopped mixed herbs (preferably lemon thyme, marjoram and basil)
Salt and freshly ground black pepper
2 tablespoons fresh breadcrumbs (preferably wholewheat)
4 tablespoons grated Gruyère or Cheddar cheese

Boil chayote whole in salted water for 12–15 minutes, until just tender. Drain and refresh under cold water, drain again and pat dry. Cut in half and remove the insides leaving a firm shell. Chop the scooped out flesh, including the flat seed if you haven't already eaten it.

Heat the oil and cook onion gently until transparent and golden. Then add the chopped chayote flesh, the tomato, herbs and seasoning to taste. Stir well together and cook for a minute or two. Divide stuffing between the four vegetable halves. Mix the breadcrumbs with the grated cheese and use to cover each chayote half. Place stuffed halves in lightly greased ovenproof dish and bake at 200°C/400°F/Gas Mark 6 for 15 to 20 minutes, until top is golden brown.

VARIATIONS: Tofu, diced, can be added for a more substantial dish. Cashew or pine nuts will help the protein element and add an interesting crunch to the dish. Or, if the animal meat aspect is not important, diced ham, bacon or cooked meats. The same recipe can be used to stuff marrow, courgettes, bell peppers, etc., adjusting the initial boiling time according to size and condition of vegetable. The stuffing can be extended by adding breadcrumbs.

MICROWAVE OVEN: Cut chayotes in half, place side by side on plate, making a neat arrangement, thinner ends next to fatter ends, add a little water, cover with cling film and microwave on HIGH for 7–8 minutes, till just tender. Remove, drain, refresh in cold water. Add chopped onion to oil in a bowl, cover with cling film, microwave on HIGH for 2 minutes. Cut chayote in half and remove insides leaving a firm shell. Chop the scooped out flesh, including the flat seed if you haven't already eaten it, mix with onion, tomato, herbs and seasoning to taste, stirring together well. Divide stuffing between the four vegetables halves. Mix the breadcrumbs with the grated cheese and use to cover each chayote half. To reheat: arrange in suitable dish as before, add a tablespoon water, cover tightly with cling film and microwave on REHEAT or 80% for 7 minutes (the cheese will not brown but brown breadcrumbs will help the look, or you can flash the dish under a grill at the end of cooking).

VEGETABLE CURRY

It seems to me impractical to cook a number of different dishes to serve two people. This curry, therefore, mixes together more vegetables than I think a genuine Indian dish would since usually they would be divided between a number of different dishes. The flavour is excellent (it is adapted from a recipe by Madhur Jaffrey) and the vegetables can be changed according to availability and personal preference.

2 tablespoons arachide/groundnut/peanut oil
1 medium sized onion, peeled and chopped
½ teaspoon cumin seeds
2 dried red chilli peppers, crushed (remove seeds if you prefer your curry mild)
1 tablespoon grated fresh ginger, peel the ginger before grating
2 fat cloves garlic, peeled and reduced to a purée with a little salt then mixed with the grated ginger to a paste
1 teaspoon ground coriander
1 teaspoon ground turmeric
1 medium sized potato, peeled and diced
1 small aubergine, diced
Small tin peeled tomatoes, chopped, and juices
½ teaspoon salt
Freshly ground black pepper

100 g/4 oz/1 cup cauliflower florets
Few mushrooms, quartered if large
1 tablespoon freshly squeezed lemon juice
Garnish: 1 tablespoon chopped fresh parsley (or coriander leaves if they are available)

Heat the oil and cook the onion gently until transparent. Raise heat slightly and add the cumin seeds, stirring for a moment or two, then add the crushed chilli pepper. Let it darken then add the ginger and garlic paste and stir over the heat for a few moments. Add the coriander and turmeric and stir for another few moments. Then add the potato and aubergine and cook gently, stirring, for a few minutes, until they have absorbed some of the spices and become well coated with the onion. Add the chopped tomato and the juices, season, stir, bring to the boil then add cauliflower, lower heat and simmer gently until vegetables almost cooked. Add the mushroom and continue cooking until all vegetables cooked. Check seasoning, add the lemon juice and serve garnished with the chopped parsley (or coriander).

ACCOMPANIMENTS: Rice, plainly boiled or cooked with raisins, and one or two of the following: chopped apple tossed in a little lemon juice, sliced banana, dry roasted peanuts, raisins (if not included in the rice), mango chutney, pickles of any sort.

VARIATIONS: Other vegetables which can be used: to be added at start of cooking, as for the potato and aubergine: carrots, turnips, kohlrabi, celery. To be added at the second stage of cooking, as for mushrooms: beans, sweet peppers, broccoli florets, peas, mange tout.

MICROWAVE OVEN: Place oil and onion in suitable sized casserole dish, cover tightly and microwave on HIGH for 2 minutes. Uncover, add all the spices, stir well and microwave, uncovered, on HIGH for 30 seconds. Add potato and aubergine, stir well with the spices. Add the tomato and seasonings, stir again, cover tightly and microwave on HIGH for 8 minutes. Uncover, add cauliflower and mushrooms, cover again, microwave on HIGH for 4 minutes. Allow to stand for 4 minutes, uncover, check seasoning, add the lemon juice and serve as above.

TOWARDS TOMORROW: Cook double quantities. Next day reheat second half of vegetable curry and serve with: 3 tablespoons grated cucumber mixed with thick yoghurt (if preparing ahead of time, degorge the cucumber by placing in a colander with a little salt, a saucer on top, and leaving to drain for 20 minutes before rinsing and patting dry). Spoon the cucumber and yoghurt on top of the curry before serving and garnish with more chopped parsley (or coriander).

OKRA WITH CELERY AND TOMATO

Okra are those slim green pods sometimes called lady's fingers because of their shape, belonging to female gardeners no doubt! Cut them and they exude a stickiness that can provide a good consistency in a dish like this. In the southern United States okra are an essential item in the gumbo range of dishes.

1 tablespoon light vegetable oil
1 small onion, finely chopped
1 clove garlic, peeled and crushed
2 stalks celery cut into lengths about the same size as the okra and blanched in boiling water for 5 minutes
225 g/8 oz okra, washed, patted dry and stalks trimmed
Small tin chopped or peeled tomatoes
Salt and freshly ground black pepper
Garnish: Little fresh basil or chopped parsley

Heat oil, add onion and garlic, cook gently until softened and transparent. Add blanched celery, the okra and tomatoes, salt and pepper, bring to the boil then cover, lower heat and simmer 15–20 minutes until okra is tender. Check seasoning and serve garnished with torn basil leaves or chopped parsley.

ACCOMPANIMENTS: Pasta and a green salad.

MICROWAVE OVEN: Place onion and garlic with oil in bowl, cover tightly with cling film and microwave on HIGH for 2 minutes. Add tomatoes, cover tightly and microwave on HIGH for 3 minutes. Uncover carefully, add okra and celery, re-cover tightly with cling film and microwave on HIGH for 7 minutes, stirring halfway through cooking. Leave to stand for 2 minutes, before adding basil or parsley and serving.

MARROW WITH GARLIC, ONION AND MUSHROOM SAUCE

If you grow courgettes, it is almost impossible to keep track of all the upcoming little vegetables before some swell into young marrows. Far too fibrous and flavourful to cook as courgette, they can be turned into a variety of successful dishes, such as this one. Don't substitute fresh mushrooms for the dried, they will not have nearly as much flavour.

3 tablespoons olive oil
10 g/⅓ oz/3 tablespoons dried ceps (mushrooms), soaked in boiling water for 45 minutes, drained (soaking water reserved) and chopped
2 cloves garlic, 1 peeled and finely chopped, 1 peeled and bruised
1 medium sized onion, peeled and finely chopped
2 tablespoons flour
150 ml/5 fl oz/⅔ cup milk plus 75 ml/2½ fl oz/5 tablespoons water mushrooms were soaked in
Salt and freshly ground black pepper
350 g/12 oz marrow, peeled and cut into large dice
Garnish: Little chopped parsley or lemon thyme

Heat two tablespoons of the olive oil in a frying pan, add the chopped mushrooms, the chopped clove of garlic and the onion and cook gently for about 20 minutes, until soft and tender. Add the flour, stir in well and cook together for a couple of minutes. Then gradually add the milk to make a lump-free sauce (it can't quite be classed as "smooth" because of the vegetables). Bring to the boil, stirring all the time, season to taste then reduce the heat so the sauce hardly simmers while you cook the marrow.

Heat the remaining tablespoon of oil with the bruised clove of garlic, then add the diced marrow and stir-fry until the vegetable looks transparent and is tender. Remove the garlic, season to taste, place in a warm serving dish, check the seasoning of the sauce then pour it over the marrow, garnish with the chopped herb and serve.

ACCOMPANIMENTS: New potatoes tossed in olive oil and a little grated lemon peel would be nice, so would almost any salad.

143

VARIATIONS: Courgettes can replace the marrow, they will need a little less cooking and taste particularly delicious. Add chopped tomato to the sauce just before pouring over the marrow. Add grated cheese to the top of the dish and brown under a grill before serving.

MICROWAVE OVEN: Place 2 tablespoons oil, the mushrooms, the chopped clove of garlic and onion in large bowl, cover tightly with cling film, microwave on HIGH for 5 minutes. Replace the flour with 1 table-spoon cornflour, stir into the onion, stir in the milk, re-cover tightly, microwave on HIGH for 2 minutes, uncover, stir well, re-cover, microwave on HIGH again for 1 more minute or until bubbling hot and lightly thickened. Check seasoning, leave covered on the side. To cook the marrow, place the sliced vegetable in a suitable sized dish, add 3 table-spoons water and the bruised clove of garlic, cover tightly with cling film and microwave on HIGH for 5 minutes. Allow to stand for 2 minutes then drain off any excess liquid, pour over the sauce and serve.

TOWARDS TOMORROW: Make double quantity of sauce and use next day with pasta, it would make a very good lasagne, the pasta layered with fresh mushrooms sliced and sautéd in a little more olive oil and topped with the sauce. OR process into a soup with additional milk, garnish with freshly fried croûtons.

FLAGEOLET GRATIN WITH CELERY AND MUSHROOMS

This recipe uses a tin of flageolet beans, making it quick and simple, but any soaked and cooked dried beans, such as haricot, butter or flageolet, can be used instead. You will need about 300 ml/ 10 fl oz/generous cup cooked beans. The cream makes this dish utterly delicious but the same quantity of a white sauce (see BASIC BÉCHAMEL sauce in the SAUCY IDEAS section on page 188) can be substituted if you prefer, have it of coating consistency.

½ standard tin flageolet beans or similar (approx. ¾ cup drained beans)

3 stalks celery, trimmed and sliced, blanched for 3 minutes, drained, refreshed and drained well

300 g/10 oz/5 cups mushrooms, halved, or quartered if large, oyster or brown button preferably but white button will do. If using field mushrooms, see COOK'S TIP below

| *Salt and freshly ground black pepper* |
| *½ teaspoon chopped fresh lemon thyme leaves, or parsley* |
| *150 ml/5 fl oz/⅔ cup double (heavy) cream* |
| *3 tablespoons fresh brown breadcrumbs* |
| *3 tablespoons grated hard cheese, Caerphilly goes well* |

Mix together the beans, blanched celery and the mushrooms. Place in a greased gratin dish. Season and scatter over the lemon thyme or parsley then pour over the cream, or white sauce. Mix together the cheese and the breadcrumbs, use to cover the top of the dish and place in a preheated oven at 190°C/375°F/Gas Mark 5 for 40 minutes.

ACCOMPANIMENTS: Noodles tossed in olive oil would go well, so do new or creamed potatoes. A green salad is also good.

VARIATIONS: Skinned, deseeded and sliced tomatoes can be used instead of mushrooms or as well as.

COOK'S TIP: Field mushrooms have lots of flavour but also give off large quantities of liquid. If you want to use these, thickly slice, cook rapidly in a little butter or oil until all the juices are evaporated then add to the gratin.

MICROWAVE OVEN: Mix blanched celery with mushrooms, beans and thyme, stir in cream or sauce, place in a shallow dish and microwave, tightly covered, on HIGH for 8 minutes. Uncover carefully, mix cheese and breadcrumbs together, brown under a hot grill and serve.

TOWARDS TOMORROW: Use other half of beans with a parsley sauce or as part of a salad.

POTATO, LEEK AND CELERIAC CASSEROLE

A warming winter dish, this. The pungent leek goes well with the two root vegetables, celeriac adding extra flavour and the parsley brightening the dish both with its colour and flavour.

1 medium sized potato, peeled and sliced
2–3 leeks, depending on size, trimmed, white and pale green parts thinly sliced, blanched in boiling water for 1 minute then drained, refreshed in cold water and squeezed dry
1 medium sized celeriac, peeled, halved and thinly sliced
Salt and freshly ground black pepper
2 tablespoons freshly chopped parsley
300 ml/10 fl oz/generous cup of vegetable stock (either from a cube, homemade or from the previous day's vegetable cooking)
Garnish: Some small sprigs of parsley

Grease a small casserole dish then layer the sliced potatoes, leeks and celeriac, seasoning with salt, pepper and the chopped parsley as you go and finishing with a layer of either potatoes or celeriac.

Bring stock to the boil, pour over vegetables, cover with tin foil and place in a preheated oven at 190°C/375°F/Gas Mark 5 and cook for 1 hour, then remove foil and allow to brown for about 15–20 minutes, or until potatoes and celeriac are cooked through. Garnish with parsley sprigs and serve.

ACCOMPANIMENTS: Green noodles will go well, tossed in a little olive oil, or serve with a crunchy salad, perhaps grated carrot and diced cucumber with raisins, seasoned well and tossed with a little freshly squeezed lemon juice or some French dressing.

VARIATIONS: Substitute milk or a mixture of milk and cream for the stock. Grated cheese, either on its own or mixed with fresh breadcrumbs, can be added to the top of the dish.

MICROWAVE OVEN: Assemble casserole as above, reduce stock by half, pour over, cover tightly with cling film and microwave on HIGH for 12 minutes, allow to stand for 3 minutes.

GRATIN OF POTATOES AND CHEESE

Any form of potato and cheese gratin I find utterly delicious and there are many, many variations possible. The more cream you use, the richer the dish. It is also excellent cold. Here is a basic recipe plus some ideas for variations.

Approx. 2 tablespoons butter
1 clove garlic, peeled
350 g/12 oz/2¼ cups waxy potatoes, peeled and sliced
Small, round goat's cheese such as Capricorn OR about 100 g/4 oz Camembert cheese, thinly sliced
Salt and freshly ground black pepper
150 ml/5 fl oz/⅔ cup milk or milk and cream or cream

Butter thoroughly a small gratin dish, rub with the garlic clove, layer half potatoes on bottom of dish, add the cheese then the second half of the potatoes, making a nice arrangement of the top layer. Season lightly.

Heat the milk, milk and cream or cream to boiling point, pour over potatoes and cheese, dot top with butter and place in preheated oven at 180°C/350°F/Gas Mark 4 and cook for 1 hour or until potato cooked through.

ACCOMPANIMENTS: A good green salad.

VARIATIONS: Grated Gruyère can be used instead of the goat's or Camembert cheese. Grated carrot or courgette can be substituted for the cheese or use sliced onion, cooked to transparent gold in butter or oil. Blanched, sliced leeks are another possibility (leeks also combine well with the cheese). A lightly beaten egg can be added to the liquid if liked.

MICROWAVE OVEN: Choose a deepish dish and assemble the gratin as above. Reduce the amount of milk, milk and cream or cream by a third then pour over, cover gratin tightly with cling film and microwave on HIGH for 12 minutes, or until potato cooked (test with tip of sharp knife through the cling film).

MUSHROOMS IN FILO PASTRY

Crisp filo parcels offer a change from pastry turnovers and pies and can be filled with a variety of stuffings. The mushrooms are succulent and tasty but some alternatives are suggested after the recipe. The parcels can be prepared an hour or so before cooking and kept on a baking tray in the fridge. Filo pastry is sold frozen, defrost, use what is needed then return the remaining sheets to the freezer for another occasion.

2 tablespoons butter or arachide/groundnut/ peanut oil
1 shallot or 6 spring onions, white and pale green parts, chopped
450 g/1 lb button mushrooms
Salt and freshly ground black pepper
1 clove garlic finely chopped with 2 tablespoons parsley
4–8 sheets filo pastry
Melted butter or more oil

Heat butter or oil, add chopped shallot or spring onions, cook gently some 3 minutes until softened. Raise heat, add mushrooms, salt and pepper to taste and cook briskly until any juices have been released and evaporated. Allow to cool. Add the garlic and parsley, stirring well.

Keeping remaining filo pastry under cling film or a damp cloth, lay on top of each other two pieces of filo pastry each approximately 15 cm/6 inches by 20 cm/8 inches (some sheets are about double this size, others nearer it so you will either need one sheet or two for each packet), brush top layer lightly with melted butter or oil. Add one quarter of mushroom mixture then bring each corner of the pastry in to make a neat envelope, or gather together like a drawstring purse. Press or pinch to close pastry then brush all over lightly with melted butter or oil. Place on oiled baking sheet.

Parcels can be prepared several hours ahead of time. When ready to cook, place in preheated oven at 200°C/400°F/Gas Mark 6, until golden brown, approximately 15 minutes. Serve immediately, garnished with sprigs of parsley; if liked, these can be fried in a little more oil.

ACCOMPANIMENTS: A salad.

VARIATIONS: Almost anything can go inside these parcels. Grated courgettes, stir-fried, seasoned and mixed with toasted pine nuts and a little

148

cheese; cooked rice mixed with a little cooked onion and some chopped fresh peppers, cucumber, apple, herbs, tomato (peeled and deseeded), blanched beans or corn niblets, etc.

CARROT CUSTARDS

Little moulds of grated carrot seasoned with fresh ginger and cooked with egg – very simple and very good.

225 g/8 oz/2½ cups grated carrots
1 teaspoon grated fresh ginger root
150 ml/5 fl oz/⅔ cup milk or cream
1 whole egg and 1 egg yolk
Salt and freshly ground black pepper
For serving: Natural yoghurt, chopped fresh parsley or mixed herbs

Add the grated carrot to boiling water and cook for 2 minutes. Drain immediately, refresh in cold water then drain again. Squeeze by hand really dry. Add the grated green ginger to the milk then beat the eggs lightly and mix thoroughly with the milk and ginger, season. Add the grated carrot and mix well together.

Grease four small ramekin dishes and fill with the mixture. Place in a small roasting tin or ovenproof dish, add boiling water to come halfway up the sides of the ramekin dishes and bake in a preheated oven at 180°C/350°F/ Gas Mark 4 for approximately 25 minutes, until the custards are firm to the touch. To turn out, run a sharp knife around the sides of each custard and ease them out of the dish on to plates, serving two per person.

While the custards are cooking, season the yoghurt, stirring well, and add chopped parsley or mixed herbs, a dash of tarragon vinegar can also add extra interest. Serve with the custards.

ACCOMPANIMENTS: Noodles or plain potatoes tossed in a little butter or hazelnut or walnut oil plus green beans or a salad.

VARIATIONS: Use grated courgettes or Jerusalem artichokes or celeriac or kohlrabi instead of the carrot. Chopped herbs can be used for flavouring instead of the grated ginger. Mushroom sauce can accompany instead of the yoghurt.

MICROWAVE OVEN: Assemble the custards as above. Tightly cover each dish with cling film and arrange the dishes in a circle in the oven. Microwave on HIGH for 2 minutes, rearranging the custards halfway through if the oven does not have a turntable. Pierce film and leave to stand for 2 minutes before uncovering and unmoulding.

CHEESE SOUFFLÉ

Choose a strongly flavoured cheese and, provided the instructions are carefully followed, the recipe should be a resounding success every time.

Little butter for greasing dish and 1–2 tablespoons dry breadcrumbs (optional)
25 g/1 oz/2 tablespoons butter
25 g/1 oz/4 tablespoons flour
150 ml/5 fl oz/²⁄₃ cup milk
3 tablespoons dry sherry
100 g/4 oz/½ cup grated cheese, Gruyère, Cheddar, Parmesan, etc., or a mixture such as Lancashire and Cheddar
2 large egg yolks
1 teaspoon Maille Dijon mustard plus a good dash of Worcestershire sauce
Salt, freshly ground black pepper, good pinch cayenne pepper
3 large egg whites

Butter very well a soufflé dish of some 1 litre/1¾ pint/4½ cup capacity and dust with dry breadcrumbs (these give a nice crusty outside to the soufflé).

Melt butter, add flour then liquids to make a smooth sauce. Remove from heat, add cheese, there will be enough residual heat in the sauce for it to melt, then beat in egg yolks well one by one. Or beat the egg yolks well in a bowl and fold into the sauce. Add seasonings to taste. Beat the egg white to stiff peaks, fold one third into the sauce, give the remaining egg whites a quick beat to reincorporate any breaking down, then add the sauce mixture on top and carefully fold in.

Place in soufflé dish, adding a greased paper collar if mixture comes too near top of dish. Place in preheated oven at 190°C/375°F/Gas Mark 5 for 30 minutes. To test if ready, give the dish a careful shake with oven-gloved hands. If soufflé wobbles dangerously, give it another few minutes, if it just trembles slightly, serve immediately by plunging two spoons back to back into the centre then ensuring each portion has a combination of soft centre, which should still be very slightly runny, and crisp outside.

VARIATIONS: The cheese can be replaced with the same quantity of a wide variety of vegetables: purée of spinach, chopped broccoli or mushrooms, grated courgette or carrot. Whatever you choose, make sure it does not need cooking before it goes into the soufflé as the only thing that gets really cooked in the oven is the soufflé mixture itself.

PANCAKE FLIPS

Don't think it isn't worth making pancake mixture for two, one batch can provide two different meals. And there are pancakes very different from crêpes that make easy and slightly different meals. Most are best eaten straight from the pan, easy when it's just the two of you.

F TWIN PANCAKES

This is the basic recipe for crêpes and should produce a dozen pancakes. Make the full amount, then use six for CARAMELISED APPLE PANCAKES now and the other six for SMOKED TROUT TWICE-FRIED PANCAKES tomorrow.

Pancakes:

100 g/4 oz/scant cup plain flour sifted with pinch salt
1 egg & 1 egg yolk, size 2
150 ml/5 fl oz/⅔ cup milk mixed with 150 ml/5 fl oz/⅔ cup water
1 tablespoon melted butter or light vegetable oil

Sift flour into bowl with salt. Make well in centre, add whole egg and the extra yolk then begin to add the liquid slowly, stirring all the time, gradually mixing in the flour. When half the liquid has been added, stir in melted butter or oil and beat well until mixture smooth. Stir in remaining liquid then cover and leave to stand for two hours before using. Batter should have consistency of thin cream, more liquid can be added if necessary.

Heat and wipe out a 15–18 cm/6–7 inches frying pan with oil and a little salt then wipe out with kitchen paper to polish surface. Set over a moderate heat and put in a few drops of oil or a flake of butter. Take enough batter in a ladle or cup to cover the bottom of the pan very thinly. Tip batter into pan and immediately roll pan round clockwise so mixture coats it evenly. If mixture cooks so quickly it won't cover pan, the pan is too hot.

Cook until underneath of pancake is a good brown. Run a palette knife under edges to loosen, slip knife underneath and flip pancake over (or toss). Cook for 10–20 seconds on other side. Turn on to rack or stack on plate over simmering water if keeping to eat as soon as all cooked. The first pancake is almost always a "trial" to test consistency of mix, temperature of pan and amount needed to coat pan thinly. It is rarely usable. Altogether the above mixture should make twelve usable pancakes. Serve half with sugar and either lemon or orange quarters to squeeze over, or with

151

homemade jam and use the other half for CARAMELISED APPLE PAN-CAKES, SMOKED TROUT TWICE-FRIED PANCAKES or HAM AND MUSHROOM PANCAKES, see below.

VARIATIONS: Pancakes can be stuffed with a variety of fillings and are good for using up small amounts of cooked fish, salmon is superb, or meat such as chicken or lamb. Mix with a small amount of white sauce or a little mayonnaise or cream or yoghurt. Season well, spices and herbs can add extra flavour, place filled pancakes in a greased dish, brush with melted butter or cover with a sauce and place in a preheated oven at 220°C/425°F/Gas Mark 7 for 10 minutes to heat through. Follow the same method for sweet pancakes, sugar can be sprinkled over after brushing with the melted butter.

F CARAMELISED APPLE PANCAKES

Normandy in northern France is famous for its apples as well as its dairy products and many of its traditional dishes, like this one, combine apples and cream, often adding Calvados or apple brandy as well.

6 crêpes made as on page 151

Apple:

450 g/1 lb Cox's orange pippins

25 g/1 oz/2 tablespoons butter

25 g/1 oz/2 tablespoons caster sugar

Caramel Sauce:

3 tablespoons water

50 g/2 oz/4 tablespoons granulated sugar

75 ml/3 fl oz/5 tablespoons double cream

Peel, quarter and take out cores of apples then cut in thick segments. Heat butter in a small pan, add apple and cook over moderate heat, carefully tossing apples until slightly transparent, then sprinkle over sugar and continue cooking until nicely caramelised. Divide between pancakes, rolling up or folding in four or flipping edges of pancake over apple

For the caramel sauce, heat water and sugar slowly until melted then bring to boil, lower heat and cook steadily until a golden brown. Remove from heat immediately and carefully stir in cream, protecting hand in case of splatters.

Pancakes can be reheated under tin foil in oven preheated to 220°C/425°F/ Gas Mark 7 for 10 minutes then served with either hot or cold caramel sauce.

MICROWAVE OVEN: Good for reheating: arrange apple pancakes on dish, cover tightly with cling film, microwave on HIGH for 1 minute.

SMOKED TROUT TWICE-FRIED PANCAKES

Crisp, succulent mouthfuls that should be eaten as soon as made.

6 crêpes made as in first recipe
1 smoked trout, approx. 225 g/8 oz, skinned and flesh flaked
2½ tablespoons natural yoghurt or cream
Freshly ground black pepper
Pinch dry English mustard powder
Little good vegetable oil for frying

Roughly mash smoked trout flakes with yoghurt or cream and seasonings. Spread on one half of each pancake. Fold over crêpes, then fold again into a tricorn shape. If preparing ahead, wrap and place in fridge until ready to cook.

Add sufficient oil to frying pan to cover base with a thin film, heat steadily until almost smoking hot, then fry the pancake parcels until crisp on each side. Serve immediately garnished with lemon wedges.

ACCOMPANIMENTS: Thick yoghurt or mayonnaise flavoured with a little lemon juice; a green salad. New potatoes are nice if a more substantial meal is needed.

VARIATIONS: Other fillings could include smoked mackerel, smoked salmon, minced cooked chicken or turkey, mushrooms, hummus, taramasalata, etc.

F HAM AND MUSHROOM PANCAKES

These pancakes are delicious and the filling nicely contrasts taste and texture.

6 crêpes made as in first recipe
25 g/1 oz/2 tablespoons butter
4–6 spring onions, white and pale green parts chopped

100 g/4 oz/2 cups mushrooms, chopped
½ teaspoon chopped fresh thyme
1 dessertspoon cream or thick yoghurt
Salt and freshly ground black pepper
6 thin slices of ham
Little Dijon mustard
Little melted butter
25 g/1 oz/2 tablespoons grated Cheddar cheese

Melt butter, add spring onions and cook gently for 1–2 minutes. Raise heat and add mushrooms, cook rapidly until moisture has evaporated. Remove from heat, add the thyme and cream or yoghurt and season to taste.

Place a slice of ham on each pancake and spread first with a little mustard then with some of the mushroom mixture, dividing it between the six pancakes. Fold or roll up each gently and place in greased ovenproof dish. Brush the filled pancakes with melted butter and sprinkle with cheese.

To reheat, place in preheated oven at 220°C/425°F/Gas Mark 7 for 10 minutes.

ACCOMPANIMENTS: A salad or a green or puréed vegetable.

MICROWAVE OVEN: Cover dish tightly with cling film and microwave on HIGH for 2 minutes. Allow to sit for 2 minutes then serve.

POTATO PANCAKES

Not all pancakes are crêpes. Grated or shredded vegetables can be mixed with egg and fried in little rounds, the results are exceedingly good. A processor makes preparation the work of a moment but a grater will work well if more slowly.

225 g/8 oz/2 cups raw potato, peeled and roughly chopped
100 g/4 oz/1 cup onion, peeled and roughly chopped
1 tablespoon flour
3 tablespoons milk
2 eggs, size 3
Salt and freshly ground black pepper

Pinch grated nutmeg

Little olive oil

Place all ingredients except oil in a food processor or blender and work until finely chopped and creamy OR grate vegetables and mix well with remaining ingredients.

Heat a heavy frying pan and cover base with a film of oil. Add a small ladle of mixture, flatten slightly, then cook over medium heat until golden brown. Turn and brown other side. Repeat, stirring mixture between each pancake and keeping cooked pancakes warm until all are prepared. Mixture makes approximately 8 pancakes.

ACCOMPANIMENTS: Pickled or spiced fruit or chutney or apple and sage sauce, vegetables to choice. Or use to accompany cold meats.

COOK'S TIP: When using processor, be careful not to overwork mixture, leave it with a little texture. Potato and onion can be minced instead of processed or grated.

CABBAGE PANCAKE

Another shredded vegetable pancake, this time cooked in one large round. Simple but very good, as all fried cabbage is – remember bubble and squeak – it can serve as a main dish or as an accompanying vegetable.

175 g/6 oz/2 cups finely shredded green cabbage

2 cloves garlic, crushed

4 tablespoons fresh wholewheat breadcrumbs soaked in 4 tablespoons milk

3 eggs, size 2, lightly beaten

Salt and freshly ground black pepper

Little grated nutmeg

2 tablespoons olive oil

2 tablespoons grated mild cheese such as Caerphilly

If you like your cabbage well cooked, it is best to parboil it for 3 minutes, then drain very well. If you prefer it slightly crunchy, use raw. Mix together all ingredients apart from the oil and cheese.

Heat oil in a medium sized frying pan, add cabbage mixture, cover with a lid or a plate and cook over a medium heat for about 12 minutes until the bottom is nicely browned, the egg cooked and the cabbage the way you like it. Sprinkle the cheese on top and put under a medium grill to brown, then slide on to a warmed plate and serve immediately.

ACCOMPANIMENTS: Very good with grilled sardines, either fresh or tinned, or grilled bacon, and a tomato salad. Or with fried or poached eggs.

VARIATIONS: A few crushed juniper berries can be added to the mixture or a little chopped and softened onion.

STARS AND
STRIPES
PANCAKES

The Americans adopted the drop pancake principle and have turned it into a national dish. No roadhouse breakfast is complete without dollar pancakes, the size of the old silver dollar, served with maple syrup and crispy grilled bacon. Nothing wrong with that, the combination is inspired. But this type of pancake is capable of many excellent variations all based on the same mixture with different additions. All work exceedingly well for two, when it's easy for the pancakes to reach the mouth almost as soon as they leave the pan.

CORN ON THE
COB S. & S.
PANCAKES

100 g/4 oz/scant cup plain flour
1 teaspoon baking powder
Pinch salt
1 large egg, lightly beaten
250 ml/8 fl oz/1 cup milk
1 small tin corn niblets
½ red pepper, trimmed of membrane, flesh diced
1–2 tablespoons arachide/groundnut/peanut oil

Sift flour with baking powder and salt. Mix together egg and milk then add slowly to the dry ingredients to make a smooth batter. Add the corn and the diced red pepper, stirring in well.

Heat a thick frying pan, barely cover the surface with oil, then add small ladles of the mixture, giving it a good stir between each, making little pancakes about 7.5 cm/3 inches across; it depends on the size of your pan how many you can fit in in one go, I usually manage three. Fry over medium heat until set and turned golden underneath, then turn and brown the other side, which doesn't take long. Keep on a plate set over a pan of simmering water until all are made, mixture should make around 10, then eat immediately.

ACCOMPANIMENTS: Good with cold meats or simply grilled chops. Or as a vegetarian meal with a tomato salad and perhaps a green vegetable.

VARIATIONS: Replace the diced red pepper with a little diced salami.

COOK'S TIP: Don't leave this sort of pancake mix to stand, the baking powder starts to work as soon as the liquid is added and the pancakes should be fried immediately they are mixed.

PARSNIP S. & S. PANCAKES

Wonderful on a cold winter's day, the tiny touch of sweetness from the honey plays up the sweetness of the parsnip.

1 tablespoon arachide/groundnut/peanut oil
1 large or 2 small parsnips, peeled and trimmed of hard inner core then grated
1 clove garlic, finely chopped
100 g/4 oz/scant cup plain flour
1 teaspoon baking powder
Pinch salt
1 large egg, lightly beaten
250 ml/8 fl oz/1 cup milk
1 tablespoon clear honey
Freshly ground black pepper
1–2 tablespoons more of arachide/groundnut/peanut oil

Heat the first tablespoon of oil and sauté the grated parsnip with the chopped garlic until soft.

Sift the flour with the baking powder and salt. Mix together the egg and milk then add slowly to the dry ingredients to make a smooth batter. Add the honey and the cooked parsnip and stir in well. Season with a little ground black pepper.

Heat a thick frying pan, barely cover the surface with oil, then add small ladles of the mixture, giving it a good stir between each, making little pancakes about 7.5 cm/3 inches across, it depends on the size of your pan how many you can fit in in one go, I usually manage three. Fry over medium heat until set and turned golden underneath, then turn and brown the other side. Keep on a plate set over a pan of simmering water until all are made, mixture should make around 10, then eat immediately.

ACCOMPANIMENTS: Superb with a good cranberry sauce. As with the CORN ON THE COB PANCAKES on page 156, these go well with cold meats or plainly cooked chops, etc. Or can serve as the main dish in a vegetarian meal. Very good also for brunch.

COOK'S TIP: See the tip for the previous recipe CORN ON THE COB PANCAKES on page 156.

DATE AND NUT S. & S. PANCAKES

A dessert version, or good for afternoon tea on a cold winter's day.

4 tablespoons plain flour
½ teaspoon baking powder
Pinch salt
1 tablespoon caster sugar
1½ tablespoons chopped dates
1 tablespoon roughly chopped walnuts
1 small egg, lightly beaten
120 ml/4 fl oz/½ cup milk
1–2 tablespoons arachide/groundnut/peanut oil

Sift flour with baking powder, salt and sugar, add the chopped dates and nuts and mix well together. Mix together the egg and the milk and add gradually to the dry ingredients to make a smooth batter.

Heat a thick frying pan, barely cover the surface with oil, then add small ladles of the mixture, giving it a good stir between each, making little pancakes about 7.5 cm/3 inches across, it depends on the size of your pan how many you can fit in in one go, I usually manage three. Fry over medium heat until set and turned golden underneath, then turn and brown the other side. Keep on a plate set over a pan of simmering water until all are made, mixture should make around 6, keep covered with a lid or tin foil if you want to eat a savoury course first but eat as soon as possible.

ACCOMPANIMENTS: Cream or Greek-style yoghurt or a fruit sauce, the liquidised contents of a small tin of apricots is very good, especially with a splash of white rum added.

COOK'S TIP: See the tip for the CORN ON THE COB PANCAKES recipe on page 156.

PEACH PANCAKES WITH HAZELNUT BUTTER

A wonderful dessert when peaches are in season.

4 tablespoons plain flour

½ teaspoon baking powder

Pinch salt

1 tablespoon caster sugar

1 small egg, lightly beaten

120 ml/4 fl oz/½ cup milk

1 ripe peach, peeled, stone discarded, flesh diced

2 drops almond essence

For Hazelnut Butter:

½ tablespoon hazelnuts, browned in the oven and skins rubbed off

25 g/1 oz/2 tablespoons unsalted butter, softened

Sift flour with baking powder, salt and sugar. Mix together the egg and the milk and add gradually to the dry ingredients to make a smooth batter. Add the diced peach and the almond essence, stirring well.

Heat a thick frying pan, barely cover the surface with oil, then add small ladles of the mixture, giving it a good stir between each, making little pancakes about 7.5 cm/3 inches across, it depends on the size of your pan how many you can fit in in one go, I usually manage three. Fry over medium heat until set and turned golden underneath, then turn and brown the other side. Keep on a plate set over a pan of simmering water until all are made, mixture should make around 6, cover loosely with tin foil or a lid if you are serving something in between, then eat as soon as possible with the hazelnut butter added to each pancake as they are put on the dessert plate.

For Hazelnut Butter: Grind the browned and skinned nuts in a processor or nut mill, add the softened butter and work together. Form into a small roll, wrap in tin foil and chill until ready to serve, then slice.

159

ACCOMPANIMENTS: Slices of fresh peach can be served with the pancakes if liked.

VARIATIONS: Peaches tinned in unsweetened juice can be substituted for the fresh fruit. Other fruit can also be used: apricots (try dried as well), apple (toss in lemon juice to prevent fruit going brown), mango, etc.

COOK'S TIP: See the tip for the CORN ON THE COB PANCAKES recipe on page 156.

ORANGE AND RAISIN PANCAKES

Grated rind and juice of 1 small orange
50 g/2 oz/4 tablespoons raisins
5 tablespoons plain flour
½ teaspoon baking powder
Pinch salt
1 tablespoon caster sugar
1 small egg, lightly beaten
120 ml/4 fl oz/½ cup milk

Mix the rind with the raisins and juice and leave to soak for one hour. Sift the flour with the baking powder, salt and sugar. Mix together the egg and the milk and add gradually to the dry ingredients to make a smooth batter. Add the raisin and orange mixture.

Heat a thick frying pan, barely cover the surface with oil, then add small ladles of the mixture, giving it a good stir between each, making little pancakes about 7.5 cm/3 inches across. It depends on the size of your pan how many you can fit in in one go; I usually manage three. Fry over medium heat until set and turned golden underneath, then turn and brown the other side. Keep on a plate set over a pan of simmering water until all are made, mixture should make about 6, cover loosely with tin foil or a lid if you are serving something in between, then eat as soon as possible.

ACCOMPANIMENTS: Slices of fresh orange can be served with the pancakes if liked. Or try the marmalade sauce on page 197. An orange sabayon sauce, see page 195, would also be lovely.

COOK'S TIP: See the tip for the CORN ON THE COB PANCAKES recipe on page 156.

MAY I ACCOMPANY YOU –
VEGETABLE DISHES

Vegetables can be made a little different without doing anything complicated. A dribble of hazelnut or walnut oil can give extra flavour and finish
and is healthier than butter. A few chopped herbs, try a little lemon thyme
or savory as a change from parsley, can bring out unexpected flavours and
even dispense with other seasoning; grated cheese mixed with dry breadcrumbs can be added to cooked cauliflower, broccoli or leeks then flashed
under the grill for a quick gratin effect. A *mélange* of vegetables can be
cooked very quickly, particularly in a microwave, try carrots, celery and
broccoli, or carrot and cucumber batons make a very good combination.

Puréeing a vegetable produces quite a different effect and is done in a
twinkling with a food processor or vegetable mill. Leeks, carrots, parsnips,
broccoli, Jerusalem artichokes are only a few of the possibilities. Any left-
overs are ideal for soup. Spices can add a different note, try coriander with
carrots, a touch of curry with parsnips, cardamom with broccoli, nutmeg
with artichokes. A little good olive, hazelnut or walnut oil will add richness
as well as flavour, as will a dribble of butter heated until it just starts to go
brown then stirred into the purée.

Sometimes instead of spending time on the main dish it's fun to do
something a little more complicated with the vegetables. Some of the
following ideas take almost no time, others are slightly more demanding.

BROAD BEAN KERNELS WITH YOGHURT

When broad beans are anything larger than the size of your first fingernail, they are better stripped of their tough outer jackets after cooking, as in the following recipe. The kernels are then reheated into a delicious purée. Cream can be substituted for yoghurt if you aren't worried about cholesterol.

600 g/1½ lb broad beans, weighed in the pod

Little light stock or water or half water/half white wine

Salt and freshly ground black pepper

2–3 tablespoons natural yoghurt, sheep's for preference.

De-pod the broad beans and cook in plenty of salted water. Drain immediately and refresh in lots of cold water then pick off the grey-green outer skin, saving the inner, brighter kernel. Reheat these, crushing with a wooden spoon, with a little light stock or water or half water and half white wine, adding a few twists of the pepper pot. For a smoother purée, you can process or pass the beans through a sieve but the rougher texture is attractive. Check seasoning then finish off by stirring in the yoghurt.

ACCOMPANIMENTS: The beans are good with cold meats as well as fish and roasted meats, particularly chicken.

VARIATIONS: The purée can also fill little pastry cases or be used to stuff trout. Cream can replace the yoghurt.

MICROWAVE OVEN: Place the pods in a dish with 2 tablespoons water, cover tightly with cling film, microwave on HIGH for 7 minutes then refresh in cold water and proceed as above.

CAULIFLOWER WITH CUMIN

A way of cooking cauliflower than is simple, unusual and delicious.

1 medium sized cauliflower, cut in smallish florets

2 tablespoons arachide/groundnut/peanut oil

½ tablespoon black cumin seed

Salt and freshly ground black pepper

4 tablespoons water

Trim the cauliflower and cut into small florets, discarding thick stem pieces. Soak in a bowl of cold water for half an hour before cooking (this improves all cauliflower whatever the method of cooking). Drain just before cooking.

Heat the oil then add the cumin seed, it should pop a little. Add the drained florets and stir-fry for a moment then season and add the water. Continue cooking, stirring the cauliflower, until the vegetable is just tender and the water has evaporated, if necessary add a little more water or a lid.

SOUFFLÉD CAULIFLOWER CHEESE

A slight variation on cauliflower gratin that gives a luscious lift to the dish. It can form the basis of a whole meal, see suggestions after the main recipe.

1 small cauliflower
25 g/1 oz/2 tablespoons butter
25 g/1 oz/4 tablespoons flour
300 ml/10 fl oz/generous cup milk
½ teaspoon French Dijon mustard
Dash Worcestershire sauce
Salt and freshly ground pepper
1 egg, separated
100 g/4 oz/1½ cups tasty Cheddar cheese, grated

Trim the cauliflower of leaves and tough stalk, cut into large florets and cook in boiling salted water for approximately 7 minutes or until just tender. Drain, refresh in cold water and drain again.

Make a smooth sauce by melting the butter, stirring in the flour and cooking over a very gentle heat for 2–3 minutes then gradually adding the milk, stirring all the time. Bring to the boil and simmer for 2–3 minutes, continuing to stir. Add the mustard, Worcestershire sauce and season to taste. Then stir in the egg yolk and two-thirds of the grated cheese. Beat the egg white to soft peak and fold carefully into the sauce.

Place the well-drained cauliflower in a suitable sized shallow ovenproof dish, which has been well buttered or oiled, and pour the sauce carefully over the top. Scatter the last third of the grated cheese over. Place in a preheated oven at 190°C/375°F/Gas Mark 5 for 25 minutes, or until topping golden brown and slightly risen. Serve immediately.

VARIATIONS: Add grilled bacon to make a complete meal. OR place sautéd field mushrooms, cut into thick slices and cooked with a little butter or oil and fresh chopped herbs, underneath the cauliflower to make another main dish. OR omit the cauliflower and pour the sauce over the mushrooms instead. OR place the mushrooms inside a pre-baked flan dish and top with the soufflé sauce for another main dish, in each case bake as above.

MICROWAVE OVEN: Use to pre-cook the cauliflower florets in a dish, the stalk ends standing up, with a few tablespoons of water, covered tightly with cling film and microwaved on HIGH for 6 minutes. Drain, refresh in cold water and drain again.

TOWARDS TOMORROW: Make double the basic sauce, halving before adding the seasonings and cheese, etc., and use second half, having seasoned it, with chopped parsley for fish or broad beans. Or serve with leeks, split in half, cleaned thoroughly, boiled until tender, refreshed in cold water, squeezed well to remove all moisture then placed in greased dish, covered with white sauce and reheated at 180°C/350°F/Gas Mark 4 for 30 minutes, or in a microwave, covered in cling film, on HIGH for 5 minutes. This is also good with cheese added to the sauce as above.

CELERY IN CIDER

A good vegetable to cook if you have the oven going, or if you can cook it in the microwave. It has a clean flavour that goes well with a variety of dishes.

1 tablespoon arachide/groundnut/peanut oil
Small onion or a shallot, finely chopped
4–6 sticks celery (about half a head), cut into small sticks
150 ml/5 fl oz/²⁄₃ cup medium dry cider
Salt and freshly ground black pepper

Heat the oil and gently cook the onion or shallot until transparent but not coloured. Add the celery sticks and toss to coat in the oil and onion/shallot mixture. Place in a small ovenproof dish. Bring cider to the boil, season to taste, pour over the celery, cover with a lid or tin foil and bake in a pre-heated oven at 180°C/350°F/Gas Mark 4 for approximately 45 minutes or until tender.

VARIATIONS: Use stock instead of water.

COOK'S TIP: One of the easiest ways to strip off the tough fibres from celery stalks is to run a potato peeler down the outside of each stalk.

MICROWAVE OVEN: Place onion or shallot with oil in a small, deep dish, cover tightly with cling film and microwave on HIGH for 2 minutes. Reduce quantity of cider to 5 tablespoons, add to celery, cover again tightly with cling film and microwave on HIGH for 7 minutes.

TOWARDS TOMORROW: Use the other half of celery head to make soup OR use several stalks to make an apple and celery salad. Peel off tough fibres then cut celery into small dice. Mix with one crisp dessert apple, Granny Smith or Cox's, diced the same way, tossed in lemon juice, then add mayonnaise to taste. A little cream or thick natural yoghurt can also be added, also a little chopped walnut. Serve any remaining celery stalks fresh with cheese.

BRAISED CHICORY

Fresh chicory has a bitter edge that is very successful in many salads. When cooked, this bitterness mellows to an interesting, slightly smoky flavour. It tastes very good with bland meats and fish.

3 small heads of chicory, trimmed of solid stalk core and split in half
50 g/2 oz/4 tablespoons butter
Salt and freshly ground black pepper
Juice from ½ freshly squeezed lemon

Use a little of the butter to grease a small fireproof dish or frying pan, be generous. Lay in the halved chicory heads, dot with the remaining butter and season. Place over a moderate heat and let the butter start to melt. When it begins to sizzle, lower the heat and cook gently until the chicory is tender, about 20 minutes. Sprinkle with lemon juice and serve.

VARIATIONS: A little chopped bacon can be added to the chicory, it should be browned first. The heads can also be cooked whole but will take a little longer. A little cream can be added just before the end of cooking. For a blander flavour, blanch the heads, whole, in boiling salted water for 5 minutes, then drain, refresh, drain again, trim out tough stalk end and proceed as above.

COOK'S TIP: If using chicory whole, use the point of a sharp knife to hollow out the tough stalk end.

MICROWAVE OVEN: Chicory braised in the microwave is best cooked with a little stock or wine rather than butter, which is also better for one's cholesterol level. Prepare heads as above, lay in a single layer in a suitable dish, add 7 tablespoons stock or a mixture of stock and white wine, cover tightly with cling film and microwave on HIGH for 9 minutes.

STIR-FRIED CARROTS AND GINGER

Very simple, very quick and gives a little zing to a vegetable that's usually available very cheaply.

1 tablespoon arachide/groundnut/peanut oil
A small piece of fresh root ginger, peeled and very finely sliced
350 g/12 oz/3 cups grated carrot
Salt and freshly ground pepper
Half a lemon

Heat the oil in a largish frying pan, add the ginger and grated carrot, season and stir-fry for 2–3 minutes, until carrot is just cooked. Squeeze the lemon over just before serving.

VARIATIONS: A little chopped parsley can also be added. Courgettes can also be cooked this way. Before cooking, sprinkle salt over and allow to stand for 20–30 minutes then squeeze out all moisture before cooking. Instead of ginger with the courgettes, garnish with toasted almonds just before serving.

F LEEKS BAKED IN CREAM

Leeks take very well to sauces (see TOWARDS TOMORROW under SOUF-FLÉD CAULIFLOWER CHEESE on page 164) and to cream as in the following recipe:

2–3 leeks, white and pale green parts, split and well washed
Little butter
Salt and freshly ground black pepper
6 tablespoons double cream
Little grating of nutmeg (optional)

Clean leeks very well then add to boiling salted water and cook for 5 minutes. Drain, refresh in cold water then squeeze out all moisture very thoroughly. Place in a well-buttered dish in a single layer. Season. Pour over cream, add a very light dusting of freshly grated nutmeg, if you like, cover with buttered tin foil and bake in preheated oven at 160°C/325°F/Gas Mark 3 for approximately 30 minutes or until well cooked.

VARIATIONS: Replace cream with a white sauce.

COOK'S TIP: To clean leeks really thoroughly, split from just above the trimmed root and right through the pale green part, give leek a quarter turn and repeat, it will look rather like an African fly whisk. Then soak for several hours in cold water, inspecting finally to see no soil has been left between leaves. Before cooking, tie the fly whisk together again. Remove the string or thread after the initial blanching.

MICROWAVE OVEN: Boil, drain and lay in dish as above, adding cream and a dusting of nutmeg but omitting other seasonings. Cover tightly with cling film and microwave on HIGH for 10 minutes.

MINTED COURGETTES

The fresh taste of mint goes surprisingly well with courgettes. This is a very simple dish that doesn't take long to do but gives a nicely different flavour to a favourite vegetable of mine.

1 tablespoon arachide/groundnut/peanut oil
250 g/10 oz/2½ cups courgettes, sliced or cut into batons
Salt and freshly ground black pepper
1 tablespoon fresh mint, chopped

Heat oil in a frying pan, add the courgettes, season to taste and stir-fry for several minutes until tender but still slightly crisp. Add the chopped mint and toss quickly to distribute evenly. Serve immediately.

VARIATIONS: Another quite delicious effect is given by a little fresh tarragon. Add a branch at the start of cooking and remove before serving.

COOK'S TIP: Mint tends to go black when chopped, leaving this to the last minute helps to preserve the colour. When preparing for mint sauce, chop with sugar, it makes the operation much easier, then pour on a tablespoon of boiling water, this restores the colour and melts the sugar, finish by sharpening with wine vinegar to taste.

MICROWAVE OVEN: The effect in a microwave is even faster, the oil can be omitted and the mint cooked with the vegetable. Place the prepared courgette and mint in a suitable dish with 2 tablespoons water, cover tightly with cling film and microwave on HIGH for 5 minutes. Drain before serving.

POTATO GRATIN WITH LEMON THYME

Potato gratins are one of the most delicious ways of serving this versatile vegetable. They do not have to be cooked with milk or cream and don't need cheese as an extra flavouring. Here is one with olive oil and lemon thyme, subtler than the ordinary herb, that is ideal to serve with a simply cooked piece of meat or fish:

4–5 tablespoons olive oil, or other good vegetable oil
3 medium sized potatoes, or equivalent (350 g/12 oz), peeled and sliced
Salt and freshly ground black pepper
1 tablespoon fresh lemon thyme, leaves removed from tough stalk

Oil a small gratin or other shallow dish. Line with 2–3 layers of the sliced potato, brushing each layer with oil, seasoning lightly and scattering with lemon thyme. Brush final layer with oil and season lightly again. Cover with oiled tin foil and bake in a preheated oven at 190°C/375°F/Gas Mark 5 for approximately 1 hour until cooked through, removing foil from top for last 10 minutes of cooking to brown top.

VARIATIONS: Instead of thyme, use parsley or add a few tiny slivers of garlic in between the potato layers. Or add a layer of peeled and sliced tomatoes with a few leaves of roughly torn basil. For a potato gratin with milk or cream, follow the recipe for GRATIN OF POTATOES AND CHEESE in the NO MEAT – NO FISH section on page 147, omitting the cheese.

MICROWAVE OVEN: I don't find the texture of potatoes cooked this way in the microwave brilliant but the saving in time certainly is. Prepare as above but omit seasoning. Cover tightly with cling film and microwave on HIGH for 11 minutes.

MARROW WITH CARAWAY

Marrow is not the most satisfactory of vegetables but it is lovely and cheap. And there are ways of cooking it that I find acceptable. This is one and another follows. Together they should deal with a medium sized marrow and are sufficiently different not to be too boring to have one day after the other. If you do still have marrow left over, try a recipe from the NO MEAT – NO FISH section on page 137.

2 tablespoons arachide/groundnut/peanut oil
½ a medium sized marrow (approx. 450 g/1 lb untrimmed, 350 g/12 oz/3 cups when trimmed), peeled, seeds discarded, flesh cut obliquely into thin slices
Salt and freshly ground black pepper
1 teaspoon caraway seeds
1 tablespoon raspberry wine vinegar

Heat the oil, add the sliced marrow, seasoning and the caraway seeds and stir-fry gently until the marrow looks faintly transparent, when it will be cooked. Add the tablespoon of vinegar and toss the slices gently for a moment or two then serve.

VARIATIONS: Instead of the caraway seeds, add a teaspoon of paprika and use ordinary wine or sherry vinegar.

TOWARDS TOMORROW: Use the rest of the marrow in the following recipe.

F MARROW PROVENÇALE

Anything cooked *à la provençale* has tomatoes, garlic and olive oil. All combine with the marrow superbly, making you forget its usual rather fibrous anonymity.

1 tablespoon good virgin olive oil
1 large clove garlic, peeled and crushed
½ a medium sized marrow (approx. 450 g/1 lb untrimmed, 350 g/12 oz/3 cups trimmed), peeled, seeds discarded, flesh cut into chunks
225 g/8 oz ripe tomatoes, peeled, deseeded and sliced OR a small tin peeled tomatoes, with juice, roughly chopped
Salt and freshly ground pepper
Freshly chopped parsley

Heat the oil, add the garlic and fry gently for a minute then add the marrow chunks, stir well to coat in the oil then add the sliced tomatoes and seasoning, stir again then cook gently, uncovered, until the marrow is cooked, approximately 20–30 minutes (according to size of chunks and age of marrow). Add the chopped parsley and serve.

VARIATIONS: Basil can replace the parsley. A little chopped bacon can be added before the marrow. A few lightly crushed coriander seeds can be added with the marrow. The recipe is also good with courgettes. OR do the following simple dish: MARROW WITH BASIL: Peel and deseed marrow, cut into thick slivers. Cook with 2 tablespoons water and a little chopped fresh basil in a microwave for 7 minutes on HIGH. Drain then serve garnished with more basil.

COOK'S TIP: Tinned tomatoes generally have more flavour than fresh unless they are very good. If liked, the tomatoes can be sieved to remove the seeds.

MICROWAVE OVEN: Omit oil. If using tinned tomatoes, omit the juices, then process tomatoes with the garlic. Mix together everything except the seasoning and parsley, cover tightly with cling film, microwave on HIGH for 8 minutes. Pierce film, uncover carefully, check seasoning, sprinkle with parsley and serve.

TOWARDS TOMORROW: Any left-over is very good cold, particularly if a little more olive oil is dribbled over. It can form the basis of a salad: add anchovies or pickled herring and a little cold cooked pasta. Hard-boiled eggs are also good with it.

PARSNIPS AND TOMATO GRATIN

Parsnips are a root vegetable I love, they are so full of sweet flavour and taste wonderful just boiled and tossed in a little olive or hazelnut oil or in butter. And they are another vegetable that combines well with tomato.

---

1 tablespoon butter or arachide/groundnut/peanut oil

---

1 clove garlic, peeled and lightly bruised

350–450 g/12 oz–1 lb parsnip, peeled, cored and cut in thick slices

---

225 g/8 oz ripe tomatoes, peeled, deseeded and sliced OR a small tin of peeled tomatoes, with their juices, roughly chopped

---

Good pinch sugar

2 tablespoons grated mature Cheddar cheese 2 tablespoons breadcrumbs	mixed together

A little extra butter or oil

Heat oil in a frying pan, add garlic clove and cook gently for 1–2 minutes. Remove garlic and add the parsnip. Season and then stir-fry gently for 5–7 minutes until parsnip becomes faintly transparent and tender. Add the tomato and the sugar, raise the heat slightly and cook, stirring gently, until tomato is reduced slightly and coats parsnips. Check seasoning and place in a shallow ovenproof dish, sprinkle over the mixed cheese and bread-crumbs, either dot with flakes of butter or dribble over a little oil. Place under a hot grill for a few minutes to brown. Serve.

VARIATIONS: Another dish in which a little bacon can be included, or some chopped ham. A little cream can also be added just before serving if liked.

COOK'S TIP: Removing the woody core from all but the smallest of parsnips improves the finished vegetable remarkably. Cut the peeled vegetable in quarters and slice out the solid centre, quite easy to recognise.

MICROWAVE OVEN: Dish will be much more liquid but the flavour is excellent. Omit salt and pepper, mix together all ingredients except the cheese and crumbs, place in a deep dish. Cover tightly with cling film and microwave on HIGH for 8 minutes, stirring halfway through. Pierce film, uncover carefully, remove garlic clove, check seasoning, sprinkle over the crumbs and cheese and place under a hot grill to brown. Serve.

CABBAGE WITH GARLIC AND JUNIPER

I first tasted this at John Tovey's delightful Miller Howe hotel, it transforms a very ordinary vegetable into something special.

2 tablespoons arachide/groundnut/peanut oil
2 garlic cloves, crushed with 5 juniper berries
½ a firm green cabbage, trimmed of stalk and outer leaves and shredded
Salt and freshly ground black pepper

Heat the oil gently, add the crushed garlic and juniper berries and stir in well. Raise heat slightly but don't allow garlic to brown before adding the shredded cabbage, season to taste. Stir-fry for several minutes until cabbage just tender.

171

COOK'S TIP: Garlic can become bitter when browned, always try to avoid this happening.

MICROWAVE OVEN: The cabbage isn't the same dish at all cooked in the microwave but a little crushed garlic and juniper berries can be added to shredded cabbage cooked with a little water, covered tightly with cling film and microwaved on HIGH for 7 minutes. Pierce film, uncover carefully, drain off excess liquid and serve.

TOWARDS TOMORROW: Serve the other half of the cabbage shredded and lightly boiled, seasoned well with freshly ground black pepper and a dusting of nutmeg. OR blanch in boiling water for 1 minute, drain and refresh, squeeze out all water and use as base for a salad. OR toss in a little finely chopped onion softened in oil, add a couple of tablespoons of white wine and braise over a low heat until cooked, 20–30 minutes. OR use for CABBAGE AND GARLIC SAUSAGE SOUP in the SOUP section on page 14 OR for CABBAGE PANCAKE in the PANCAKE FLIPS section on page 155.

SALAD BOWLS

Most salads don't need cooking and need never be dull; a bowl filled with imagination can be a journey into the unknown and a meal in itself.

Almost anything can form the basis for an uncooked meal and neither lettuce nor tomato is essential: lamb's lettuce or corn salad (or *mâche* as the French, and so most chefs, call it), Chinese cabbage, chicory, radicchio, finely sliced cabbage, grated root vegetables, celery, peppers, herbs, avocado pear, apples and other fruit, including sliced dried fruits, nuts, these are only some of the possible ingredients. Really crunchy vegetables such as mange tout, cauliflower florets and beans can be quickly blanched. Left-over cooked vegetables, in moderate proportions, can sometimes be added with great effect. When preparing for two, keep unused portions of saladings in a plastic bag in the bottom of the fridge so they stay crisp and fresh and can be used to ring the changes.

Cold meat or fish, perhaps acquired ready cooked from a good delicatessen counter, can be accompanied by many different sorts of salad and can provide more than one meal: match a small selection of sliced meats with a green salad. Next day slice up some of the left-overs and mix with a cooked and sliced potato in a good dressing and serve with a grated vegetable salad. Still some meat left over? Chop and mix with avocado pear and grapes in yoghurt dressing for a completely different effect. Or try an open sandwich (see TIME FOR A SNACK section on page 248) or use to upgrade a soup into a complete meal (see SOUP section on page 10).

A salad can also be much more than an accompaniment, this section is devoted to what could be called complete "meals in a bowl". Though it starts off with one which has to be individually plated, it is an excellent example of the comprehensive approach to salads. Remember that a large jar of French dressing can be kept ready made in the fridge so that one lot of mixing will do many meals.

SALADE TIÈDE

I am very fond of these "warm salads". They make an excellent lunch or light supper dish, or a starter for a more formal meal, especially good if the main dish is to be cold. The base should be varied but there is no need to buy three or four different lettuces then feel condemned to salad for the rest of the week. One good head plus a few blanched green beans or mange tout, or both, plus a small head of chicory or radicchio, some fresh herbs and a few very fresh sliced button or oyster mushrooms will do well, or some supermarkets provide small packets of mixed saladings, remember to wash them thoroughly before use, even if they claim to have been washed already, to avoid any possible Listeria problem.

This recipe uses chicken livers but is followed by suggestions for other possibilities.

A small selection of saladings: see introduction
1 tablespoon good vegetable oil
225 g/8 oz/1 cup chicken livers, strings and any green parts removed, large pieces cut into two
50 g/2 oz/grapes, halved and deseeded
3 tablespoons good French dressing

Arrange the saladings nicely on two plates. When ready to eat, heat the oil, briskly sauté the livers, leaving them pink (they will still feel slightly soft when pressed lightly), add the grapes and continue cooking for a moment or two then pour in the dressing and heat. Finally spoon the pan contents over each plate of salad, the slight wilting of the greens under the impact of the hot liver and sauce is all part of the charm of the dish.

VARIATIONS: Instead of chicken livers, sauté a plump chicken or duck breast then slice thinly across and divide between two plates, heat dressing and pour over. Bacon and croûtons form another possibility, so does a small but thick piece of grilled steak, sliced into thin strips. Or scampi or large uncooked prawns, etc.

HAM, CHEESE AND BEAN SALAD

A very simple salad made with easy to acquire ingredients.

Small tin butter, flageolet or haricot beans
100 g/4 oz/2–3 slices mild ham, cut in strips
50 g/2 oz/½ cup Emmenthal or Gruyère cheese, cut in strips
2 tomatoes, skinned, deseeded and cut into slivers
French dressing made with 1 tablespoon wine vinegar, little French mustard, salt and freshly ground black pepper, pinch soft brown sugar, 4 tablespoons olive oil

Some crisp lettuce leaves
Fresh basil leaves, if available

Mix together beans, ham, cheese and tomato. Moisten with the French dressing, using just enough to leave the ingredients glossy. Arrange on the lettuce leaves on a large plate or a shallow dish or bowl. Just before serving, tear the basil leaves and scatter over.

VARIATIONS: Hard-boiled eggs also go well with this salad.

COOK'S TIP: Basil leaves start to go black as soon as they are chopped or torn so must be left until the last minute.

CHICKEN, CHICORY AND WALNUT SALAD

A great salad for autumn, particularly if you can get hold of some "wet" walnuts, straight off the tree, there is a world of difference between these and older, dryer specimens. Chicory, with its astringent, deliciously bitter flavour, like an attractive man or girl who proves to have a bitingly witty tongue, goes well with the earthy flavour of the nuts and the clean, sweet taste of the chicken. The pale colours and fresh green of the watercress are extremely chic. The exact blend of mayonnaise and yoghurt can be adjusted according to taste.

Approx. 225–275 g/8–10 oz/1⅓–1⅔ cups cooked chicken, cut in bite-sized pieces
1 head chicory, sliced
Approx. 50 g/2 oz/½ cup walnut halves or pieces
150 ml/5 fl oz/⅔ cup natural yoghurt
2 tablespoons thick mayonnaise
Salt and freshly ground black pepper
Small bunch watercress, cleaned
Small head of lettuce

Mix chicken with the chicory and walnuts. Add the yoghurt gradually to the mayonnaise, making a smooth sauce to your taste, and season. Remove

175

leaves from half the watercress and chop roughly, mix with the sauce. Pour the sauce over the chicken mixture and stir together. Place the lettuce leaves round the outside of a dish or shallow bowl and pile the chicken salad in the centre. Garnish with the reserved watercress and serve.

VARIATIONS: Turkey can substitute for chicken and a bulgar salad (see page 179) for the lettuce. Lightly whipped cream can be substituted for the yoghurt.

COOK'S TIP: Don't mix the watercress with the sauce too soon before eating or it may lose its colour. If no cooked chicken is on hand, wrap a large chicken breast, or two small, in tin foil, dosing it first with a dash of white wine or stock or dry vermouth and some seasoning, and cook in a moderate oven at 180°C/350°F/Gas Mark 4, for half an hour. Allow to cool, then cut into suitably sized pieces.

CHICKEN, APPLE AND BEAN SALAD

This is a fruity salad with the beans adding a particularly fresh note. See above recipe for cooking breast of chicken if no left-overs available.

Approx. 225–275 g/8–10 oz/1⅓–1⅔ cups cold cooked chicken, cut in bite-sized pieces
Approx. 150 ml/5 fl oz/⅔ cup well-flavoured French dressing
Handful runner beans, trimmed, sliced, boiled for 2 minutes, drained, refreshed in cold water then tossed in a little of the dressing
4 tablespoons brown rice, well washed and cooked in salted water then drained and tossed in a little of the dressing
1 crisp eating apple, cored, diced and tossed in juice of a lemon
Handful of grapes, halved and deseeded
1 orange, segments released without pith or membrane (see BACK TO BASICS section on page 280)
Few leaves of mint
Lettuce (optional)

Mix together chicken with the beans, rice and fruit. Chop several leaves of mint and add with sufficient French dressing to give a gloss to each ingredient. If using lettuce, arrange leaves round the outside of a dish or shallow bowl and heap the salad in the middle. Or serve without lettuce if you prefer. Garnish with a few extra leaves of mint and some slices of lemon or a small branch of grapes.

VARIATIONS: Cold turkey or duck can be substituted for the chicken. A little fresh pineapple can be substituted for the orange if available and cucumber can also be added. Instead of rice use a handful of cooked pasta shapes, see recipe below.

COOK'S TIP: A mean hand in adding dressing is best, too much leads to soggy ingredients sitting in sad pools.

PASTA, MUSHROOM, BACON AND WATERCRESS SALAD

Pasta makes excellent salads. Use the shapes that hold sauces and dressings well – the shells, spirals or *penne* (quills). The pasta needs to be well moistened and goes best with ingredients that are succulent and juicy, such as tomatoes, melon, etc. In the following recipe, each ingredient adds its own texture and flavour to make a totally pleasing effect.

1 tablespoon olive oil
3 slices smoked streaky bacon, de-rinded and cut into strips
100 g/4 oz/2 cups mushrooms, sliced
5 tablespoons red wine
75 g/3 oz/1 cup pasta twirls
Salt, freshly ground black pepper
Small bunch watercress, half leaves removed and roughly chopped
Curly endive leaves

Heat oil then cook bacon gently. Add the mushrooms and cook, stirring constantly, until moisture has been evaporated off. Add the red wine, bring rapidly to boil then simmer for 5 minutes. Remove from heat and cool.

Cook the pasta in salted water until just tender then drain and toss with the mushroom mixture. Add freshly ground black pepper and check to see if salt is needed (bacon may have added enough). Cool then add the chopped watercress and mix well.

Arrange the curly endive leaves over the base and sides of a shallow dish or bowl, then add the salad. Garnish with the reserved watercress and serve.

VARIATIONS: Diced Edam, Gouda, Samsoe or Jarlsberg cheeses also go well with this salad.

COOK'S TIP: Be careful not to overcook the pasta, it is ready when *al dente*, still with a tiny bit of resistance when bitten into, it will soften just a little bit more after removing from the heat. Don't leave sitting in the hot water, it will continue cooking.

TOWARDS TOMORROW: Use the rest of the curly endive for a mixed salad with some more lettuce, some briefly blanched mange tout and/or French beans. Or for a SALADE TIÈDE, see page 173.

SMOKED MACKEREL SALAD

This salad is very quick to make, tinned butter beans are excellent and there is no point in cooking such a small quantity. The smoked mussels can be left out if you prefer but they add considerable flavour, a tin is an excellent storecupboard standby.

1 smoked mackerel, skinned and flaked
1 tin (350 g/12 oz) butter beans, drained
Small head fennel, trimmed and chopped
1 small tin smoked mussels, drained
150 ml/5 fl oz/⅔ cup natural yoghurt
Salt and freshly ground black pepper
1 lettuce, washed
Garnish: 1 lemon, cut into wedges

Place the mackerel, beans, fennel and mussels into a bowl. Add the yoghurt and seasonings, go lightly with the salt, and mix together carefully, keeping the fish flakes as intact as possible. Arrange lettuce around the edge of a bowl or dish, pile salad in the middle and garnish with the lemon wedges plus any fronds the fennel head may have yielded.

COOK'S TIP: This salad is best prepared just before eating. Left to stand, the beans start to absorb the smoky flavour of the fish and the dish becomes unbalanced.

BULGAR SALAD

Bulgar, or bulghur, is wheat that has been boiled and baked then cracked. A soaking softens the tiny grains and allows them to swell, after which the wheat is ready to eat. Bulgar wheat is very popular in the Middle East, where it forms the basis of a number of salads such as the very popular tabbouleh, this salad is somewhat similar.

4 tablespoons bulgar wheat, thoroughly washed and drained
2 tablespoons extra virgin olive oil
1 small onion, or 2 shallots, peeled and finely chopped
½ large or 1 small lemon
Salt and freshly ground black pepper
Good pinch each of ground coriander, cumin and allspice and a tiny pinch cayenne pepper
1 large carrot, or 2 small, scrubbed and coarsely grated
1 stalk celery, finely diced
2 tomatoes, skinned, deseeded, diced
2 tablespoons freshly chopped fines herbes (parsley, chervil, tarragon, chives)
1 tablespoon dry roasted peanuts
2–3 tablespoons diced tofu or feta or Caerphilly cheese
Garnish: A slice of lemon

Place washed bulgar wheat in clean water and soak for five minutes then drain again, squeezing out as much moisture as possible. Heat olive oil and gently fry onion or shallot until soft.

Place the drained wheat in a large bowl and pour over the onion and oil. Add seasoning, the lemon juice and all the spices and mix very well. Then add all the remaining ingredients except half of the tofu or cheese, toss to mix. Place in a serving bowl, scatter over the reserved cheese, garnish with a slice of lemon and serve.

VARIATIONS: Lots of different possibilities for this type of salad: the vegetables can be mixed and matched according to taste. Cooked meat or fish can be added, the spices and herbs varied. Served with just spices and herbs, the bulgar wheat makes a good accompanying salad.

CAULIFLOWER, BEAN AND POTATO SALAD

A very tasty vegetable salad.

1 small cauliflower, cut into florets
Handful runner or French beans, trimmed and cut into 2.5 cm/1 inch lengths
Handful broad beans, measured out of the pods
100 g/4 oz/1 cup potatoes, scrubbed
Little French dressing (see SAUCY IDEAS section)
4–5 spring onions, white and pale green parts finely chopped
Small bunch chives, chopped
Salt, freshly ground black pepper
Approx. 150 ml/5 fl oz/⅔ cup mayonnaise, preferably homemade
Some crisp lettuce leaves

Blanch the cauliflower and the beans in boiling water for two minutes, drain. Refresh briefly in cold water, drain thoroughly again and toss in French dressing. Cook the potatoes, drain, refresh briefly in cold water, drain and toss in French dressing. When vegetables are cold, drain off excess dressing. Mix vegetables with chopped spring onions and two-thirds of the chives, check seasoning. Then mix with sufficient mayonnaise to coat lightly. Arrange the lettuce leaves around a large plate or a shallow dish, add the salad in the centre, garnish with the remaining chives and serve.

VARIATIONS: A little chopped ham or cheese can be added if liked. Sliced carrots can also be added for extra flavour and a nice colour contrast.

COOK'S TIP: Tossing the vegetables in dressing while they are still hot means they absorb some of the dressing and have more flavour.

TOWARDS TOMORROW: Blanch a large cauliflower then reserve the cooking water and half of the vegetable to make soup or a cauliflower cheese for the next day.

CHINESE CABBAGE SALAD

Another vegetable salad. Chinese cabbage, with its long, prettily veined leaves wrapped as tightly as a well-furled umbrella, has a subtle flavour. The upper end of the leaves, sliced carefully across so the whorled arrangement of leaf and stalk remains intact, is both decorative and nicely crisp for a salad.

6–8 slices from the top end of a Chinese cabbage
2 carrots, grated
1 large or 2 small oranges, segments released without pith or membrane, halved
1 tablespoon raisins, soaked in any juices released from the oranges whilst segmenting
Few grapes, halved and deseeded
4 tablespoons natural yoghurt, Greek-style
1 teaspoon clear honey
Salt and freshly ground black pepper

Arrange the Chinese cabbage slices prettily round the edge of a serving dish or plate. Mix together the grated carrot with the halved orange segments, the raisins and grapes. Pile in the middle of the rings of cabbage. Mix the yoghurt with the honey, season to taste and dribble over the salad.

VARIATIONS: Use black olives instead of the grapes.

COOK'S TIP: Never cook Chinese cabbage in water, however brief the immersion, it seems to reduce the cabbage to limp disaster. A very quick stir-fry is the best option.

TOWARDS TOMORROW: Thickly slice the remaining, stalk end of the cabbage then stir-fry in a little oil with a crushed clove of garlic, plus a little finely grated fresh ginger root for a vegetable dish to accompany simply grilled meat or fish.

SAUCY IDEAS

If there's one thing more time consuming to make for two than anything else, it's a sauce. But there are quick and easy ways to provide a finishing touch to simple cooked meats and fish. And a sweet sauce can cheer up commercial ice cream or turn fresh fruit into an almost instant pudding.

BASIC GLAZED SAUCE WITH BUTTER
F (without butter)

A quick and easy sauce to accompany anything that has been sautéd, when the pan juices can be used as a base. The quality will depend on the liquid used. Strongly reduced stock is what is needed, just what the cook catering for two is unlikely to have on hand! Instead try a little alcohol. Medium dry sherry, wine, vermouth, Pernod, even a dash of Angostura bitters, can all form the basis of a tasty little sauce but use with either a little stock or water, or with cream, or yoghurt that has been stabilised and thickened with cornflour (1 teaspoon to 150 ml/5 fl oz/⅔ cup is about right). The stronger the flavour of the alcohol, the less is required. The other great sauce secret is a dash of wine vinegar, which sharpens and adds depth, sherry or balsamic vinegar can add even more interesting notes. A little butter added at the end gives a lovely sheen and rounds off the flavour but it is not essential if you are watching cholesterol levels. Don't use a stock cube, it will be far too salty and roughly seasoned.

---

150 ml/5 fl oz/⅔ cup reduced stock OR half wine and half stock or water OR
2 tablespoons medium dry sherry or dry vermouth or Pernod made up to full quantity in light stock or water OR 1 tablespoon Angostura bitters in light stock or water OR substitute double cream or stabilised yoghurt (see above) for the light stock or water

---

Salt and freshly ground black pepper

25–50 g/1–2 oz/2–4 tablespoons unsalted butter, chilled and diced (optional)

Skim or pour off any excess fat from the pan juices then deglaze with chosen alcohol (if using), scraping bottom of pan well to incorporate all flavoursome bits and allowing heat to evaporate off spirit. Add remaining liquid, bring to boil and simmer gently, reducing quantity slightly. Check seasoning, add a dash of vinegar if required, strain if necessary. Just before serving, swirl the chilled butter pieces into the sauce to thicken slightly and give a glossy finish and a rounded, enriched flavour to the sauce.

F TOMATO SAUCE

Excellent for a wide variety of dishes, chops, chicken, vegetables, even some fish. Very quick and easy to make.

Little olive oil
1 shallot, finely chopped
1 small tin peeled tomatoes, roughly chopped
1 teaspoon fresh basil leaves or ½ teaspoon dried
Salt and freshly ground black pepper
Pinch sugar (optional)

Heat the oil, add the chopped shallot and cook gently for a few minutes to soften. Add the chopped tomatoes with their juices, the dried basil (if using fresh, keep on one side), season well and cook gently, stirring from time to time, until sauce has well amalgamated and thickened slightly. Just before serving check seasoning, add a pinch of sugar if liked, tear fresh basil leaves into small pieces and add, stirring well.

VARIATIONS: Instead of shallot, a small onion can be used but it will need longer cooking. A little garlic can also be added. Sauce can be sharpened with a little lemon juice. A couple of tablespoons of olive oil added at the end will give extra depth of flavour and richness.

COOK'S TIP: Basil leaves darken as soon as they are torn or cut so leave this until the end. If making sauce ahead of time, or freezing, leave adding fresh basil until just before serving.

MICROWAVE OVEN: Microwave can be used for cooking shallot or onion. Place in small bowl with oil, cover tightly with cling film and microwave on HIGH for 1 minute. It can also be used for cooking complete sauce, uncovered, but will not achieve reduction so easily.

F LEEK OR MUSHROOM SAUCE

A useful sauce to accompany meat or fish can be made from small amounts of puréed vegetables.

100 g/4 oz/2 cups trimmed leeks or mushrooms, finely sliced
Small knob butter
5 tablespoons water or stock
Salt and freshly ground black pepper
Little additional water, stock or white wine
½ teaspoon arrowroot, slaked with little water
1 tablespoon fresh herbs, chopped very finely (optional)

If using leeks, make sure they are washed very thoroughly in lots of cold water, then drained well. Heat the butter, gently sauté the leeks or mushrooms for a moment or two, then add the water or stock and season to taste. Cook gently until vegetables soft. Drain, reserving liquid.

Reduce vegetable to purée in either a blender or a processor or push through a food mill. Add sufficient liquid to make a good sauce consistency, with additional hot water, stock or wine if necessary. Add a little of the hot sauce to the slaked arrowroot, then pour that into the sauce and heat gently, stirring constantly, until sauce comes to the boil and is slightly thickened. Add the herbs if liked and serve.

VARIATIONS: Any vegetable that will purée well can be used, i.e. carrots, celeriac, courgette, squash, etc. Follow the same basic method above. A little cream or yoghurt can also be added.

COOK'S TIP: The arrowroot stops the sauce separating, it is not absolutely essential.

MICROWAVE OVEN: Omit butter and seasoning. Place prepared vegetable in a bowl with the liquid. Cover tightly and microwave on HIGH for 7 minutes. Then purée as above and thin with the reserved liquid adding more as necessary. Add the slaked arrowroot, cover tightly and microwave on HIGH for 3–4 minutes, until sauce hot and thickened, timing will depend on temperature of sauce before being microwaved again.

ℱ MUSTARD AND HONEY RAISIN SAUCE

This is a quick sauce that is delicious with plain ham or cold chicken or turkey, or with simply cooked poultry or ham.

50 g/2 oz/¼ cup soft brown sugar
½ tablespoon cornflour
1 teaspoon dry English mustard
1 tablespoon cider vinegar
225 ml/7½ fl oz/1 cup liquid made up of juice of 1 orange and stock or water
Grated rind ½ orange
3 tablespoons raisins
Salt

Place sugar in a saucepan, stir in the cornflour and mustard, then slowly add the liquids, stirring well. When all smooth, heat gently until sugar has melted, then add grated orange rind and raisins and cook gently until the raisins are plump and the sauce the consistency of clear honey.

COOK'S TIP: Always grate orange peel before squeezing out the juice. Citrus fruits grate more easily when chilled in the fridge.

TOWARDS TOMORROW: Use the grated rind from the other half of the orange to flavour skin on chicken or a custard or a sabayon sauce, etc.

ℱ RED PEPPER SAUCE

This is one of the most beautifully coloured and clear flavoured of sauces. The down side is that the initial peeling of the pepper is fiddly. Using tinned red pepper, which is already peeled, is easier but the flavour won't be quite as good. The up side is that grilling and peeling one red pepper is not nearly so bad as several! The sauce is delicious with delicately flavoured foods like chicken or fish or vegetables such as salsify, Jerusalem artichokes or celeriac, or with pasta.

1 red pepper
Little fish or meat stock or white wine
Salt and freshly ground black pepper

Either heat grill to its hottest and place red pepper underneath, on tinfoil paper, and turn it over until all the surface is charred black OR blacken over a gas burner, holding pepper on a fork OR place on a foil-lined baking tray in the top of a very hot oven until well blackened. Then pop the pepper in a piece of newspaper, wrap up loosely and leave for about 5 minutes. After that, rinse the pepper under cold running water, peeling off the skin. The pepper will now be softened and partially cooked. Cut in half, discard stem, seeds and white pith. Cut flesh into small pieces, place in a saucepan with a little stock or white wine and cook gently for a few minutes with a little seasoning until completely tender then process or blend into a sauce, adding a little more liquid if necessary. Sieve for a completely smooth effect. A little lemon juice or a dash of wine vinegar can enliven the flavour. Reheat gently before serving.

VARIATIONS: Other coloured peppers can also be used exactly as above. Chefs adore using two different coloured pepper sauces either side of a prettily presented main dish.

COOK'S TIPS: 1) The peeled peppers can be de-cored and deseeded then sliced and kept submerged in really good olive oil ready for serving alone or for mixing with a few prawns or with anchovies for an instant first course or adding to quickly sautéd chopped chicken livers for a sauce for pasta and a great many other ideas that will occur to you once you have them on hand. 2) Use a soup ladle to push any purée through a sieve, its shape conforms to that of the sieve and does the job in no time.

TOWARDS TOMORROW: Peel some extra peppers, see above.

F **APPLE SAUCE**

This is especially good with pork but it is also delicious with a variety of cold meats, savoury pancakes, etc. The amount of sage can be adjusted to taste.

1 cooking apple, Bramley or similar, peeled, cored and roughly chopped
2 tablespoons water
A little salt and pepper
10–14 sage leaves, chopped

Place all ingredients in a small saucepan and cook gently until apple is reduced to pulp. Check seasoning and consistency, a little more water can be added if liked, or the sauce reduced by further cooking.

VARIATIONS: Add a tablespoon or two of white wine.

MICROWAVE OVEN: Omit seasoning, place all other ingredients in a bowl or jug, cover tightly with cling film, microwave on HIGH for 4 minutes, pierce film with a knife, uncover carefully, beat with a whisk or wooden spoon to reduce to smooth sauce. Season to taste.

SAVOURY SABAYON SAUCE

There is nothing particularly tricky about this sauce if you remember that it must never approach boiling temperature otherwise the egg will start to coagulate and a nasty scrambled mess will result. Always cook the sauce in a bowl set above simmering water and you can hardly go wrong. It only takes a few minutes to cook such a small amount. It is very good with bland meats, fish and vegetables.

1 egg yolk

5 tablespoons stock, cider or wine, OR a mixture of water plus a dash of wine vinegar (only good if using a flavouring – see below)

Salt and freshly ground pepper

Place the egg yolk in a bowl that will fit nicely over a saucepan of simmering water, add the liquid and a little seasoning and beat until pale and very frothy. Place over the simmering water and keep whisking until the sauce has thickened and the whisk is leaving trails. Take the pan off the heat and keep whisking the sauce for a little longer, then serve. The flavour of this sauce can be varied according both to the liquid used and additional flavourings, as below.

VARIATIONS: CURRY SABAYON: Gently fry a teaspoon of curry powder in a little melted butter for several minutes then whip into the egg yolk with the liquid. **TOMATO SABAYON:** Whisk a little tomato purée in to finished sabayon, which is good made with white wine or a dash of white wine vinegar. **TARRAGON SABAYON:** Add a dash of tarragon vinegar to the liquid plus a teaspoon of sugar, very good with trout. **ANCHOVY SABAYON:** Add a little anchovy essence to taste to finished sabayon, very good with fish or with spinach stuffed pancakes or flan.

COOK'S TIP: When making any egg-based sauce, keep a bowl of cold water by the stove. If the sauce seems as though it could be overheating and appears on the point of curdling, plunge the sauce bowl into the cold water. The heat will immediately drop and the danger be averted. Just removing from the simmering water may mean there is sufficient heat left in the bowl to continue the curdling process.

F BASIC BÉCHAMEL

A classic béchamel sauce will be made with milk infused with a slice of onion, some slices of carrot, a little chopped ham and a small bunch of herbs. Probably more fiddly than you want to bother with on most occasions but it does make a wonderfully flavoured sauce. However, you can make a very reasonable version with plain milk and some good seasoning, particularly if you are using other flavourings as well, such as cheese or chopped parsley. It is worth making double quantities of a white sauce such as this and keeping one half for tomorrow, or even the next day, it is so versatile. The following quantities are for half a pint of sauce, which will usually do two meals for two. The flavourings given at the end are for half the amount of sauce.

25 g/1 oz/2 tablespoons butter
25 g/1 oz/3 tablespoons flour
Salt and freshly ground black pepper
350 ml/generous 10 fl oz/1½ cups milk
Optional: 2–3 tablespoons cream

Melt the butter, add the flour, season, and cook gently over a low heat, stirring from time to time, for several minutes. Then gradually add the milk, stirring in between each addition, over the heat, to make a smooth sauce. Simmer very gently for 10–12 minutes, without stirring, then skim off the skin that has gathered on top, this removes all the impurities and leaves you with a smooth, well-cooked sauce. Stir in the cream if using.

Divide the sauce in half and place cling film over one half and refrigerate for later use. Add chosen flavouring to the half for immediate use. Flavourings (for half above amount):

PARSLEY SAUCE:

2 tablespoons chopped parsley

Serve with fish, eggs, vegetables, especially broad beans.

PRAWN SAUCE:

2 tablespoons chopped prawns, a little tomato purée or anchovy essence

Serve with fish or hard-boiled eggs.

CHEESE SAUCE:

2 tablespoons grated tasty Cheddar, a little French mustard and a dash of Worcestershire sauce

Serve over cauliflower (adding grilled bacon can make it a complete meal), or eggs, or vegetables, or with stuffed pancakes.

MUSHROOM SAUCE:

2 tablespoons chopped fresh mushrooms cooked with a little butter or oil and sharpened with a squeeze of lemon

Serve with fish, beef, chicken, butter beans, pancakes, etc.

ONION SAUCE:

1 medium sized onion, peeled and chopped, blanched in boiling water, drained, then softened in a tablespoon butter, puréed and added to béchamel.

Serve with lamb, eggs, vegetables, pancakes, etc.

VARIATIONS: The consistency of the sauce can be regulated by altering the amount of butter and flour. A thin sauce uses half the above amount as a basis for soups; for a coating sauce use double the amount of butter and flour given and treble the above quantities for a *panade* that will bind minced meat or fish for croquettes.

REHEATING FOR TOMORROW: Heat very gently, stirring all the time. It may be necessary to add a little more milk to achieve the correct consistency after the sauce has returned to the boil.

MICROWAVE OVEN: The microwave doesn't deal kindly with wheat-based sauces but it can produce an excellent sauce using cornflour instead and without the fat, making it ideal for slimmers. And the process is so quick there is not much point in making double quantities. Use 1 tablespoon of cornflour to 150 ml/5 fl oz/generous ½ cup milk. Slake the cornflour with a little cold milk in a large jug, stir in the hot milk, cover tightly with cling film and microwave on HIGH for 4 minutes, then whisk, being careful the sauce doesn't foam up over the edges of the jug. Season, add flavourings as above, heating through again for 30 seconds, on HIGH if necessary, then stir again and serve.

MAYONNAISE

Mayonnaise is one of the most useful sauces in the cook's repertoire. It can top soups, mix together cooked ingredients for a pancake filling, form the basis of a wide variety of sauces to accompany fish, pies and meats as well as various salads. There is no need to worry about the chance of Salmonella in eggs. If you use the following proportions of vinegar to oil and egg, the acid in the vinegar will kill any Salmonella bacteria, provided you leave the mayonnaise at room temperature for 24 hours rather than refrigerating it. The flavour of mayonnaise can be varied according to the oil used. The very strongly flavoured olive oils will dominate whatever you use the mayonnaise with, for most purposes you need something blander. A good arachide/ground-nut/peanut oil or grapeseed or sunflower oil can be used on its own or mixed with a little olive oil for a mayonnaise with character that will take to any number of different flavours; vary the choice and proportions according to the end use.

1 egg yolk, size 3
Salt and freshly ground black pepper
150 ml/5 fl oz/⅔ cup good oil
1 tablespoon wine vinegar

This amount of mayonnaise is easy to make with a wooden spoon and this really does produce the best result, the texture is unbeatable. But a hand-held electric beater certainly speeds the process and the result is very acceptable. The method is exactly the same in both cases. Beat the yolk with a little seasoning until it is pale and has increased in volume, this gives a greater volume for the first of the oil to be added to and lessens the danger of separation. Then beat in the oil drop by drop. When the mixture gets very thick, thin with a little of the vinegar then continue with the oil, dribbling it in a little faster after about half has been incorporated. The vinegar plays a triple role, as well as thinning, it sharpens the mayonnaise and provides the vital acidic element. If your mayonnaise is to your taste but still a little thick, a spoon or two of hot water can be used to thin it further. Other sharpening agents, such as lemon or lime juice are great on taste but will be less effective in killing bacteria. Finally, check seasoning.

VARIATIONS: Use flavoured vinegar, such as tarragon, chilli, etc. Or, if you are sure of your eggs, substitute lemon juice for the vinegar. Flavour with grated orange or lemon rind (allow to mature for several hours or overnight for best results), colour and flavour with spinach purée.

AIOLI: The classic French garlic mayonnaise so good served with slivers of fresh vegetables, *crudités*, with drinks or as a first course, is made by crushing a fat clove, or two or three, of garlic with salt, then beating that into the yolk before proceeding as above but leaving out the vinegar, the garlic will thin the oil sufficiently to produce a rich, thick, golden mayonnaise.

TARTARE SAUCE: Served with fried or grilled fish: add to above quantity of mayonnaise: 2 teaspoons chopped capers, 3 finely chopped cocktail gherkins, 1 teaspoon finely chopped chives and 1 tablespoon double cream.

EXTRA LIGHT MAYONNAISE: For serving with cold salmon, etc.: whip the egg white/s left over to stiff peak and fold into mayonnaise.

HERB MAYONNAISE: Use 2 tablespoons freshly chopped herbs to above quantity mayonnaise and blanch in boiling water, refreshing in cold and squeezing quite dry before adding to the mayonnaise. This prevents the colour going grey if the mayonnaise isn't used immediately.

COOK'S TIP: Have all your ingredients, egg, oil and vinegar, at room temperature before you start. This helps the emulsification process. If your mayonnaise does curdle, start again with another egg yolk and dribble in the curdled mixture bit by bit, beating all the time, before continuing with the rest of the oil. You will need to add another tablespoon of vinegar so it is best to increase the quantity of oil as well. Don't bring mayonnaise out of a very cold place into a very warm room, let it adjust to changes in temperature gradually, otherwise it may separate.

TOWARDS TOMORROW: Make twice as much as you think you will need and keep the rest ready to hand, you will find any number of uses for it, particularly in the summer. Keep in a cool place for at least 24 hours to ensure the vinegar's acid has killed off any bacteria before eating or placing in the fridge.

FRENCH DRESSING

Another most versatile dressing that can be used on hot vegetables and other ingredients, either for serving warm or cold, or to toss with any combination of saladings. Or it can be used as a sauce, with artichokes or avocados, for instance. The classic recipe is 1 part of vinegar to 3 parts of oil, seasoned with salt and pepper, but this produces a very sharp dressing that is seldom used outside France. The following recipe is one to get you started. Experiment with oils and seasonings (herbs, mustards, etc.) until you find exactly what suits which dish and your own taste. The main rule is that the better the ingredients, the better the dressing. Don't buy cheap olive oil, it is processed with heat and has a nasty raw edge to it. There are good olive oils with a wide range of flavours, from very light to green and powerful. Look for "cold pressed" and "virgin" on the label, best of all is "extra virgin" with an acidity of below 1 per cent. Other oils can also be used, or a mixture, but try and choose unrefined oils where possible, the flavour is much, much better.

½ teaspoon French mustard

---

1 teaspoon–1 dessertspoon caster or soft brown sugar or honey

---

1 small clove garlic, crushed (optional)

Salt and freshly ground black pepper

---

2 tablespoons wine vinegar

---

10 tablespoons good oil (see above)

Mix the mustard with the sugar, add the garlic, if using, and seasoning, then the vinegar. Finally whisk in the olive oil. The resulting emulsification will not remain long so it is best to prepare the dressing at the last minute or keep in a screw-top jar so it can be well shaken just before using. However, a processor produces a creamy emulsion which will keep together for much longer than one shaken or whisked.

VARIATIONS: Lemon or orange juice can replace the vinegar, especially good for salads containing citrus fruits. A low-calorie salad dressing can be made with a small tub of natural yoghurt, 1 teaspoon tarragon wine vinegar or lemon juice, 1 teaspoon oil, 1 teaspoon clear honey, salt and freshly ground pepper. Mix all together. Freshly chopped parsley or green pepper can be added as well.

COOK'S TIP: French dressing keeps well in a screw-top jar in the fridge, ready for instant use.

TOWARDS TOMORROW: Make two or three times what you need for today and keep the remainder in the fridge, all ready for the next occasion.

SWEET SAUCES

F FRUIT SAUCE

A quick fruit sauce can provide an instant pudding with a few meringue shells, fresh or poached contrasting fruit, ice creams, sweet pancakes, and I am sure you can think of more uses.

100 g/4 oz/1 cup frozen fruit – raspberries, strawberries, apricots, peaches, etc.
Approx. 2 tablespoons icing sugar (if fruit not frozen in syrup or with sugar)
A squeeze fresh lemon juice
1 tablespoon kirsch or white rum or brandy (optional)

Push the fruit through a nylon or stainless steel sieve. Beat in the icing sugar, if used, until completely dissolved, adjust quantity to taste. Sharpen with the lemon juice and optional alcohol. OR place everything in a processor or blender and work until puréed, adjusting lemon juice and alcohol to taste. Sieve if necessary.

VARIATIONS: Instead of frozen, fruit canned in unsweetened juice can be used, this will probably be sweet enough without additional sugar, the flavour will not be as fresh but certain fruits work very well. Apricots processed with a good slurp of rum produce an excellent sauce.

HOT FUDGE SAUCE

This wonderfully simple sauce will turn any commercial ice cream into a dish fit for the gods, or it can be used with fruit-stuffed pancakes or meringues or apple tart or a slice of cake. In fact, it can turn a wide variety of foods into an instant, scrummy pudding.

50 g/2 oz/4 tablespoons soft light brown sugar
1½ tablespoons unsalted butter
1½ tablespoons golden syrup
1½ tablespoons cream

Place all ingredients in a heavy saucepan, heat gently, stirring every now and then, until the sauce is boiling. Simmer for a couple of minutes. Serve hot.

SWEET WINE SAUCE

This is another, easy, instant sauce that can make a pudding out of odds and ends, such as bananas, or apples cooked in a little filo pastry, stuffed pancakes, sponge cake with fruit, etc. Although it has a very modern feel, it was in fact popular with a wide variety of puddings in the eighteenth century and goes back a long way beyond that.

5 tablespoons medium sweet white wine
1 tablespoon soft light brown sugar
2 tablespoons unsalted butter, diced

Heat wine with sugar gently until melted, bring to boiling point and simmer for 2 minutes. Remove from heat, add butter all at once, swirling round the pan to melt and meld with the wine. Use immediately, warm rather than hot. If you reheat this sauce, the butter will separate out from the wine.

F CHOCOLATE SAUCE

Another simple sauce that's great with ice cream or meringues (or both) and is an inspired combination with pears, either fresh or poached in wine.

50 g/2 oz plain chocolate, broken into pieces
4 tablespoons double cream
1 tablespoon rum
Small nut of butter

Place all ingredients in a bowl over a pan of simmering water and allow to heat gently until chocolate has melted, stirring to achieve a shiny sauce. Use while still warm.

COOK'S TIP: Do choose good quality chocolate: Chocolate Menier in the green packets, Terry's dark or Bournville plain chocolate. So called "cooking chocolate" does not have a sufficiently high proportion of cocoa butter for a satisfactory flavour or texture.

MICROWAVE OVEN: Place all ingredients into deep bowl, cover tightly and microwave on HIGH for 2 minutes. Stir well and serve.

SWEET SABAYON SAUCE

This sauce is basically the same as the savoury one given on page 187, the method is repeated here for ease of reference. It is perfect with fruit, with sweet flans, pancakes, etc.

1 egg yolk
5 tablespoons sweet white wine or sweet cider
1 tablespoon caster sugar
Pinch salt

Place the egg yolk in a bowl that will fit nicely over a saucepan of simmering water, add the wine, or cider, the sugar and salt and beat until pale and very frothy. Place over the simmering water and keep whisking until the sauce has thickened and the whisk is leaving trails. Take the pan off the heat and keep whisking the sauce for a little longer then serve. If liked, a spoonful of cream can be whisked into the sauce after it has thickened, continuing to cook until the cream has heated through.

VARIATIONS: Substitute freshly squeezed orange juice for the wine or cider, or any other fruit juice. Grated orange or lemon peel can be added. An orange sabayon sauce is wonderful with strawberries.

COOK'S TIP: This sauce will keep warm over a pan of hot water for 30–40 minutes. Whisk well before using.

CRÈME ANGLAISE

There are few sauces more versatile than an egg custard, it can accompany almost any fruit, tarts, many different puddings, be used with sponge cake, jam and some cream for trifle. And an amount for two is so quickly made it isn't a chore, it is particularly easy in a microwave.

150 ml/5 fl oz/⅔ cup milk
1 vanilla pod or 2 drops vanilla essence
2 egg yolks, size 3
2 tablespoons caster sugar

Heat the milk with the vanilla pod to just below boiling point then leave, covered, to infuse for 20 minutes. Or heat and add vanilla essence. Beat egg yolks, first on their own, then with the sugar, until thick and pale. Whisk in the warm milk then strain into a clean bowl and place above a pan of simmering water or directly on a very low heat and stir continuously until the custard has thickened enough to coat the back of a spoon.

COOK'S TIP: Vanilla pods can be used more than once. Wash after use, allow to dry then keep in jar of caster sugar, which will become beautifully perfumed with the flavour of the pod. Use the sugar for cakes, biscuits, custard, etc. Slitting the pod to release the tiny black flecks will produce a much stronger flavoured sauce. If buying vanilla essence, make quite sure it is made from the vanilla pod and is not "flavouring", which has a quite different and definitely inferior taste.

MICROWAVE OVEN: Place milk in a litre jug, add the vanilla pod, cover tightly and microwave on HIGH for 3 minutes. Leave for 5 minutes to infuse. Beat yolks, first on their own, then with the sugar, until thick and pale, then whisk in the warm milk. Strain back into the cleaned jug and add the vanilla pod again. Microwave on HIGH, uncovered, for 1 minute. Stir. How much further cooking the sauce needs depends on how hot the milk was when you started. Give it 30 seconds, stir again then finish cooking in 10-second blasts, stirring in between and assessing progress of the sauce. When cooked, give a final stir and pour immediately into a cold jug, removing vanilla pod.

MARMALADE SAUCE

This is the easiest of sauces. Any marmalade can be used to taste but I like the thick-cut and preferably home-made. It's wonderful with vanilla ice cream, and very good with a sweet omelette, LEMON KNIGHTS (see page 205) or ORANGE AND RAISIN PANCAKES (see page 160).

---

1 tablespoon marmalade

---

3 tablespoons amontillado or medium sweet sherry or whisky

Heat together, stirring, until marmalade melted and sauce slightly syrupy, then serve.

SIMPLE WHITE SAUCE

A useful sauce for any number of puddings, perhaps when you haven't the time to make a proper custard. It is particularly simple to make in a microwave oven.

---

225 ml/7½ fl oz/scant cup milk

---

1 dessertspoon cornflour

1–2 tablespoons caster sugar

Few drops vanilla essence

Small knob butter (optional)

Take a tablespoon of the cold milk and mix with the cornflour to a smooth paste. Add the sugar to the remaining milk and heat to just below boiling point. Add a little of the hot mixture to the slaked cornflour, mix well, return this to the hot milk and bring to boil, stirring constantly, until thickened and smooth. Add the vanilla essence and stir in with butter if using, it will give the sauce a lovely shine.

MICROWAVE OVEN: Blend the cornflour with a little of the milk in a jug (or bowl) of at least 1 litre/1¾ pint/4½ cup capacity, then add the rest of the milk, sugar to taste and the vanilla essence. Cook, uncovered, on HIGH for 3 minutes or until thick, whisking carefully every minute. If using butter, add this at the end.

VARIATIONS: Grated orange or lemon rind can be added, or 1 tablespoon cocoa powder. Or substitute half the milk with strong black coffee.

SWEET TALK

I have to admit that my husband and I don't often have puddings, weight seems to adhere to our frames on the most spartan of meals so including sweet dishes too often is a recipe for Michelin-figure qualification, a full set of spare tyres in no time! But every now and then a pud rounds off the meal and it needn't take great effort. Meringues are a great standby, they keep extremely well and can be used with ice cream, fruit or a sweet sauce for a very easy pudding.

Fresh fruit is delicious as well as healthy, a simple fruit salad for two doesn't take long to prepare and is so much more attractive and appetising than an apple straight from the bowl.

Baby bread puddings are fun, Lemon Knights and a jam omelette delicious and very little trouble to do. Yoghurt can be mixed with ready-to-eat dried fruit or fresh fruit for another instant pudding, a session in the fridge with demerara sugar on top will produce a mock brûlée (see below for recipes).

Pastry can provide another set of puddings. Don't think it's a bore to make, one batch can provide two meals, see suggestions after the following recipe for ways of using the other half.

TARTE TATIN

One of the nicest of all puddings, the combination of the buttery fruit and crisp pastry is sensational, and the tart itself is very simple. Lots of variations are possible, see at the end of the recipe. Remember when choosing the baking dish that the tart will be served turned out and that you will need a similarly shaped but slightly larger dish for its presentation.

50 g/2 oz/4 tablespoons butter

50 g/2 oz/4 tablespoons sugar, fine demerara is nice

3 crisp eating apples, cored, peeled and cut into thick sections

Half quantity basic shortcrust pastry (see recipe in BACK TO BASICS section on page 274 but make full quantity and use other half for another dish, see below for suggestions)

Little icing sugar (for presentation)

Butter thickly the base and sides of a small gratin or other suitable oven-proof dish or tin and sprinkle with half the sugar. Arrange apples neatly inside, packing close together. Flake the remaining butter over and sprinkle with rest of sugar. Roll out pastry and fit over the fruit but inside the dish or tin rather than over the edge, trim roughly to shape then tuck in excess pastry neatly. Place in preheated oven at 190°C/375°F/Gas Mark 5 for 40–45 minutes.

Remove from oven, allow to cool slightly then turn out on to a fireproof dish the same shape as the baking dish. The tart is now upside down. It should be nicely caramelised at the bottom but hardly ever is. So sprinkle over some icing sugar and finish off under a hot grill.

ACCOMPANIMENTS: Egg custard or cream.

VARIATIONS: Use pears instead of apples, or apricots, dry off well if you are using soaked dried ones, or peaches, or try anything that takes your fancy, popular with some chefs is mango served with a raspberry sauce.

TOWARDS TOMORROW: Use second half of pastry for a quiche, see NO MEAT NO FISH section, or to top a fruit or savoury pie. Or make one of the following sweet flans:

F PEAR FRANGIPANE

A most delicious tart, rich but light.

Half quantity basic shortcrust pastry (see BACK TO BASICS section on page 274)

Frangipane:

50 g/2 oz/4 tablespoons butter
50 g/2 oz/4 tablespoons caster sugar
2 egg yolks, beaten
1½ teaspoons rum
50 g/2 oz/3 tablespoons ground almonds
1½ tablespoons flour

2 dessert pears (Williams, etc.), ripe but firm
1½ tablespoons preserve jelly such as quince or redcurrant
1 tablespoon rum

Use pastry to line a 15–18 cm/6–7 inch flan tin, chill for 30 minutes then bake blind in a preheated oven at 190°C/375°F/Gas Mark 5 for 15 minutes. Cool.

Cream butter, beat in sugar until pale and soft, beat in egg yolks, then the rum and finally stir in flour and ground almonds. Or process butter and sugar until pale and soft, trickle in egg yolk with machine running. Add other ingredients with machine off then give a very quick whizz to blend together. Pour frangipane into the cool pastry case and spread evenly.

Peel pears, cut in half, remove core with a teaspoon and cut out stalk. Place flat on chopping board and slice through length of pear into thin segments, keeping pear half together. Press slightly to ease pieces of pear into fitting one quarter of the tin, then lift in with a spatula. Repeat with other pear halves.

Place in a preheated oven at 190°C/375°F/Gas Mark 5 for 15 minutes, reduce heat to 180°C/350°F/Gas Mark 4 for a further 15–20 minutes until flan browned and frangipane set. Heat jelly to melt with the rum then use to brush over the top of the cooked tart.

Serve at room temperature.

ACCOMPANIMENTS: Whipped cream, Greek-style yoghurt or *crème fraîche*.

COOK'S TIP: Several layers of well-scrunched tin foil gently fitted into the pastry case are excellent for baking blind, the foil transmits the heat to the pastry base and helps it become crisp at the same time as the edges. Keep the foil ready shaped for future bakings.

MICROWAVE OVEN: Can be used to melt jelly and rum, place in a bowl, cover tightly with cling film and microwave on HIGH for 1 minute.

F   FIG FLAN

Forget nursery jokes about figs. As long as you can deal with the pips, these rich, succulent fruits have a lot to offer. Here they are used for a delicious flan.

Half quantity basic shortcrust pastry (see BACK TO BASICS section on page 274)
7–8 dried ready-to-eat figs
1 medium sized egg, lightly beaten
75 ml/2½ fl oz/5 tablespoons milk or single cream
1 tablespoon caster sugar
2 drops vanilla essence

Use the pastry to line a 15–18 cm/6–7 inch flan tin, or two individual flan tins, and bake blind at 190°C/375°F/Gas Mark 5 for 20 minutes if you have time as this will give a crisper finish. Otherwise go straight to the filling stage: trim any hard stalk off the soaked figs, cut in half lengthwise and arrange in the flan case with the seeds uppermost. Beat egg into milk or cream with the sugar, add the drops of vanilla essence then pour over the figs. Place in preheated oven at 190°C/375°F/Gas Mark 5 for approximately 30 minutes, until custard set. Best eaten warm.

ACCOMPANIMENTS: Cream or thick yoghurt.

VARIATIONS: Fresh figs can be used if these are available.

COOK'S TIP: Always buy vanilla essence, made from the beans, rather than vanilla *flavouring*, which only pretends to taste like the beans. It does, in fact, bear very little resemblance to the real thing.

FUDGE BANANAS

Bananas are such a useful fruit to have around, so easy to peel and slice. Added to a little left-over dried fruit salad they can change its whole character, or mixed with thick yoghurt or whipped cream they make an instant dessert. My husband likes a banana with his porridge. Mashed with lemon they make a good sandwich filling. Here they are cooked to make a pudding that is as quick and easy as it is good tasting.

2 bananas
2–3 tablespoons demerara sugar
Walnut-sized knob of unsalted butter
5 tablespoons natural yoghurt mixed with ½ teaspoon cornflour OR 5 tablespoons double cream
A little freshly squeezed lemon juice
Little additional demerara sugar

Heat grill. Place sugar and butter in saucepan and heat to melt. Add yoghurt or cream and bring to boil, stirring constantly until smoothly amalgamated and slightly thickened. Sharpen with lemon juice to taste and simmer for 2–3 minutes.

Slice bananas into shallow, fireproof dish, pour over fudge sauce, sprinkle with a little more sugar and place under hot grill for about 5 minutes, when bananas should be heated through and sauce slightly caramelised. Serve immediately.

VARIATIONS: Instead of fudge sauce, place peeled bananas in small ovenproof dish, splash over 3 tablespoons rum plus a squeeze of lemon juice, dot with a little butter, sprinkle with a tablespoon or two of demerara sugar and place in a preheated oven at 190°C/375°F/Gas Mark 5, for 10 minutes, baste once during cooking if convenient, then serve accompanied by cream or Greek-style yoghurt.

MICROWAVE OVEN: Place sauce ingredients in a small jug or basin, cover tightly with cling film and microwave on HIGH for 2 minutes. Uncover carefully, stir well then pour over bananas, sprinkle over the sugar, cover tightly again and microwave on HIGH for 1 minute 30 seconds if sauce is hot, 2 minutes if sauce only lukewarm. For the bananas with rum, place rum, lemon, butter and sugar in a jug or bowl, cover tightly and microwave on HIGH for 2 minutes. Uncover very carefully, pour over the peeled bananas placed in a suitable dish, re-cover tightly with cling film and microwave on HIGH for 3 minutes. Serve as above.

TOWARDS TOMORROW: Make double the quantity of fudge sauce and save half to reheat and serve with vanilla ice cream.

RASPBERRY RICE CREAM

*Start preparation several hours before serving
This is a delicious way to make a few raspberries go a long way. It is as good with frozen as with fresh berries.

40 g/1½ oz/3 tablespoons round pudding rice
300 ml/10 fl oz/generous cup full cream milk
50 g/2 oz/4 tablespoons caster sugar
1 egg, separated
75 g/3 oz/¾ cup raspberries

Wash rice thoroughly, place in pan with milk, bring to boil then lower heat, cover and simmer very gently until rice is very tender. By then all the milk should have been absorbed, if not, remove lid and cook a little longer until it is. Stir in half the sugar. Beat the egg yolk until pale, remove rice from heat, stir in the yolk then return mixture to a very gentle heat and stir until slightly thickened. Allow to cool, stirring occasionally to prevent a skin forming, or cover with cling film. Whip egg white to stiff peak, whip in remaining sugar then fold into cooled rice mixture. Reserve a few nice raspberries for garnish then fold remaining berries into rice. Fill either one dish or two individual glasses and place reserved berries on top.

VARIATIONS: Instead of the raspberries, fold in chopped orange segments removed without membrane (see BACK TO BASICS section on page

280), garnish with a segment or two. Other possible fruits are other berries, cherries, mango, passion fruit, pineapple, etc.

COOK'S TIP: Watch the rice, it can get very sticky if allowed to cook too long.

TOWARDS TOMORROW: Cook double quantities of rice and mix with some other fruit for a pudding a day or so later. Or serve with fresh fruit on the side. The second half can also be reheated (without the egg) with raisins for a hot pudding. Serve with a little cream on the top.

YOGHURT CHEESE AND FRUIT DESSERT

As well as being very healthy, yoghurt is wonderfully versatile. Apart from using it as it comes, yoghurt can be drained in muslin overnight, when it will turn into a simple curd cheese. Here it is used for a dessert with a Middle Eastern flavour.

300 ml/10 fl oz/generous cup natural yoghurt drained overnight in a piece of muslin or similar

25 g/1 oz/3 tablespoons chopped dates

6 kumquats, cut in quarters, skin left on, seeds removed OR segments removed from 1 orange without the membrane

1 small eating apple, cored, diced and tossed in freshly squeezed lemon juice

1 tablespoon sunflower seeds, lightly toasted

1 tablespoon clear honey heated with 1 tablespoon freshly squeezed lemon juice and allowed to cool

Divide the yoghurt cheese between two small dessert dishes, arrange fruits around. Sprinkle over the sunflower seeds then dribble over the honey and lemon mixture.

VARIATIONS: The fruits can be anything you like, summer berries are delightfully fresh, just sprinkle with lemon juice and only use sugar if you have a really sweet tooth.

COOK'S TIP: J-cloths are great for any culinary use that calls for muslin. Sterilise before use by boiling in water.

TOWARDS TOMORROW: Prepare double the amount of yoghurt cheese, roll remainder in chopped walnuts and serve with cheese biscuits.

BREAD AND BUTTER PUDDING

Anton Mosimann and Michel Bourdin have both brought new chic to this nursery favourite. It can be as rich or plain as you like. This version has lots of flavour and is creamy without being sinful.

2 slices bread, granary, brown or white according to taste, spread generously with unsalted butter
1 tablespoon each sultanas, raisins and chopped candied peel
1 whole egg and 1 egg yolk, lightly beaten
150 ml/5 fl oz/⅔ cup milk
Good pinch cinnamon mixed with 1 tablespoon sugar (optional)
1–2 tablespoons soft brown sugar

Cut bread in quarters and layer or overlap in a buttered ovenproof dish, scattering the dried and candied fruits in between the layers. Beat egg into milk with the cinnamon sugar, if using, and pour over the bread. Allow to stand for at least 30 minutes, one hour is better, then sprinkle over the sugar, place dish in a pan, add hot water to halfway up dish and bake in a preheated oven at 180°C/350°F/Gas Mark 4 for 40–45 minutes, until custard is set. Serve warm.

ACCOMPANIMENTS: Apricot sauce made by liquidising a small tin of apricots in natural juices, a tablespoon of rum can be added if liked OR single cream.

VARIATIONS: Individual puddings can be made in large ramekin dishes, bake *au bain-marie*, in a bath of hot water, in the oven as above. Apricot jam can be spread on bread instead of using the dried and candied fruit.

COOK'S TIP: Bridge rolls or brioche will make an incredibly light version.

LEMON KNIGHTS

Another good way of using left-over bread, a version of Poor Knights, or French Toast. It uses items usually on hand and, like so many simple things, it tastes wonderful. To make it really special, serve with a strawberry or raspberry sauce (see FRUIT SAUCE in SAUCY IDEAS section on page 193).

1 egg, lightly beaten
1 tablespoon milk
2 tablespoons caster sugar
1 teaspoon freshly grated lemon rind
2 large or 4 small thickish slices white bread
½ oz butter, 1 tablespoon arachide/ groundnut/peanut oil

Mix together the beaten egg, the milk, one tablespoon of the sugar and the lemon rind. Dip the bread in the mixture, first on one side, then the other. Heat the butter and oil then fry each slice of bread on both sides until golden and crisp. Put on serving plate and sprinkle with remaining caster sugar.

ACCOMPANIMENTS: A strawberry or raspberry sauce is spectacular but jam will do instead, use a good, low-set variety like Bonne Maman. Maple syrup is also good. At the other end of the sweetness spectrum, thick yoghurt is lovely. Fresh fruit also goes well.

VARIATIONS: Omit the lemon, mix the sugar with a little ground cinnamon or mixed spice for a spicy flavour OR substitute orange for the lemon. Use fruited bread instead of plain.

APRICOT CLAFOUTIS

A pudding that is warming and delicious, ideal for serving when the oven is being used for another course as well. Use the ready-to-eat dried apricots, then the soaking is the only preparation needed before cooking. Otherwise the fruit will need to be precooked.

75 g/3 oz/⅓ cup sliced dried ready-to-eat apricots, boiling water poured over and fruit left to soak several hours
1½ tablespoons plain flour
2 tablespoons demerara sugar
1 large egg and 1 egg yolk
150 ml/5 fl oz/⅔ cup milk

Sift flour into a bowl, stir in the sugar, add the egg and the yolk in a little well then gradually stir in the milk, drawing in the flour and mixing all together into a smooth batter. If possible, leave to sit for a couple of hours.

Drain the soaked apricots and place in a buttered gratin dish with a capacity of just under 600 ml/1 pint/generous 2 cups. Give batter a good stir and pour over, bake in a preheated oven at 180°C/350°F/Gas Mark 4, for about 40 minutes, until puffy and golden brown. Serve hot or warm.

ACCOMPANIMENTS: Cream or thick yoghurt.

VARIATIONS: Any fruit can be used instead of the apricots, black cherries are traditional but try also sliced apples or pears, any soft fruits, apples and blackberries, etc.

COOK'S TIP: Letting the batter sit allows the starch cells in the flour to absorb the liquid and so gives a little lighter effect to the finished dish.

F DRIED FRUIT SOUP

*Start preparation several hours before serving

This is a traditional favourite in Sweden. It is light on the digestion and has a very good flavour.

100 g/4 oz/1 cup mixed dried fruit, well washed and soaked overnight in 750 ml/1¼ pints/3 cups water
1 piece lemon peel removed without any pith
1 tablespoon sugar
1 tablespoon potato flour or arrowroot

Add the peel to the fruit in its soaking water, bring to the boil then lower heat and poach very gently until tender. Add the sugar and allow to dissolve. Slake the potato flour or arrowroot with a little water, add a little of the hot poaching liquid then stir into the pan of fruit. Bring back to the boil and stir gently until the juices are transparent and slightly thickened. Serve warm or cold.

ACCOMPANIMENTS: Cream or Greek-style yoghurt.

VARIATIONS: The thickening agent can be omitted and the soup served just as it is OR the fruit can be nicely arranged on a flat dish then brushed with the thickened juices and finished with a few toasted almonds for a dried fruit *salade compote*.

COOK'S TIP: To avoid any possibility of breaking up the fruit while the soup is thickening, the juices can be drained off the cooked fruit and thickened on their own, then poured back over the fruit.

MICROWAVE OVEN: The dried fruit will cook beautifully in the microwave without any need to presoak. Place in a large container with 350 ml/ 12 fl oz/1½ cups water, plus the piece of lemon rind, cover tightly with cling film and microwave on HIGH for 10 minutes, turning fruit over halfway through cooking. Arrowroot and potato flour don't cook very well in the microwave so either do this operation on the stove or substitute ½ tablespoon cornflour, slake with cold water, add the hot liquid from the fruit, stir well, cover tightly with cling film and microwave on HIGH for 1½ minutes, stir, then add to fruit.

TOWARDS TOMORROW: Cook more fruit than is needed and use part, without thickening the juices, for the PARADISE SOUFFLÉ (see TONIGHT'S SPECIAL – DESSERTS section on page 243), or eat for breakfast with or without cereal.

RHUBARB NUTTY CRUMBLE

Crumble mixtures can make a substantial dessert of many fruits. Here nuts are added and used with rhubarb for a warming spring pud.

225–350 g/8–12 oz rhubarb, trimmed, cut into short lengths, washed
Grated rind and juice 1 orange
2 tablespoons soft brown sugar
40 g/1½ oz/3 tablespoons butter
6 tablespoons wholewheat flour
Pinch salt
3 tablespoons demerara sugar
1½ tablespoons toasted hazelnuts, roughly chopped

Mix together the washed rhubarb with the grated orange rind, place in a shallow ovenproof dish and sprinkle over the orange juice and the soft brown sugar. Rub the butter into the flour seasoned with a pinch of salt, add the demerara sugar and hazelnuts and mix together. Cover the rhubarb with the crumble mixture and place in a preheated oven at 225°C/425°F/Gas Mark 7 for 30 minutes, turning down the heat towards the end of cooking if the crumble mixture browns too quickly.

ACCOMPANIMENTS: Cream or thick yoghurt.

VARIATIONS: The topping can be used on all sorts of fruit such as apple, pears, apricots, plums, etc. The hazelnuts can be omitted or replaced with other nuts. Chopped dried fruit can be used in the crumble mixture instead of nuts.

BAKED APPLES WITH RUM AND RAISINS

Who was it who said that a millionaire's favourite pudding was a baked apple? A good one is, indeed, neatly wrapped perfection. Two things determine the quality of any baked apple, the first is the fruit itself, I think nothing beats a Bramley, the second is the flavour given by the filling. This recipe is delicious but some alternatives are suggested below. Choose your apples carefully, checking for imperfections and finding a good shape.

2 medium sized Bramley apples
2 tablespoons large raisins, soaked several hours in 2 tablespoons light rum
Knob butter
2 tablespoons water
2 tablespoons clear honey

Wash the apples, core them, score a line round their equators (this helps prevent them splitting in the cooking), place them in an ovenproof dish then stuff the holes with the soaked raisins. Pour any remaining rum over the apples, add a knob of butter on top of the raisins, sprinkle over the water then spoon over the honey. Place in a preheated oven at 200°C/400°F/ Gas Mark 6, for 45–60 minutes, until cooked.

ACCOMPANIMENTS: Custard, cream or thick yoghurt.

VARIATIONS: Use chopped dried apricots soaked in little orange juice instead of the raisins. Add chopped almonds, walnuts or hazelnuts. Just fill the centres with demerara sugar and omit the rum and honey. Cook the apples in a little wine instead of water, or in a mixture of orange and lemon juice, add grated zest to the filling. Mix candied fruit with the raisins or use instead of the dried fruit.

COOK'S TIP: If use of the oven makes it suitable, apples can be cooked at a lower temperature for a longer period.

MICROWAVE OVEN: Prepare apples as above, place in a suitable dish so they are not touching, cover tightly with cling film and microwave on HIGH for 3½ minutes. Slip point of knife into cling film to pierce then allow to stand for 5 minutes.

F BAKED PEARS WITH HONEY AND CARDAMOM

Baked pears are as good as baked apples. The effect is different because the fruit is peeled before cooking but, once again, lots of variations are possible. The cardamom gives a spicy flavour with a green edge that goes well with the buttery pear flesh. Acacia is the sweetest of all honeys but you can substitute any other as long as it's clear.

2 pears, Conference or similar
4 cardamom pods, seeds released and crushed
2 tablespoons acacia honey
Knob of butter
3 tablespoons water

Peel pears, cut in half, remove core with a teaspoon, cut out the threads of stalk, place fruit in an ovenproof dish. Mix together the cardamom and the honey and pour into the holes left by the removal of the cores. Top with a few flakes of butter. Add the water to the dish, cover either with a lid or a piece of tin foil and place in a preheated oven at 180°C/350°F/Gas Mark 4 for 45–60 minutes, until pears are cooked through, if they were very unripe, they may take even longer.

ACCOMPANIMENTS: Cream, vanilla ice cream, thick yoghurt.

VARIATIONS: Omit cardamom, use chopped crystallised ginger instead, or leave plain. Cook in a mixture of half white wine and half water.

COOK'S TIP: Choose pears that are firm, ripe ones will disintegrate in the cooking.

MICROWAVE OVEN: Prepare as above, arrange in single layer in suitable dish, cover tightly with cling film, microwave on HIGH for 5 minutes. Pierce film and allow to stand for 5 minutes. Test tenderness with the point of a knife and give a minute or two longer cooking if necessary, patching holes in the covering with more cling film.

CITRUS FRUIT SALAD

*Start preparation several hours or night before serving

A very refreshing pudding that has an attractive *mélange* of sweet and sharp flavours. It is also very healthy.

1 orange, segments removed without membrane
1 small or ½ large grapefruit, segments removed without membrane
2 dried apricots, ready to eat, sliced thinly
1 passion fruit
To Serve: Greek-style yoghurt

Place the orange and grapefruit segments with the sliced apricots and leave to marinate for several hours or overnight. Before serving, divide fruit between two dishes. Cut the passion fruit in half and add the pulp and seeds over the top of each portion. Serve with thick yoghurt.

ACCOMPANIMENTS: Crisp little dessert biscuits.

VARIATIONS: For those with a really sweet tooth, a little honey can be added to the yoghurt.

COOK'S TIP: Seeds of the passion fruit can be sieved out but I think they look interesting and add to the textural quality of this dish.

TOWARDS TOMORROW: Use the other half of the grapefruit for AVOCADO SURPRISE (TONIGHT'S SPECIAL – STARTERS section on page 213).

JAM SOUFFLÉ OMELETTE

Very easy but very effective and quite delicious, this simple pudding makes a good ending to any meal.

2 large eggs, separated
1 dessertspoon caster sugar
1 tablespoon single cream or milk
1–2 tablespoons good jam: strawberry, apricot, black cherry, etc.
Small knob butter
Little sifted icing sugar

Beat egg yolks with sugar until pale, beat in the cream or milk. Warm jam in a small saucepan. Heat grill or set oven at 200°C/400°F/Gas Mark 6. Whip egg whites to soft peak and fold into the yolk mixture carefully but thoroughly.

Heat small frying pan (approximately 18 cm/7 inches diameter), add the knob of butter, let it melt and as it foams, add the egg mixture. Cook on a moderate heat for 1 minute to set and brown the bottom. Then place under the grill or in the oven to cook the top. Spread the warm jam over the top, fold one side over the other and slide on to a warm plate. Sift icing sugar over the top and serve immediately.

ACCOMPANIMENTS: Cream if liked.

VARIATIONS: Jam can be replaced with a little ripe fruit such as berries or cooked apple, etc. OR sliced bananas heated in a little butter then sprinkled with lemon juice or rum are very good, so are strawberries heated with a little redcurrant jelly.

COOK'S TIP: The icing sugar can be marked with red-hot skewers, caramelising the top into diamonds.

TONIGHT'S SPECIAL

Cooking a special meal for two can be great fun. Buying a luxury item is not such a burden as it is for more and every once in a while it is interesting to attempt something a little more complicated than normal. A full-scale dinner party for two need not, in fact, call for enormous effort or vast expense.

STARTERS

AVOCADO SURPRISE

The surprise here is that the avocado is served hot. Baking can be tricky as the fruit can turn both watery and bitter if overcooked. But flashed under the grill with bacon across the top, the flesh is warmed into melting butteriness. The combination of avocado, bacon and grapefruit is particularly good, the acidity of the fruit providing a good contrast to the richness of the pear and bacon.

1 ripe avocado pear
Few segments grapefruit, without membrane, cut into chunks
4 rashers smoked streaky bacon, cut into strips
Freshly ground black pepper

Just before eating, cut avocado pear in half. Remove the stone and fill the centre of each half with the grapefruit chunks. Lay the strips of bacon across the top, covering the surface of the pear. Place under a hot grill until the bacon is sizzling. Serve immediately.

VARIATIONS: Place mussels under the bacon instead of the grapefruit, or prawns OR use a little diced salami sausage in the hole and cover with grated cheese.

COOK'S TIP: Cut the avocado with a stainless steel knife. Silver knives used to be advocated but who has one of those these days? Anyway, stainless steel is just as effective but carbon knives can turn the flesh black.

SEAFOOD AND MELON

Small Charentais or Galia melons cut in half and stuffed with prawns or any other seafood are delicious. I'm not a great one for fancy effects, partly because I lack the dexterity to achieve them successfully but also because I prefer food to look what it is. However it is quite easy to cut melon in a simple serrated pattern that helps create the impression of care having been taken. Insert a sharp, small knife in a series of angled cuts around the middle of the melon, slanting the knife first one way then the other, linking up the cuts. Then pull the two halves of the fruit apart, *et voilà*!

For slimmers, approximately 100 g/4 oz/ ½ cup good prawns each dressed with a squeeze or two of fresh lemon juice and a couple of turns of the pepper mill, is perfect. But the dressing in the following recipe gives a little more flavour and the fennel offers an interesting contrast, both in flavour and texture, with the prawns and melon.

---

1 small Charentais or Galia melon, cut in half and seeds removed (if the melons are very small, use one per person, cutting off each top and removing seeds)

---

100 g/4 oz/1 cup frozen shelled prawns, defrosted

---

50 g/2 oz/⅓ cup diced fresh fennel

½ tablespoon freshly squeezed lemon juice

---

2 tablespoons olive oil

¼ teaspoon Maille Moutarde au Poivre Vert

½ tablespoon mixed fines herbes (chives, chervil, parsley, tarragon, as are available)

Salt and freshly ground black pepper

Mix together the lemon juice, olive oil, mustard, herbs and seasoning. When completely emulsified, check seasoning then add the prawns and fennel and mix well together. Pile into the melon halves (or the whole melons), top with a slice of lemon cut butterfly style and serve.

214

VARIATIONS: Many variations are possible. Reduce the amount of prawns and add small dice of cucumber and slivers of peeled tomato flesh and add some mussels, freshly cooked or preserved in brine. OR substitute flaked, cooked fish for the prawns, perhaps diced monkfish, lightly poached in a little court bouillon, then cooled. OR use scampi or lobster meat OR diced ham mixed with French beans is very good. OR, for a vegetarian version, use a mixture of French beans cut into 2.5 cm/1 inch lengths of sliced fresh fennel, mix with diced cucumber and tomato plus diced apple tossed in lemon juice. The same dressing will do for all these variations though with the vegetarian version substituting tarragon vinegar for the lemon will add extra flavour.

COOK'S TIPS: 1) Grapefruit, oranges and tomatoes can be cut in the same way as suggested for the melon in the introduction above. 2) To butterfly a slice of orange or lemon, cut from the centre through the skin, pull the cut edges apart and sit the slice on food or a plate.

TROUT SMOKIES

Really good smoked trout needs nothing more than a segment of lemon and thinly sliced brown bread and butter. But there are times when simple perfection is not enough, or the trout is not quite as good as hoped. Then try this:

1 small smoked trout, skin and bones removed
1 tomato, peeled and deseeded, the flesh cut into segments
Freshly ground black pepper
1 teaspoon tarragon vinegar
1 teaspoon caster sugar
4 tablespoons double cream

Divide the smoked trout between two small fireproof ramekins. Add the segments of tomato plus a couple of grinds of black pepper to each. Whip together the vinegar, sugar and double cream until it holds its shape, spread on top of the trout then place in a preheated hot oven, 200°C/400°F/Gas Mark 6, for 5 minutes. Serve immediately.

ACCOMPANIMENTS: Thinly sliced brown bread and butter.

VARIATIONS: Use smoked mackerel instead of the trout, the flavour is more full bodied and the result equally delicious.

215

EGGS MIMOSA

Really simple, this, bu... and it tastes excellent.

2 hard-boiled eg...	
50 g/2 oz/4 tablespoons	
1 tablespoon thick...	
1 tablespoon single cr...	
4 fillets ancho...	
Garnish: Watercr...	

Cut the hard-boiled eggs in half, remove yolks and set as... with prawns and turn both halves of each egg upside down on either one serving dish or two individual plates. Mix together the mayonnaise with the cream or yoghurt to achieve a coating consistency, check seasoning. Spoon over the eggs. Place the yolks in a small sieve or Mouli cheese grater and sieve or grate over the eggs (this is the Mimosa bit). Split the fillets of anchovy and cross two halves over each egg. If liked, a little watercress can be used to add a final garnish to each plate.

COOK'S TIP: Don't keep homemade mayonnaise in the fridge, it can separate when brought back to room temperature. Also the acidity in the vinegar will be hindered from killing off any Salmonella bacteria.

TOWARDS TOMORROW: Use the remaining anchovy fillets in the tin with scrambled eggs OR for a garnish on an open sandwich OR use in the recipe for STUFFED DUCK'S LEGS (see TONIGHT'S SPECIAL – MAIN COURSES section on page 231). OR pound or process with black olives and a little good olive oil for a good spread that will keep well in the fridge (see HELP FOR MOTHER HUBBARD section on page 263).

CAMEMBERT PACKETS

Another very simple starter that is spectacularly good, the crisp filo pastry contrasting beautifully with the melting cheese.

2 sheets filo pastry
2 triangles of Camembert cheese (individual or cut from a larger piece), ripe but not at all runny
Little Maille Moutarde au Poivre Vert
Approx. 1 tablespoon unsalted butter, melted

Fold filo pastry sheet in half, keeping other sheet under cling film to prevent it drying out. Brush pastry with melted butter, turn over. Spread a smidgeon of mustard on either side of the cheese, place in the middle of the doubled-over pastry and wrap neatly, or bring pastry up and pinch together, making a sort of draw-string purse. Repeat with second piece of pastry and cheese. Place in fridge for 1 to 3 hours then bake in preheated oven at 200°C/400°F/Gas Mark 6, for 10 minutes, until pastry is golden and crisp.

VARIATIONS: There are many fillings possible with these little parcels: cooked mushrooms are very good and can be mixed with diced ham for a more substantial dish. The cheese can be diced and mixed with toasted pine nuts. Shellfish are another option, no need to cook first, toss in lemon juice or a little French dressing and add some chopped herbs. Rounds of goat's cheese can be used instead of the Camembert. Puff pastry can be used instead of filo but will take approximately 25 minutes to cook.

COOK'S TIP: Unused filo pastry can be refrozen for another day. The size of sheets varies, with small ones, use two sheets for each packet.

GRILLED GOAT'S CHEESE

Goat's cheese of the Brie variety, such as Capricorn, has a combination of firmness and creaminess that is ideal for this dead-simple treatment. Really good olive oil is essential for the best result.

1 round goat's cheese, Capricorn or similar
Little extra virgin olive oil, cold pressed
Few black peppercorns, crushed OR few fresh basil leaves

Cut the cheese into four slices, trimming off the white skin at top and bottom but not on sides. Brush each piece of cheese with olive oil then press it into the crushed black peppercorns, if using. Place on a tin-foil lined grill pan and set under a preheated grill until the cheese starts to melt. Remove from heat, use a spatula to place each piece on a serving plate and either serve immediately OR leave to cool then place on a Nasturtium or vine leaf and garnish with Nasturtium or borage flowers, or use watercress. If using the basil leaves, tear these over in small pieces immediately before serving.

ACCOMPANIMENTS: Good granary or slightly malted brown bread spread with unsalted butter.

COOK'S TIP: As soon as basil leaves are cut or torn they will start to go black, always prepare just before serving.

SPICY GRILLED GRAPEFRUIT

Another very simple starter, fresh and light but ideal for a chilly autumn or winter day.

1 grapefruit, preferably a ruby variety
1 tablespoon soft brown sugar
Good pinch ground cinnamon
3 pods cardamom, seeds released and crushed

Cut the grapefruit in half then cut round each segment with a grapefruit knife so that the flesh can be lifted out easily. Mix together the sugar, cinnamon and cardamom. Thoroughly heat the grill on its highest setting. Sprinkle the spiced sugar mixture over each grapefruit half, set under the grill, leave till bubbling hot then serve immediately.

VARIATIONS: Omit the spices and pour a dessertspoonful of medium sherry over each grapefruit half, add the sugar and grill as above. A little chopped crystallised ginger can be added before serving.

F DRUNKEN KIPPERS

*Start preparation 24 hours before eating
This is an old favourite I used to do when I was first married, it is no less good for that and very easy. Do choose good kipper fillets, preferably those smoked without artificial colouring.

4 small kipper fillets, or a pair of small kippers, de-boned and filleted
2 shallots, peeled and finely sliced, OR 4 spring onions, white and pale green parts sliced
150 ml/5 fl oz/²⁄₃ cup dry white wine
½ teaspoon each black peppercorns and coriander seeds, 6 juniper berries and 6 allspice berries, all lightly crushed, half a bay leaf
½ tablespoon lemon juice
Garnish: 2 slices lemon

Skin kipper fillets by slipping a sharp, flexible knife blade between the kipper's skin and flesh then, keeping the angle nicely flat and firmly holding the end of the skin, push the blade quickly away from you, stripping the flesh off (it's much easier than it sounds!). Cut into 2.5 cm/ 1 inch slices and place in a single layer in a shallow dish. Scatter over the slices of shallots or spring onions.

Place the wine in a pan, add the spices, bring slowly to the boil, simmer for 2 to 3 minutes, then cool. Add the lemon juice and pour the dressing over the fillets, cover with cling film and leave to marinate overnight. Garnish with lemon slices before serving.

ACCOMPANIMENTS: Crusty brown bread with unsalted butter.

VARIATIONS: Substitute chunks of smoked haddock, uncooked, for the kippers. Don't use smoked trout, the spices will swamp its delicate flavour, and I think smoked mackerel is too oily for this treatment.

MARINATED MUSHROOMS EN CROÛTE

Another old favourite brought up to date with a crisp case of filo pastry.

175 g/6 oz/3 cups button mushrooms
150 ml/5 fl oz/⅔ cup extra virgin olive oil, cold pressed
1 tablespoon red wine vinegar
1 clove garlic, crushed
½ teaspoon each coriander seeds and allspice berries
Salt and freshly ground black pepper
Juice 1 lemon
4 pieces filo pastry approx. 20 cm/8 inches square
Little unsalted butter, melted
Little grated lemon peel
1 tablespoon chopped parsley.

Rub any clinging compost off mushrooms but do not peel. Trim off ends of stalks, cut large mushrooms into four. Bring the olive oil, wine vinegar, garlic, coriander, allspice, salt and ground pepper gently to the boil then allow to simmer for 2 minutes. Add the mushrooms and simmer for 5 minutes. Remove from heat, add the lemon juice and marinate for at least 4 hours.

To make the filo cases: Choose a couple of small ramekin dishes or other ovenproof containers and butter the outsides very well, place upside down on a buttered baking sheet. Brush filo pastry each side with melted butter.

Drape two pieces over each container, pressing the pastry lightly against the sides. Place the second piece of pastry at an angle to the first so that the points form a petal effect round the container. Bake in a preheated oven at 200°C/400°F/Gas Mark 6 for 10 minutes, or until golden brown and crisp. Remove from oven, carefully take off the pastry from each container, remove containers from baking sheet then place the pastry other way up back on the baking sheet and return to the oven for a few minutes so that the insides become crisp.

Mix together a little grated lemon peel with the tablespoon chopped parsley.

Just before eating, place each pastry container on a serving plate, drain the mushrooms and divide between them. Dribble a little of the cooking liquid over, sprinkle over the mixed lemon peel and parsley and serve immediately.

VARIATIONS: The mushrooms don't actually need to be placed in pastry cases, they can be served just as they are in a little dish, or on a vine or Nasturtium leaf, with some fresh brown bread and unsalted butter. Or with croûtons of fried bread. Other vegetables can be prepared in the same way. Try very young leeks or small, quartered, leaf artichokes (trim tops of leaves and remove stem and hairy choke first), both will need longer cooking.

COOK'S TIP: Much of the flavour of the mushrooms depends on the quality of the oil, don't stint on this, go for a good green flavour. The pastry cases will start to go soggy as soon as you add the mushrooms so don't keep the prepared dish hanging around.

MICROWAVE OVEN: Place marinade ingredients in suitable bowl, cover tightly with cling film and cook on HIGH for 3 minutes. Uncover carefully, add mushrooms, re-cover tightly with cling film, cook on HIGH for 3 minutes. Allow to cool and proceed as above.

TOWARDS TOMORROW: Cook and marinate double quantities, the remaining half will keep well for several days in the fridge and can be used as part of a salad. Good accompaniments would be hard-boiled eggs and crisp lettuce hearts such as Little Gem. Split anchovy fillets are good as a final garnish.

MAIN COURSES

SALMON WITH HAZELNUT OIL, ORANGE AND CORIANDER

Another of my favourite recipes, very quick and capable of lots of variations. Escalopes are quicker to cook than cutlets with less risk of overcooking and so becoming dry.

2 escalopes of fresh salmon, approx. 100–175 g/4–6 oz each
1–2 tablespoons hazelnut oil
½ teaspoon coriander seeds, crushed or ground / *Grated rind of ½ small orange* } *mixed together*
Salt and freshly ground black pepper
Little arachide/groundnut/peanut oil
Garnish: 2 slices orange, little watercress or parsley

Brush each side of each salmon escalope with a thin film of hazelnut oil. Press each side into the mixture of crushed coriander seeds and grated orange rind. Season lightly.

Heat a large pan with a thin film of hazelnut oil. When hot, sear each side of each escalope, reduce heat and cook for no more than 1–2 minutes, according to thickness of the fish, they should look still slightly underdone when removed from the pan, cooking will continue away from the heat. Remove, garnish with slices of orange and a little watercress or parsley.

ACCOMPANIMENTS: Freshly cooked noodles or tagliatelle or new potatoes, plus a green salad or vegetable. A little homemade mayonnaise flavoured with grated orange rind and lightened with a tablespoon or two of cream or yoghurt provides a good sauce.

VARIATIONS: Oils and flavourings can be varied, try virgin olive oil with a few crushed green peppercorns OR walnut oil with a little cumin seed. OR just add a few drops of truffle-flavoured olive oil to the pan before sautéing. OR don't bother with any particular flavourings, just use a little good olive oil or a mixture of butter and oil. OR brush with oil, season and wrap in filo pastry (see the TROUT IN FILO PASTRY recipe in the SOMETHING FISHY section on page 23), bake at 200°C/400°F/Gas Mark 6 for 10 minutes, pastry will be golden brown and salmon cooked; herbs can add flavour or place on a little cooked spinach or fennel.

COOK'S TIP: Keep hazelnut and walnut oils in the fridge and use within six months of opening, they can go rancid quite quickly. Mayonnaise flavoured with orange or lemon rind improves with being allowed to stand for several hours. If your fishmonger won't cut escalopes for you, buy a small whole fish, ask him to fillet it out and cut your own, just like very thick slices of smoked salmon, slicing them off the skin as you work. Wrap the spare escalopes in cling film and freeze, use within three months.

MICROWAVE OVEN: Prepare escalopes, place in dish, add a tablespoon of water, cover tightly with cling film, microwave on HIGH for 2 minutes. Leave to sit for 2 minutes then serve as above.

SCALLOPS WITH FENNEL

The only scallops really worth bothering with are fresh, freezing does something to the texture and renders them practically tasteless. And for two it is possible to afford the extravagance of buying them when in season. With the scallops beg some fish bones off the fishmonger to make a good stock (see BACK TO BASICS section at the end of the book on page 277). Cooked fennel is much subtler than when it is aniseed fresh and is an ideal partner for the sweet scallop flesh. Briefly frying the corals in a little butter, or hazelnut oil if you have it, brings out a nicely nutty flavour.

225 g/8 oz/1½ cups fennel, trimmed and chopped (reserve any fronds for garnish)
8 large scallops
300 ml/10 fl oz/1¼ cups fish stock
150 ml/5 fl oz/⅔ cup dry white wine
Salt and freshly ground black pepper
Little grated lemon peel
Little butter or hazelnut oil

Bring a pan of salted water to the boil, add chopped fennel, cook until soft, drain well and then purée, either through a food mill or in a processor, to a smooth and thick sauce.

Remove the corals from the scallops and reserve. Trim off opaque white muscle and any discoloured membrane from the scallops then slice each horizontally through the middle. Reduce the fish stock and white wine by half in a shallow pan, season lightly then reduce heat to a mere shimmer and poach scallop rounds for 1 minute each side. Remove scallops and keep warm. Reduce cooking liquid a little further then add to the fennel purée until a good consistency sauce is reached. Reheat gently, check seasoning and enliven with a little grated lemon peel.

Meanwhile, in a small pan, melt a little butter or a dash of hazelnut oil and sauté the corals for about 1 minute, tossing gently.

Place sauce on bottom of serving dish or plates, arrange the scallops on top, garnish with the corals and fennel fronds and serve immediately.

HOSTESS NOTES: Prepare the fennel purée, reduce stock and wine. Have everything else ready and it will not take more than a few minutes to finish off the dish. It really does need to be cooked at the last minute, ideal when there is only two of you.

ACCOMPANIMENTS: New potatoes or pasta and a green salad.

VARIATIONS: Scallops can be left whole, fennel omitted and sauce finished with a little cream.

MICROWAVE OVEN: The dish is so quick to cook it seems madness to use a microwave, except that poaching fish works so well this way. Place chopped fennel in dish with a little water. Cover with cling film and microwave on HIGH for 7–8 minutes, until soft. Drain well and purée. Reduce wine and stock on hob to a third of original quantity. Add 3 tablespoons to scallops arranged in a circle around a suitable sized dish with the corals in the middle. Cover tightly with cling film. Microwave on HIGH for 1 minute, allow to stand while preparing sauce but drain off juices. Use these together with as much of the remaining reduced liquid as necessary to adjust consistency of fennel purée to a pouring sauce. Add a little grated lemon peel to enliven. Cover tightly and cook in microwave on HIGH for 1–2 minutes to reheat. Serve as above.

TROUT ROULADE WITH SPINACH AND SMOKED SALMON

This dish looks spectacularly pretty and tastes exceptionally good. All the preparation can be done well ahead of time and the fish cooked at the last minute with almost no demands on the cook.

4 fillets trout, skinned
50 g/2 oz smoked salmon
Freshly ground black pepper
Freshly squeezed lemon juice
4 large spinach leaves, or more smaller ones, blanched in boiling water for 1 minute, drained and refreshed in cold water, dried on kitchen paper
Little dry white wine

Lay each fillet of trout with the side that was the skin side on the work surface (to check how to skin fish, see BACK TO BASICS section at the end of the book on page 278). Lay a slice of smoked salmon on each, trimming and folding to match the shape of the fish, slip any odd bits into the middle. Add a grating of black peppercorns and a squeeze of lemon juice. Roll up then wrap each roll in spinach leaves, folding the leaves so they also match the shape of the fish and leave the ends of each roll free. Place two rolls on a piece of greaseproof paper or tin foil, loose ends underneath, splash over a little dry white wine and either secure the paper with a series of small folds, or gather up the foil loosely, in either case making an airtight parcel that gives plenty of room to the fish. Place each parcel on a baking sheet. Preparation can be done ahead of time and fish kept in fridge until ready to cook. Then place in a preheated oven at 190°C/375°F/Gas Mark 5, for 20 minutes. Unwrap each roulade, cut in half horizontally and arrange on a serving dish. OR serve the fish still wrapped in its packets, the aroma rising as the packets are opened is wickedly good. The fish is also good cold.

ACCOMPANIMENTS: Noodles then follow the dish with a salad.

VARIATIONS: Omit the smoked salmon and spread the fillets with a little crab meat instead OR chopped prawns. Fillets of sole or plaice can be used instead of trout, when the white flesh provides an extra contrast in colour with the smoked salmon and spinach.

COOK'S TIP: The juices can be made into a sauce if liked: reduce slightly, add a little double cream, heat through, check seasoning and serve.

MICROWAVE OVEN: Place rolls in a circle round a suitable dish, add 3 tablespoons white wine, cover tightly with cling film and cook on HIGH for 2 minutes 30 seconds. Allow to sit for 3 minutes then serve as above.

KULEBYAKA À LA RUSSE

A Russian recipe and one of my favourites. For a large party, a huge salmon pie is dramatic and delicious. No less delicious are these individual pies bursting with fresh salmon, rice, egg and mushroom. A good recipe for preparing ahead of time.

375 g/13 oz packet puff pastry

Filling:

1 thick cutlet fresh salmon

40 g/1½ oz/3 tablespoons butter

3 spring onions, chopped

50 g/2 oz/1 cup sliced mushrooms

1 hard-boiled egg, diced

2 fillets anchovy, chopped

40 g/1½ oz/3 tablespoons rice or buckwheat, cooked OR twice quantity of ready cooked rice

1 tablespoon chopped fresh herbs (parsley, chervil, dill, whatever is available)

Salt and freshly ground black pepper

Egg or milk for glazing

Cut the salmon into large dice, discarding skin and bone, leave uncooked. Melt the butter in a pan, add the spring onion and cook gently for a few minutes, then add the mushrooms and sauté briskly until all liquid evaporated off. Gently toss together the onion and mushroom mixture with the hard-boiled egg, anchovy, rice and herbs and season to taste. Then mix in the cubes of salmon.

Roll out the pastry to a thickness of 2 mm/⅛ inch and divide into four. Using a side plate as a guide, cut out two circles and pile half the mixture on each. Brush the edges with water, lay the two remaining pieces of pastry over the top of each pile of filling and gently mould the pastry into shape, pressing round the edge of the circles. Then trim off the excess and use the back of a knife to knock up the edges. Cut a steam hole in the top of each pie. Use trimmings to decorate, you can be as fanciful as you like. Refrigerate for at least 45 minutes before baking, pies can be left for several hours or even overnight.

When ready to cook, preheat oven to 220°C/425°F/Gas Mark 7. Remove pies from fridge, brush with a little beaten egg or milk and bake until well risen and golden brown, approximately 25 minutes.

ACCOMPANIMENTS: In Russia the Kulebyaka would be served with a fish consommé but either a light mayonnaise or a SABAYON SAUCE (see SAUCY IDEAS section on page 187) go extremely well. All that is needed in addition is a good salad.

VARIATIONS: The salmon can be replaced with breast of chicken but this should be precooked. The flavour will not be so fine but it is still a good dish.

TOWARDS TOMORROW: Cook three times the amount of rice and reheat excess next day in a greased dish covered with foil in a moderate oven, or with a little liquid in a microwave, to accompany another dish. Soaked raisins can be added plus a little infused saffron for greater flavour.

SHASHLYK PO KARSKI

*Start preparation 8 hours or day before serving

Another Russian recipe, this time for a lamb kebab. The marinating is important to allow the flavours to permeate the meat, they combine into a subtly unusual result.

---

350 g/12 oz top leg of lamb or shoulder fillet, weighed without skin or bones

---

Marinade:

Half a medium sized onion, peeled and grated

---

1 dessertspoon brandy

Good grating black peppercorns

Salt

---

8 dill seeds *½ teaspoon coriander seeds* *4 allspice berries*	*all crushed together*

---

2 cloves

Few fresh basil leaves or ½ teaspoon dried
1 dessertspoon wine vinegar
1 thick slice lemon, juice squeezed into marinade, peel cut into chunks

Mix together all ingredients for marinade. Cut lamb into 2.5 cm/1 inch cubes, place inside a plastic bag and place bag inside a suitable sized jug or bowl. Pour marinade over the meat and fasten bag so marinade covers all the meat. Leave some eight hours or overnight in a cool place, turning bag from time to time when convenient.

When ready to serve, thread meat on to skewers then place under a grill preheated to its hottest and cook for 4–5 minutes each side, basting with marinade halfway through cooking.

ACCOMPANIMENTS: Rice and a salad or green vegetable.

VARIATIONS: Chicken or turkey breast can be used instead of lamb. The kebabs can be barbecued instead of grilled.

COOK'S TIP: The marinade does not contain any oil and the meat can become dry if it is overcooked so watch carefully.

BOEUF STROGANOFF

A dish that completes a Russian trio and one that betrays its French origins. Many chefs found new homes with aristocratic Russians after the French revolution. They brought their tradition of *haute cuisine* to the mainly peasant cuisine they found but also absorbed many of its flavours. Before the advent of *nouvelle cuisine*, Boeuf Stroganoff could be found on many a restaurant menu, often with criminally irresponsible results. It is ironic that a dish exemplifying many of the tenets of the new cooking fashion should have been buried under the onslaught of chicken breasts and kiwi fruit and it is time it was resurrected. This version is quickly made, ideal for an occasion when there isn't much time before the meal is needed on the table, say after the theatre or a day out somewhere. Everything can be left ready, then the meal produced in under 15 minutes.

225–275 g/8–10 oz fillet or rump steak, cut across the grain in small strips

---

Knob of butter and tablespoon arachide/ groundnut/peanut oil

---

2 shallots, finely chopped (or substitute 4–5 spring onions, white and pale green parts finely sliced)

---

100 g/4 oz/2 cups button mushrooms, sliced

Salt and freshly ground black pepper

---

1 teaspoon tomato purée

---

3 tablespoons medium sherry

---

5 tablespoons sour cream or smetana

Garnish: Chopped parsley

Heat the butter and oil then quickly brown the strips of beef on all sides. Remove immediately from the pan, lower the heat, add the shallot or spring onion and cook gently for couple of minutes. Add the mushrooms, raise the heat and cook for several minutes until tender and moisture evaporated. Add the seasoning and tomato purée, then the sherry and the sour cream, keep the temperature below boiling. When all smoothly amalgamated, add the beef, which is now cooked and merely needs reheating in the sauce for a few minutes. The dish can be kept in a warm oven or cupboard for a little while but is best eaten immediately.

ACCOMPANIMENTS: Rice and a green salad or perhaps a vegetable such as mange tout or French beans.

COOK'S TIP: The rice can be cooked beforehand and reheated in a steamer over simmering water, boil the water in an electric kettle first to hasten the process and get the rice started before commencing the Stroganoff, or reheat in the microwave with a little water.

ESCALOPE OF PORK NORMANDE

Little escalopes of pork tenderloin are quick to cook, tender to eat and lend themselves to a variety of treatments. See introduction to PORK WITH ORANGE AND LEMON on page 68 for how to prepare the meat. The following recipe is a delicious combination of pork, apple and cream, rich and smooth but still quite light. It will sit happily keeping warm for the 20 minutes or so needed to finish a drink and eat a first course and can also be reheated with care. Instructions for preparing ahead of time follow the recipe.

25 g/1 oz/2 tablespoons butter
1 large crisp eating apple, Cox's or Granny Smith are ideal, peeled, cored and diced
1 tablespoon butter and ½ tablespoon arachide/groundnut/peanut oil
225–275 g/8–10 oz pork tenderloin (one tenderloin) trimmed of any fat and membrane and cut obliquely into 1 cm/½ inch thick slices then beaten out into escalopes
75 ml/2½ fl oz/5 tablespoons dry cider or chicken stock
1 small clove garlic, crushed with a little salt
3 tablespoons double cream
Freshly ground black pepper
1 tablespoon Calvados or brandy, optional
Garnish: Freshly chopped parsley

229

Melt the first lot of butter in a heavy based pan, add the diced apple, stir well to mix with the butter, cover pan and cook gently until golden, stirring from time to time.

Meanwhile, heat remaining tablespoon butter and the oil in a frying pan over a brisk heat and quickly sauté the little escalopes for about 1 minute on each side, dusting with a little salt as you turn each. They should be nicely browned. Remove as soon as cooked and keep warm. After all the meat has been cooked, drain any remaining fat from pan then add cider or stock and the crushed garlic. Scrape the bottom of the pan well, stirring in any little crusty bits, these will add extra flavour and can be strained out at the end if liked. Raise the heat and boil, reducing liquid by half. Add the cream, check and adjust seasoning, stir well and bring back to the boil then slightly reduce again to a good consistency. Add the Calvados or brandy if using. Give a final check to the seasoning, adding a little black pepper if liked.

Place the apple on the base of a warm serving dish, arrange the meat over then pour over the sauce, straining if necessary. The dish can be covered with tin foil and kept warm in a very low oven for 20–30 minutes. Garnish with a little chopped parsley before serving.

NOTES FOR HOSTESS: To prepare ahead of time and reheat: arrange cooked apples and meat in ovenproof serving dish, a gratin dish is ideal, cover and refrigerate. Keep sauce separate. To reheat: reheat sauce and pour over meat and apples, cover dish with tin foil, place in a preheated oven at 180°C/350°F/Gas Mark 4 for approximately 35 minutes, until bubbling hot. Remove foil, garnish with parsley and serve.

ACCOMPANIMENTS: New potatoes or tagliatelle and a green vegetable such as mange tout or broccoli.

VARIATIONS: Instead of the pork, beat out escalopes of breast of chicken or turkey, sliced across the grain. There are a number of other recipes using these little pork escalopes in the CHOPS WITH EVERYTHING section.

COOK'S TIP: The meat can easily be overcooked, running the danger of becoming tough and dry, remember that it will continue cooking slightly after being removed from the heat, it's enough to brown well each side.

MICROWAVE OVEN: Can be used very successfully to reheat dish: prepare as for eating immediately, cool rapidly and refrigerate. When ready to reheat, cover dish tightly with cling film, place in microwave and microwave on HIGH for 5 minutes or until bubbling hot, changing position of dish halfway through if oven doesn't have a turntable. Allow to sit for 3 minutes before serving, then garnish with chopped parsley.

ℱ STUFFED DUCK'S LEGS

It is possible now to find duck portions, breasts and legs, sold separately but it is better value to buy the whole bird then joint it yourself, freeze the bits not needed immediately and make stock from the remains of the carcass.

Boning out duck or chicken legs is not at all difficult, see below, two take very little time and the meat can then be stuffed with all manner of delicacies, turning a somewhat plebeian portion into another class of dish altogether. The following recipe may sound a little odd but the prunes, anchovies and duck flesh meld together into a subtle and truly delicious whole.

2 duck legs, boned out
Salt and freshly ground black pepper
6 prunes, soaked and stoned
½ tin anchovies, soaked in milk for 45 minutes then drained
1 dessertspoon arachide/groundnut/peanut oil
150 ml/5 fl oz/⅔ cup dry white wine
1 tablespoon brandy
Garnish: Watercress or parsley

Bone legs by grasping the ball joint then use a sharp little knife to scrape down the leg bone, pulling the flesh away as you work. Be careful not to leave the knee-cap in with the flesh as you work round that joint. When you reach the ankles, yank the flesh inside out and sever it from the end of the bone. Finally turn the flesh back inside its skin. Season inside the flesh lightly. Stuff each prune with half a fillet of anchovy, divide between the legs, insert in the gap left by the bone then tie or sew up or use cocktail sticks or small skewers to secure the flesh.

Heat oil in fireproof dish, brown legs well then remove. Discard remaining oil, pour in white wine and bring to boil, scraping bottom of pan well to incorporate all brown sediment into sauce. Replace legs in wine, bring back to boil, season lightly, cover and cook in preheated oven at 180°C/350°F/Gas Mark 4 for 1½ hours, or until tender. Large legs may need a little longer.

Remove legs and keep warm. Degrease juices and reduce slightly. Flame brandy and add, stirring in well. Check seasoning. Remove all string from legs, slice across obliquely, exposing the glossy inside, arrange on a serving plate. Spoon over the sauce, garnish with watercress or parsley and serve.

NOTES FOR HOSTESS: To prepare ahead of time and reheat: remove from oven halfway through cooking, cool rapidly. Remove all string from legs but leave whole. Remove any fat from sauce. Reheat in sauce in preheated oven at same temperature for 1 hour to finish cooking.

ACCOMPANIMENTS: Pasta such as tagliatelle or noodles or creamed potatoes and a green salad or vegetable such as peas.

VARIATIONS: Legs can be stuffed with roll of sliced ham seasoned with Maille's Moutarde au Poivre Vert OR with very young, cooked leeks wrapped round toasted pine nuts OR with pâté de foie gras (very rich) OR with grated apple mixed with a little chopped sage. Chicken legs can be treated in exactly the same way but will not need nearly so long to cook, 50 minutes should be ample.

COOK'S TIP: Make the most of the oven by baking a cake at the same time or a custard dish or baked fruit (see pudding sections) OR by making stock in the oven instead of on top of the stove: roast bones for 10 minutes on a high heat, scrape into a fireproof casserole dish, add a few vegetables, onion, carrot, celery, a bouquet garni, plus a very little salt and a few peppercorns. Bring slowly to the boil then cover tightly and cook in oven for 1½ to 2 hours.

MICROWAVE OVEN: The legs won't be nicely browned but otherwise the dish works extremely well. Prepare legs as above but omit seasoning. Reduce wine to a half. Place legs and wine in suitable dish, cover tightly with cling film and microwave on HIGH for 8 minutes. Remove legs and keep warm. Degrease juices (the duck fat will have rendered down beautifully), add brandy, cook on HIGH, uncovered, for 30 seconds. Check seasoning, adding salt and freshly ground black pepper if necessary. Remove all string from legs, cut across obliquely, arrange on a warm serving dish, pour over the sauce, garnish with watercress or parsley and serve.

TOWARDS TOMORROW: See below for suggestion for cooking breasts.

DUCK BREASTS WITH GREEN PEPPERCORNS

A succulent, luxury dish. The clean, sweet flavour of the kiwi fruit, marinated in white wine, contrasts nicely with the soft pungency of green peppercorns and the rich flesh of the duck. Like steaks, duck breasts are best served pink. Slicing each breast into a fan of rosy slivers makes a nicely elegant presentation.

2 small kiwi fruit
2 duck breasts, skin and bone removed
150 ml/5 fl oz/²⁄₃ cup dry white wine
Knob butter, 1 dessertspoon arachide/ groundnut/peanut oil
¼ teaspoon green peppercorns preserved in brine, lightly crushed
Salt and freshly ground black pepper
½ teaspoon potato flour or arrowroot, mixed to thin paste with little wine

Peel kiwi fruit and slice thickly. Place with the duck breasts in the white wine and leave in a cool place for several hours. When ready to eat, heat butter and oil over a medium heat, remove breasts and fruit from wine, pat breasts dry, season and brown briefly on both sides. Discard remaining fat from pan, add the wine used for marinating and the green peppercorns, season, cover pan and cook gently for 5 minutes or until meat just gives when lightly pressed. Remove and keep warm.

Raise heat and reduce cooking juices by a third. Remove pan from heat, add a little of the hot juices to the slaked potato flour or arrowroot, then pour all into the pan, stirring well, replace on heat and bring back to boil. When slightly thickened and clear, add the kiwi fruit slices and any juices that have run out of the breasts while they have been standing. Simmer very gently for 1 minute.

Slice each breast obliquely, arrange in a fan shape, garnish with the kiwi fruit, spoon over sauce and serve immediately.

NOTES FOR HOSTESS: If serving a first course, prepare the breasts, cover with tin foil and leave sitting in a very low oven or a warming cupboard. Have sauce ready but do not add kiwi fruit until just before serving, then bring sauce back to boil, slip in the kiwi fruit and allow to warm through while you are slicing the breasts.

ACCOMPANIMENTS: New potatoes or pasta and a salad.

VARIATIONS: Chicken breasts can be prepared in the same way but need a little longer cooking, they should not be served pink. The duck breasts can be cooked in butter or oil without the wine then served with a homemade jelly or a sauce. If cooking breasts with the skin on, cook in a very hot pan, skin side down, for several minutes before reducing heat and turning the breast to finish cooking. Kiwi fruit can be replaced by grapes or slices of peach or mango.

COOK'S TIP: Duck breast meat is very lean and if it is overcooked it will become dry and tasteless.

MICROWAVE OVEN: Marinate fruit and breasts as above, omit seasoning. Place breasts side by side in a suitable sized shallow dish so a thin end is next to a fat end, pour over two thirds of the wine and add the lightly crushed green peppercorns. Cover tightly with cling film and microwave on HIGH for 5 minutes. Mix potato flour or arrowroot with remaining wine. Carefully remove film from cooked breasts. Remove breasts and keep warm. Pour hot juices into slaked potato flour or arrowroot, return to microwave oven and microwave, uncovered, on HIGH for 3 minutes, or until lightly thickened. Slip in kiwi slices, cover tightly and cook on 30%/DEFROST for 30 seconds. Slice breasts, arrange on serving plates, add kiwi slices, pour over sauce and serve.

TOWARDS TOMORROW: See above for a recipe for the legs.

HONEYED QUAIL

Quail are perfect for small numbers. They are meaty little birds and for appetites that are less than hearty, one per person is usually adequate. However, two per portion is the usual allotment and the meat is very good cold.

A bird opened out by cutting through the backbone then flattened slightly with the heel of the hand, is known as spatchcocked. The word is apparently Irish in derivation, a shortened form of "dispatched", from the practice of quickly killing a cock and splitting it open before grilling to feed unexpected visitors. The cooked quail can quite easily be cut completely in half with kitchen scissors, making it possible to serve one and a half per person if you feel that is the perfect portion.

2–4 quail (see above)

2–4 tablespoons set honey
1–2 teaspoons Dijon mustard
1 teaspoon light olive oil
Good dash Worcestershire sauce
Salt and freshly ground black pepper

Using kitchen scissors, cut quail open down backbone, place on working surface and press down on breastbone to flatten slightly. Mix together remaining ingredients. Set quail breast side down on a foil-lined grill pan and spread half honey dressing over inside of quail. Place under a grill preheated to its highest point, cook for 5 minutes then turn birds over, spread remaining dressing over other side and grill for another 5 minutes. Keep warm until serving. Birds can also be cooked in an oven preheated to 200°C/400°F/Gas Mark 6, for 10–15 minutes, cook breast side up and baste with second half of dressing halfway through.

The birds look nice arranged on a dish lined with vine leaves, or with half birds placed in a circle, the middle filled with watercress.

ACCOMPANIMENTS: Green salad or a green vegetable such as broccoli, mange tout or beans, or miniature corn on the cob. Either new potatoes or GRATIN OF POTATOES AND CHEESE (see NO MEAT NO FISH section on page 147) would go well.

VARIATIONS: Small poussin can be cooked the same way, they may need a little longer cooking time.

MICROWAVE OVEN: Arrange birds with breasts up and legs pointing towards centre of dish. Pour over half dressing, cover tightly with cling film, microwave on HIGH for 2 minutes. Allow to stand 2 minutes then uncover, pour over second half of dressing, re-cover tightly and microwave on HIGH for a further 2 minutes (timings are for 4 birds; cook for 1 minute second time for 3 birds; cook for 1½ minutes each time for 2 birds). Serve as above.

GIGOT QUI PLEUT

Half a leg of lamb will provide a generous meal for two with plenty of left-overs for another day. Choose the shank end and try this traditional French way of roasting lamb that also provides golden potatoes rich with the flavour of the meat. The garlic melts into the lamb and perfumes the potatoes. It can be left out but much of the charm of the dish will disappear. If you can't get hold of fresh herbs, omit them, the dried ones will not add much to the dish.

1 kg/2¼ lb half leg of lamb, shank end
Little olive oil
2 cloves garlic, peeled and cut in slivers
Good pinch each chopped fresh rosemary and thyme
Salt and freshly ground black pepper
225 g/8 oz/2 cups potatoes, peeled and sliced
1 small onion, finely chopped
225 ml/7½ fl oz/1 cup light stock

Rub lamb with oil then, with a small, sharp knife, make a series of incisions into the meat all over the joint, slipping a sliver of garlic into each as you go. Sprinkle the herbs over the meat and season.

Lightly oil a small roasting pan, add the potato slices mixed with the onion and lightly season. Bring stock to the boil and pour over.

Have oven preheated to 220°C/425°F/Gas Mark 7 and place the lamb directly on to the rack, arranging the pan of potatoes underneath so that the meat juices drip straight on to it. Roast for around 1 hour to 1 hour 10 minutes, which should give lamb still a little pink inside. Stir potatoes once or twice during the roasting time. Allow lamb to sit in a warm place for 20 minutes before carving, this allows the meat to relax and gives a little extra cooking time for the potatoes if they need it.

ACCOMPANIMENTS: A good, preferably homemade, fruit jelly plus a green vegetable or salad.

VARIATIONS: The meat can also be roasted in a pan with a little wine and basted from time to time. Instead of the garlic, the skin can be laced with a few fillets anchovy (the flavour is delicious and not at all aggressive) or sprigs of rosemary.

COOK'S TIP: Remember that the meat will continue cooking a little while it rests so leave it slightly less done than you actually want.

TOWARDS TOMORROW: Cold lamb has a succulence and flavour that is hard to beat and I think it is a waste to serve left-overs from this joint other than plainly. A baked potato goes very well plus either a salad or cooked vegetable. OR, for a hot dish if you insist, try the LAMB AND AUBERGINE GRATIN from the POT POURRI section on page 76. If the pieces are really small and raggedy, mix with cooked and sliced new potatoes and a light mayonnaise to make a salad, a few chopped lemon thyme leaves can be added for extra zing, serve on a bed of lettuce. A really small amount of meat can be made into an omelette, see the TIME FOR A SNACK section on page 258.

DESSERTS

Dessert, even for a special meal, does not have to be a big production number. After two courses very often the palate only wants a little cheese and some fruit. Perfect peaches, a fragrantly ripe mango, a bunch of sweet, seedless grapes, a slice of fresh pineapple, all these are treats in themselves. But there are times when a pudding does round off a meal. Here is a small selection of special desserts that should not cause either the cook or the budget too much strain.

F CHOCOLATE AND ALMOND GÂTEAU

A scrumptious dessert, sinfully wicked and just right for a very special occasion when the extra effort it demands is worth every minute. Since the cake is best left for 24 hours to allow the almond meringue to soften and the chocolate covering to mature, it can be done well ahead of time.

75 g/3 oz/¾ cup icing sugar
75 g/3 oz/¾ cup ground almonds
3 large egg whites

For chocolate cream:

75 g/3 oz plain chocolate, Menier, Terry's Dark or Cadbury's Bournville
4 tablespoons double cream
20 g/¾ oz/1 generous tablespoon butter
1 tablespoon rum
Garnish: 3 tablespoons almonds, blanched and chopped

Using a loaf tin as a guide, draw two oblongs on two sheets of non-stick paper 11 cm/4 inches × 21.5 cm/8½ inches and lay on a baking sheet.

Sift sugar and ground almonds together into a bowl. Whip egg whites to stiff peak then carefully fold in sugar and almond mixture. Divide the mixture between the two oblongs and gently spread over each rectangle. Place in preheated oven at 150°C/300°F/Gas Mark 2 and bake for approximately 45 minutes or until golden brown and set. Remove from oven, run a palette knife underneath each rectangle to prevent it sticking to paper then place on racks to cool.

To make chocolate cream: place broken-up chocolate in bowl with cream and butter and heat over pan of simmering water until melted, stirring gently from time to time. Remove from heat, add rum, stirring in well, then refrigerate for 2–3 hours until set. Beat with an electric beater until mixture has appreciably paled and increased in volume.

Use one-third of chocolate mixture to cover one rectangle then place the other on top, trimming if necessary to match. Cover top and sides with remaining chocolate cream. Use chopped almonds to outline edge of rectangle. Place somewhere cool, but not in fridge unless weather is very hot, for 24 hours before serving.

ACCOMPANIMENTS: Single cream.

VARIATIONS: Shape can be varied, a heart if you like, or use two sandwich tins. Instead of using chopped nuts, halved almonds can be arranged down the middle of the rectangle. Individual portions are another possibility if appetites are very robust.

TOWARDS TOMORROW: Use the egg yolks to make a caramel custard or mayonnaise. But you may have spare egg whites stored in a screw-top jar in the fridge (where they will keep for two to three weeks), allow 30 g or just over 1 oz for 1 egg white.

ℱ CHOCOLATE MOUSSE

Chocolate mousse has to be one of the most popular sweets ever. It is really very little trouble to make and will sit quite happily in the fridge for at least 24 hours and maybe a bit longer, ideal for a special meal.

100 g/4 oz dark chocolate, Menier, Terry's Dark or Cadbury's Bournville
2 egg yolks
2 egg whites
25 g/1 oz/2 tablespoons caster sugar

Break up the chocolate into small pieces and melt in a small bowl over a pan of gently simmering water. Add the egg yolks to the melted chocolate, still over the heat, and whisk until mixture is smoothly amalgamated. Remove from heat. Whip the egg whites to soft peak, sprinkle over the sugar and whip to stiff peak stage. Carefully fold one-third into the chocolate mixture, then add this on to the remainder of the egg white mixture and finish folding in carefully. Divide between two glasses or dishes.

ACCOMPANIMENTS: Mousse can be finished with curls of chocolate or with some whipped double cream.

VARIATIONS: Flavour the chocolate with 2 tablespoons of Grand Marnier, or 1 tablespoon Crème de Cacao. A little chopped crystallised orange peel can be added to the mousse: remove peel from an orange without any of the pith, cut into small diamond shapes, or just chop roughly, blanch for 5 minutes in boiling water, drain and refresh. Make a heavy sugar syrup with 150 ml/5 fl oz/⅔ cup water and 100 g/4 oz/½ cup granulated sugar, allowing the sugar to melt before bringing the water to the boil, then simmering for 2 minutes before adding the orange peel and simmering for 5 minutes. If the peel is cut into julienne strips it provides a superb finish to a simple salad of orange slices.

COOK'S TIP: To make curls of chocolate, run a potato peeler down the edge of a bar of chocolate OR melt chocolate, spread over a flat tin or marble slab and allow to cool, then push the blade of a sharp knife over it at a very flat angle.

ZABAGLIONE

This is one of those puddings that has to be made at the last moment, quite nice to do with just one guest when they can happily chat to you as you whisk the delicious foamy custard over hot water, perhaps with both of you sipping a glass of the Marsala that has gone into the pudding, or of a well-chilled sweet wine.

2 egg yolks
3 tablespoons caster sugar
4 tablespoons Marsala

Place the egg yolks and sugar in the bottom of a bowl that will fit over a pan of simmering water and, away from the heat, beat until pale and increased in volume. Beat in the Marsala then put the bowl on top of the pan of gently simmering water and whisk steadily until the mixture is soft, foamy and thick enough for the whisk to leave trails when picked up. Pour into two glasses and serve immediately.

ACCOMPANIMENTS: Amaretti, Boudoir or langue de chat biscuits.

VARIATIONS: Sweet sherry can be substituted for the Marsala, though the flavour will not be quite as good. OR turn the Zabaglione into an ice cream by folding in 100 ml/3½ fl oz/6 tablespoons double cream whipped with 1 tablespoon icing sugar until it will just hold its shape. Freeze for about 4 hours and eat within 24 hours.

TOWARDS TOMORROW: Keep the egg whites in a screw-top jar in the fridge for 2–3 weeks to use for any recipe requiring just whites OR make meringues.

CARAMEL CUSTARD

Very easy and a universal favourite.

75 g/3 oz/6 tablespoons caster sugar
75 ml/6 fl oz/¾ cup milk
Vanilla pod or few drops vanilla essence
1 whole small egg and 2 small egg yolks

Place half the sugar in a heavy based pan with a tablespoon water, place over a medium heat and, without stirring, allow sugar first to melt then caramelise to a dark golden brown. Pour into the bottom of two 150 ml/5 fl oz/⅔ cup ramekins and swirl round to coat.

Heat the milk with the vanilla pod to just below boiling point, cover and allow to infuse for 15–20 minutes.

Lightly beat the egg and yolks with the remaining sugar then stir in the infused milk. Strain into a jug then pour into the ramekin dishes. Place dishes in a small roasting pan, add hot water to halfway up the ramekins and place in a preheated oven at 180°C/350°F/Gas Mark 4, for 30–40 minutes, until set.

Allow to cool then run a thin blade round edge of each dish, place plate on top, then quickly flip over and give a little sideways shake to unmould.

ACCOMPANIMENTS: Nothing needed but a crisp biscuit would be nice.

VARIATIONS: Orange liqueur can be added to the custard and orange segments removed without membrane (see BACK TO BASICS section on page 280) can be served as well.

COOK'S TIP: Try to make sure there are no bubbles on the surface of the custard before it is cooked, prick any that are there with the point of a sharp knife so that the custard is completely smooth.

TOWARDS TOMORROW: Keep egg whites in a jar in the fridge for meringues or other dishes. They will keep well for 2–3 weeks or can be frozen.

CABINET PUDDING

Though commonly thought of with nursery steamed puddings, Cabinet Pudding is a much lighter and superior article. There is something very comforting about its gentle custard base and it looks very attractive with its dried and crystallised fruits. It is as different from ordinary steamed puddings as, one imagines, the meetings of back benchers are from those of the cabinet. Also known as Diplomat Pudding, it conjures up the worldly sophistication and sybaritic outlook I associate with ambassadors.

1 tablespoon each of raisins and currants
1 tablespoon brandy
150 ml/5 fl oz/⅔ cup milk
1 vanilla pod or few drops vanilla essence
1 tablespoon each chopped candied peel and halved glacé cherries
6 sponge fingers, broken in pieces
2 egg yolks

Soak raisins and currants in brandy. Heat milk with vanilla pod to boiling point then leave, covered, to infuse for 20 minutes or so. Butter well two ramekin dishes of 150 ml/5 fl oz/⅔ cup capacity and place a circle of non-stick or buttered greaseproof paper in the bottom. Arrange some cherry halves and dried fruit attractively on this. Fill the dishes, or dish, with broken sponge fingers layered alternately with the fruits.

Beat the egg yolks lightly, add any remaining brandy not absorbed into the fruit, plus the vanilla essence if using. Whisk the hot milk in lightly then pour custard slowly over the sponge finger mixture and leave to stand for 30 minutes. Place in a pan of cold water and bake in a preheated oven at 180°C/350°F/Gas Mark 4 for approximately 35–40 minutes or until set. Remove the pan from the oven and let the pudding stand for 5 minutes before carefully turning out. Serve warm.

ACCOMPANIMENTS: Cream or a fruit sauce.

COOK'S TIP: If the pudding gets too hot in the oven, bubbles will form in the custard and it will not be so smooth and creamy, cooking *au bain-marie*, in a pan of water, helps to prevent this. The water bath also provides a steamy atmosphere which assists the texture of the pudding. Allowing the pudding to rest before cooking means that the sponge fingers absorb some of the custard and become lighter.

TOWARDS TOMORROW: Keep the spare egg whites in a screw-top jar in the fridge to make meringues or to use when egg whites are wanted. They will last 2–3 weeks. Egg whites freeze well.

PARADISE SOUFFLÉ

This is luscious and light. The dried fruits are quite sweet so you may like to cut down on the sugar.

100 g/4 oz/1 cup dried fruit, mixture of peaches, apricots and pears
150 ml/5 fl oz/⅔ cup apple juice
2 large egg whites
3 tablespoons caster sugar
5 almonds, blanched and roughly chopped

Soak fruit in apple juice for several hours then cook gently until soft. Chop finely or process (but try and leave some texture rather than reducing to a purée). Whisk egg whites to stiff peaks, whisk in sugar then fold in the fruits and almonds. Mixture should be thick and glossy. Pile into a buttered gratin dish (this soufflé is best cooked in a shallow rather than the traditional round, ridged dish) and bake in a preheated oven at 180°C/350°F/Gas Mark 4, for approximately 30 minutes, until well risen and golden brown. Serve immediately.

NOTES FOR HOSTESS: Soufflé can be prepared several hours before baking and kept in the fridge. Place in oven as main course is served, or before cheese course, and introduce a nicely contentious or scintillating item of conversation that will carry over the cooking time. If there are any left-overs, they taste very good cold.

ACCOMPANIMENTS: Single cream or Greek-style yoghurt.

VARIATIONS: All prunes can be used instead of the mixed fruits and caster sugar substituted for the light brown sugar.

COOK'S TIP: Whip the egg whites until they become shiny and thick before whisking in the sugar but don't whip whites beyond the shiny stage as they will start to collapse.

APRICOT GLORY

Many different fruits can be used for this pudding but I love the subtle flavour of Hunza apricots set off by the tarter flavour of the ordinary dried apricots soaked in orange juice. Hunza apricots look nothing very much in the packet, rather like little hunks of compacted clay, but once soaked and cooked they are delicious.

100 g/4 oz Hunza apricots, soaked overnight
150 ml/5 fl oz/⅔ cup Greek-style yoghurt
50 g/2 oz/¼ cup dried apricots ready to eat, chopped and soaked overnight in freshly squeezed juice of:
½ orange
A few toasted flaked almonds

Cook the Hunza apricots in soaking water until tender, strain off juices, remove stones and purée flesh, cool. Stir yoghurt until really smooth then layer with the apricot purée and chopped apricots, ending with a few chopped apricots on top of a layer of yoghurt. Sprinkle with a few flaked almonds and serve.

ACCOMPANIMENTS: A shortbread type of biscuit would be nice.

VARIATIONS: The yoghurt, or whipped cream, can be mixed with any sort of fruit. Soft fruits are delicious, crisp eating apples tossed in lemon and mixed with a little chopped date are very good. Grapes are elegant as well as good, see the YOGHURT BRÛLÉE below.

TOWARDS TOMORROW: Cook twice as many Hunza apricots as needed and serve the rest for breakfast or purée as above and mix with an equal quantity of whipped double cream and a third as much icing sugar, sharpen with a squeeze of lemon juice and freeze for an excellent ice cream.

MICROWAVE OVEN: The microwave can be used to cook the Hunza apricots without presoaking: Place the fruit in a bowl, add 250 ml/8 fl oz/1 cup water, cover tightly with cling film, microwave on HIGH for 10 minutes, giving apricots a shake halfway through cooking. Pierce film and allow to cool.

YOGHURT BRÛLÉE

*Start preparation several hours before serving

A very simple and most refreshing dessert capable of many variations.

100–175 g/4–6 oz/¾–1¼ cups grapes, halved and seeded
150 ml/5 fl oz/⅔ cup thick natural yoghurt
3–4 tablespoons demerara sugar

Place grapes in bottom of shallow dish, or two individual dishes. Stir yoghurt to make completely smooth and spread over the fruit. Refrigerate for at least 1 hour. Heat the grill to its highest. Sprinkle the surface of the yoghurt thickly with the demerara sugar, place under the grill just long enough for the sugar to melt, bubble and caramelise. Then remove and replace in the fridge. Serve within an hour, otherwise the crisp topping may start to melt.

ACCOMPANIMENTS: A crisp little biscuit would go well.

VARIATIONS: Grapes can be replaced with any other fruit, soft berries are very successful, exotic fruits such as mango and pineapple are also good. Peaches, apricots and plums are also excellent. Instead of caramelising the sugar, it can be sprinkled on the yoghurt immediately and the dish refrigerated for a couple of hours, when the sugar will melt and provide an attractive finish.

COOK'S TIP: Peeling the grapes is preferred by some. Prepared grapes can be frozen for a short time.

F PEACHES WITH WINE AND LEMON

Peaches, with their golden and rosy flushed flesh, are pretty special in themselves. Gently poached in a light wine syrup with a piece of lemon peel, they can provide a perfect end to any meal.

150 ml/5 fl oz/⅔ cup half white wine and half water
75 ml/2½ fl oz/4 tablespoons granulated sugar
Piece lemon peel removed without pith
2–3 peaches, halved and with stones removed
Flaked and browned almonds

Place the wine, water and sugar in a pan with the piece of lemon peel, heat gently until sugar has melted, then bring to boil and simmer for a couple of minutes. Add the halved peaches and poach very gently 10–15 minutes, until peaches tender and cooked. Remove fruit with a slotted spoon and place in a bowl. Bring syrup to boil and reduce by a half, remove lemon peel. Carefully remove skins from peach halves, place in a serving dish or dishes and pour over the thickened syrup. Just before serving, scatter the toasted flaked almonds over the top.

ACCOMPANIMENTS: Best of all with *crème fraîche* but also good with cream or with Greek-style yoghurt. Meringues, almond tuiles, langue de chat biscuits or puff pastry triangles (as with the FRUITS WITH SAUTERNES) would all go well.

VARIATIONS: Other fruits such as pears, pineapple, plums or apricots can be cooked this way. A few fresh berries can be added before serving.

COOK'S TIP: Use a potato peeler to take off a thin piece of citrus peel without any pith. Allowing the sugar to melt before the water boils prevents any danger of crystallisation as the syrup cooks.

MICROWAVE OVEN: For the syrup: place sugar, wine, water and lemon peel in a large jug, cover tightly with cling film, microwave on HIGH for 4 minutes. Carefully remove film (the steam will be very hot), stir, re-cover and cook again for further 4 minutes. Repeat stirring, re-cover and cook for another 2 minutes. Prick peaches with a fork, add to syrup, cover tightly and cook on HIGH for 1 minute. Allow to cool and finish as above.

TOWARDS TOMORROW: Cook twice as much syrup as needed and keep excess in a screw-top jar in the fridge ready to add to a fresh fruit salad if you need extra sweetness. Cook twice as much fruit and, next day, arrange on top of sliced Swiss roll topped with whipped cream OR with plain vanilla ice cream and meringue OR serve with poached chicken, adding a little of the syrup to some homemade mayonnaise with a little cream and using to coat the cold chicken.

FRUITS WITH SAUTERNES

This is a spectacular dessert in the summer but lovely versions can be made throughout the year using exotic fruits of various kinds. Sauternes is not cheap but half bottles are often available and will yield enough to make the pudding and provide two glasses of wine to accompany the end of the meal. Serve the wine well chilled.

246

350 g/12 oz mixed ripe fruits (in summer: strawberries, raspberries, cherries, peaches, etc., in winter: mango, grapes, kiwi fruit, pineapple, etc.)

A quarter bottle good Sauternes

Small packet puff pastry

Little beaten egg

Little caster sugar

To serve: Crème anglaise *flavoured with grated lemon rind OR single cream*

Marinate fruit in wine for at least one and preferably several hours. Roll out puff pastry to thickness of 5 mm/¼ inch and cut into two diamond shapes. Brush top of each with little beaten egg, sprinkle with caster sugar. Chill for 45 minutes in fridge then bake in a preheated oven at 200°C/400°F/Gas Mark 6 for approximately 10 minutes until well risen and golden brown. Place on a wire rack to cool.

When ready to serve, cut through each pastry diamond horizontally, place bottom half on a plate. Heat the fruit in its marinade, either in a pan over a gentle heat or, best of all, in a microwave, giving it 1 minute on HIGH. Fruit should be nicely warm rather than hot. Spoon over the puff pastry bottom, place sugar glazed half on top and serve accompanied by the *crème anglaise*, cream or ice cream. OR serve in a glass bowl and hand the pastry diamonds on a separate plate, or replace these with almond tuiles or langues de chats.

COOK'S TIP: Don't let the egg dribble down the side of the pastry or the layers will stick together and not rise properly. Layer up any left-over puff pastry bits and make into cheese or sugar palmiers: roll out pastry left-overs into a rectangle, either brush with egg and sprinkle with Parmesan or Cheddar cheese OR sprinkle with sugar. Fold side nearest you to the middle of the pastry then bring farther side to the middle also. Fold the doubled lengths together, roll out again and repeat folding and doubling but this time, instead of rolling out again, wrap the roll of pastry in tin foil or cling film and place in the fridge for at least 30 minutes. Then cut into slices, place on a greased baking sheet allowing room for the palmiers to spread, and bake in a preheated oven at 200°C/400°F/Gas Mark 6 for 10–15 minutes, turning over halfway through cooking, when the underside is golden brown. The little cheese versions are ideal for serving with drinks, the sweet ones lovely with desserts. Palmiers can be frozen sliced ready to bake then placed in the oven straight from the freezer.

TIME FOR A SNACK

Snacks are for the second meal of the day, or when a little something is required but the stomach is not up to a full-scale dish.

Soups can be ideal. If no homemade is on hand, commercial tins can be cheered up with a good slurp of sherry, Madeira or brandy; cream or yoghurt can be another improver, so can chopped herbs. Curry sauce or Tabasco can add a little bite to some varieties.

Eggs are a great standby, if you have a source you feel you can rely on to be Salmonella free, they can be combined with bits of this and that to make excellent snacks, see some suggestions below.

A well-stocked storecupboard can usually offer the makings of a vast variety of snacks: dried pasta, tins of tuna fish, sardines and anchovies, tins of prepared vegetables such as tomatoes, pulses, asparagus, etc., see the HELP FOR MOTHER HUBBARD section for ideas.

In our house Open Sandwiches are very popular, my mother comes from Sweden and she often produces a delicious selection when entertaining but I find them just as good for a quick snack, they are often used for lunch or a quick bite in Scandinavia.

OPEN SANDWICHES

Open sandwiches can be quite simple. Left-overs can provide the toppings or they can be acquired specially, a good delicatessen will provide a rich array. Basic ground rules are:

1) All ingredients *must* be first-class quality. Which is not to say that left-overs can't be used but they must be fresh, not raked out from a forgotten limbo at the back of the fridge. The bread can be white or brown, wheat or rye or anything else but, again, must be fresh. If hard bread is used, it should be really crisp.

2) Choose ingredients that will complement or contrast in taste and texture. And will look good.

3) Spread bread first with butter, it helps keep it from going soggy as well as tasting good. It can be salted or unsalted according to the topping. Scandinavians prefer unsalted or very lightly salted and the Danes are very fond of using lard or dripping for certain assemblies.

4) The bread should be completely covered with the topping.

5) Prepare as shortly before eating as possible, cover with cling film if there is to be any delay in serving.

6) Size can be varied, as large or small as you like or the ingredients dictate. They are meant to be eaten with knife and fork.

Suggestions for toppings:

PRAWN SALAD: Place lettuce leaves on top of buttered bread, spread centre with mayonnaise. Arrange prawns down middle. Season with salt and pepper. Garnish each sandwich with slice or slices of cucumber, each slice cut halfway through then the edges pulled gently in alternate directions so it can sit on prawns like a butterfly.

CHEESE AND GRAPE: Place thin slices of round goat's cheese or Edam or Jarlsberg cheese on buttered bread. Arrange grape halves prettily on each sandwich and garnish with sprig of parsley.

ROAST BEEF, HORSERADISH AND GHERKIN: A slice of rare roast beef topped with a little mound of creamed horseradish and garnished with a slice of pickled gherkin or a tiny one sliced through ⅞ths of its length then fanned out.

SMOKED SALMON WITH LEMON CREAM: A slice of smoked salmon garnished with a small mound of whipped double cream flavoured with grated lemon rind garnished with a slice of lemon OR with a little scrambled egg scattered with chopped parsley OR with dill sauce (very Swedish).

SALAMI WITH ONION RINGS: Thin slices of salami circled on a slice of bread topped with a few onion rings and a sprig of parsley.

HERRING WITH SOUR CREAM AND CHIVES: Slices of pickled herring on rye bread garnished with sour cream seasoned, and chopped chives.

CHICKEN WITH FOIE GRAS: Spread liver pâté on buttered bread, rye is best, top with sliced chicken, garnish with wedges of tomato and parsley.

EGG WITH ANCHOVY: Slices of hard-boiled egg topped with fine fillets of anchovy.

We'll stop here, by now you have the idea and can see almost anything can serve. Small amounts of FRESH left-overs: cold roast potatoes, a little cooked vegetable, peas, beans, carrots, etc., mixed with a little mayonnaise, some mushrooms cooked with chopped onion, slices of cold sausage, etc., can be used for excellent garnishes. The remains of roasted meats, poultry or cooked fish can also be pressed into service. With a little imagination almost anything can be made into a tempting open sandwich.

Scandinavians usually serve lager with the sandwiches, sometimes as a chaser to ice-cold schnapps (a frost-encrusted bottle brought straight from the freezer), or excellent coffee. One really good sandwich will do for a snack, two for a light meal, three to four for more substantial eating. Afters are seldom served, then usually confined to fruit or homemade biscuits, pastries or cake with coffee.

SARDINES ON TOAST DE LUXE

Sardines, like all oily fish, are extremely healthy and really good sardines are one of my favourite standbys. By really good I mean canned in olive oil. The taste is wildly superior to those immured in vegetable oil or even arachide or tournesol (sunflower) and the little fish also seem to be fatter, no doubt a personal prejudice exerting a little wishful thinking here. In Portugal they are treated like vintage wine, kept to mature, turned over carefully every few months.

Just dumping sardines on toast and pushing under the grill for a few minutes produces a quick snack that rates pretty highly, but done the following way they should prove acceptable to the most demanding gourmet. Opinion is divided over the advisability of removing the bones from the middle. I think they taste better without but for leaving them in there is the argument that the fish then provide more calcium, most desirable for keeping bones and teeth strong (also saves a fiddly task). The lemon thyme gives a nicely fresh flavour but parsley is almost as good.

2 slices good bread
1 can sardines in olive oil
Maille Moutarde au Poivre Vert
1–2 tomatoes, skinned
Salt and freshly ground black pepper
Garnish: Freshly chopped lemon thyme or parsley

Toast the bread lightly, remove crusts, spread with a little oil from the sardine can, add a scraping of mustard then slices of tomato, try and cover the edges of the toast as otherwise these can get unacceptably brown under the grill. Dust with salt and pepper then add the sardines, with or without their bones. Dust with another grinding or two of pepper and slip under a hot grill. Leave until skins are crisp and slightly bubbling. Remove, garnish with the chopped herbs and serve immediately.

HERRING ROES ON TOAST

When the fishmonger has fat, soft herring roes, buy them, they are creamily delicious and very healthy. If necessary, keep for a few weeks in the deep freeze. They make wonderful snacks, again on toast or, even better but sinfully fattening, on fried bread. Frying in olive oil won't lessen the calories but will improve the health rating.

1 tablespoon olive oil
6–8 soft herring roes, washed and drained
Salt and freshly ground black pepper
2 slices toast or fried bread
Freshly chopped parsley

Heat the oil moderately, add the roes, if they stick to the pan, lower the heat a little, and toss around for 1–2 minutes until the roes lose their slightly transparent quality. Don't overcook, they should have a really creamy texture inside. Season with salt and pepper, pile on the bread, sprinkle the chopped parsley over and serve immediately.

SMOKED MACKEREL FILLETS WITH ZESTED YOGHURT

Another very healthy fish, mackerel takes to smoking like teenagers to pop music, its flesh succulent and redolent with the subtle flavour of oak chips. Try and find fish that are smoked without additional colouring; there is a delicious variety by the Cornish Smoked Fish Company, who provide a version with cracked black peppercorns that is particularly good. The flavoured yoghurt cuts the oily quality of the fish and provides a nice extra note.

1–2 fillets smoked mackerel
Grated zest of ½ orange or lemon plus 2 slices of the fruit
4 tablespoons thick natural yoghurt
Little salt and freshly ground black pepper
Garnish: Little parsley
Brown bread and butter

Lift the smoked mackerel off its skin and place neatly on two plates. Add the grated zest to the yoghurt, stirring in well and checking for strength of flavour. Season lightly. Add a slice of the fruit to each plate, garnish with some sprigs of parsley and serve with brown bread and butter.

COOK'S TIP: The flavour of the yoghurt will deepen if you let it stand for an hour or two. Don't use ready bought orange fruit yoghurt, it will have sugar added and not taste at all the same.

BAKED POTATOES

Baked potatoes are another healthy snack, they only zoom up the coronary graph if you smother them with butter. In fact, the biological value of potato protein is higher than any other plant protein and nearly as high as egg protein. Potatoes are a most important source of vitamin C in the diet and provide a valuable contribution of vitamin B, fibre and other essential nutrients.

I think a microwave really helps on time for baked potatoes but there is no doubt that a potato cooked this way does not taste the same as one baked in the oven. A useful compromise is to microwave on HIGH for about 5 minutes then finish off with half an hour or so, depending on size, in a hot oven. Sticking a metal skewer through the length of the potato helps to reduce the amount of time needed in the oven (don't use in the microwave!). The variety of the fillings is only limited by availability and imagination. Here are a few suggestions.

First cook your potatoes, choosing nice sized Murphys with no green areas (always cut these out, they are toxic). Medium sized potatoes with skewers through their length will take about an hour in a hot oven or two unskewered potatoes should take 10–12 minutes in a microwave oven on HIGH (but check with your instruction book, they all give times for baked potatoes). When cooked cut them open, either with two cross cuts or one long one, and rough up the inside flesh a little, dribble a tiny bit of arachide/ groundnut/peanut or olive oil over and season well. Then add your filling. With a microwave, this can be a raw vegetable such as carrot, courgette or kohlrabi just grated straight in, the filled potato covered with cling film then put back in the microwave and, for two potatoes, given another two minutes on HIGH. Or less if you like your vegetables really crunchy. Indeed, there is no need to cook them at all if you would rather not.

Sometimes it is best to cook the vegetable before adding to the potato; mushrooms and leeks come into this category, they both give off a great deal of liquid. Either is delicious mixed with a little diced ham or cooked bacon.

Cheese, either grated or diced, can be added on its own or mixed with diced or grated apple tossed in a little lemon juice to prevent it going brown, or with tomato, skinned, deseeded and cut in dice or slivers. Prawns or tuna fish and sweetcorn mixed with mayonnaise are another possibility.

BAKED SOUFFLÉ POTATOES

For a change take a little extra trouble and produce soufflé potatoes. They sound and look *haute cuisine* but are really very easy.

2 medium sized potatoes
1 tablespoon butter or olive or arachide oil
Salt and freshly ground black pepper
Approx. 150 ml/5 fl oz/⅔ cup hot milk
Approx. 3–4 tablespoons chopped ham, bacon, grated cheese, cooked meat or flaked fish, etc. OR 2 tablespoons chopped fresh herbs
1 egg white

Bake potatoes in their skins (difficult to do completely in the microwave for this recipe as the skins don't become crisp enough). With skewers through their length, the potatoes should take approximately 1 hour in a hot oven,

200°C/400°F/Gas Mark 6. Cut in half, scrape out cooked potato, leaving skins intact. Mash with the butter or oil and seasonings (also the yolk of the egg if you use a whole one rather than a spare white from the fridge) then beat in sufficient hot milk to make a loose purée. Mix in the chosen filling or flavouring and season. Whip egg white to stiff peak and fold in carefully. Pile mixture into shells and bake at 180°C/350°F/Gas Mark 4 for about 20 minutes until puffy and nicely browned on top. Eat immediately.

COOK'S TIP: Potato halves can be prepared ahead of time and left in the fridge for several hours before cooking.

SPANISH TORTILLA

This is not exactly a Spanish Tortilla, rather an anglicised version that is an excellent way of using up ready cooked meat and vegetables to provide a tasty snack. Very useful when the fridge provides odd goodies but not enough to do anything really constructive with. The only essentials are onion, potato and eggs. Even the cheese is optional, except as far as my husband is concerned.

1 tablespoon olive oil
1 small onion or 2 shallots, finely chopped
1 raw potato, diced
Few cooked vegetables such as peas or beans, mushrooms, carrots, etc., cut into smallish pieces
Little cooked and diced meat
3 eggs, lightly beaten with 3 tablespoons water
Salt and freshly ground pepper
Grated cheese

Put on the grill. Heat oil in a medium sized frying pan and add the chopped onion or shallot and cook gently until soft. Add the potato, increase the heat and fry until cooked and golden. Add the cooked vegetables and meat and continue cooking until heated through. Season the beaten eggs and water and add to the pan, stirring to mix well with the other ingredients. Allow the bottom to set. Cover top with grated cheese, place under hot grill until golden and puffy and serve at once.

VARIATIONS: For a more unusual dish try AVOCADO TORTILLA. To the onion and potato add a small avocado pear, peeled and sliced, a few florets of broccoli and a handful of broad beans, both either cooked or blanched for several minutes. Arrange with the avocado on top of the potatoes and onion, pour over the egg mixture then finish cooking as above, adding grated cheese before placing under grill. OR, instead of fried vegetables, use some diced ham and chopped chives, mix the beaten eggs with 150 ml/5 fl oz/⅔ cup single (light) cream, season and bake in a well buttered or oiled fireproof dish as above. This is a popular Scandinavian dish.

COOK'S TIP: Instead of cooking omelette on top of stove, the beaten eggs can be added to the fried vegetable mixture, either in the frying pan or in a gratin or other shallow dish, and the cooking completed in the oven preheated to 180°C/350°F/Gas Mark 4 for about 20–25 minutes.

STIR-FRIED CHICKEN WITH EGGS

A good way of using up odd bits of un-cooked chicken, perhaps after you have been jointing a whole bird, or another good home for a little cooked chicken.

1 tablespoon arachide/groundnut/peanut oil
100–175 g/4–6 oz/⅔–1 cup shredded chicken, either cooked or uncooked

1 large egg, beaten 1 teaspoon sesame oil 1½ tablespoons chicken stock or water 1 teaspoon dry sherry or rice wine Pinch salt 1 teaspoon light soy sauce Pinch sugar	all mixed together

Garnish: 1 tablespoon finely chopped chives or parsley

Thoroughly heat a wok or frying pan, add half the oil and stir-fry the shredded chicken, either to warm through or until flesh is just cooked, which is as soon as it has lost its transparent quality and looks opaque, a matter of a minute or so. Remove with a slotted spoon and keep warm. Clean out the pan, add the other half of the oil and then the egg mixture, stir-frying for a minute. Just as the egg begins to set, replace the chicken in the pan and continue to stir-fry for another minute, until the egg is cooked. Place in a serving dish or divide between individual plates, garnish with the chives or parsley and serve.

ACCOMPANIMENTS: A little fried rice would go well, or warm pitta bread, or brown bread and butter.

VARIATIONS: Use prawns instead of chicken, adding to the egg without the prior cooking, they will only need heating through if already cooked.

SCRAMBLED EGGS PLUS

Scrambled eggs can be another dish in the luxury class and partners various other ingredients brilliantly to make a substantial snack. Too often, though, the eggs are a less than appetising combination of watery liquid and hard curds. The secret of really good scrambling is not being in a hurry. If you only have a few minutes, make an omelette, it takes time to achieve real creamy bliss, requires your undivided attention and, like an omelette, the result should be served immediately. So have everything else ready, see suggestions below, and prepare for a relaxing stay at the stove. A moment of decision before you start, are you going to use milk with the eggs or add a touch of cream at the end? The latter not only adds extra richness but helps arrest the cooking at a vital stage. But you can make good scrambled eggs without either – and can use oil instead of butter, the flavour of olive oil may be a little unfamiliar in this dish but a light variety is very pleasant, arachide or sunflower would be less obtrusive.

4 eggs
2 tablespoons milk or 1 tablespoon cream
Salt and freshly ground black pepper
Knob of butter or tablespoon light olive or arachide/groundnut/peanut or other light oil

Beat the eggs well with the seasonings (go easy with the pepper, it can decide to lump together) and the milk, if using cream it is best to leave this until the end. Heat the butter or oil gently then add the egg mixture. With a flat-ended spatula or spoon gently stir the eggs over a slow heat. Gradually they will start to thicken, almost like a custard, then to form embryonic

256

flakes. The process is slow and you may eventually lose patience and turn up the heat a little so the flakes form much more quickly and then find yourself removing the pan from the heat to incorporate the rapidly thickening egg from the bottom of the pan with the runnier mixture above. The eggs are cooked when they form thick and creamy flakes that look as though they should have just a moment's more cooking. This will be received in the time it takes to spoon the mixture from the saucepan on to the plates. Unless you are going to add the tablespoon of cream now. In which case, cook for just a little longer then stir in either single or double cream. Or even a little yoghurt.

VARIATIONS: Add chopped fresh herbs or diced ham or cooked bacon to the eggs before cooking or a little grated cheese at the end, stirring in carefully. Everything else is, I think, better put beside the eggs rather than in them. See below for suggestions.

MICROWAVE OVEN: I have never achieved really successful scrambled eggs in the microwave and have yet to be convinced they are possible.

ACCOMPANIMENTS:

1) **SMOKED FISH** goes brilliantly with scrambled eggs. The class combination is smoked salmon. You can sometimes get end bits quite cheaply and you only need a little to scatter over the eggs to make a most impressive snack or first course. Smoked trout or mackerel are also excellent. Both are available cold smoked and sliced like smoked salmon and, though not quite as good as the very best salmon, are much superior to some of the cheaper varieties I've tasted. Either scatter in strips over the top of the eggs or serve arranged prettily beside and garnished with sprigs of parsley or watercress and a segment of lemon.

2) **MUSHROOMS** cooked plainly or with a tablespoon of cream or with *fines herbes*, or finished with a tablespoon of parsley chopped with a small clove of garlic added at the end of cooking, which gives a zingily fresh effect.

3) **SAUSAGES, KIDNEYS, BACON,** etc., as for an old-fashioned English breakfast, any or all can stretch the snack proportions to those of a hefty meal but never mind.

4) **TOMATOES,** skinned, deseeded and flesh chopped. Add just before serving to a little onion cooked slowly until transparent.

5) I am told by those lucky enough to have sampled them that a few shavings of fresh truffle on just cooked scrambled eggs are unbelievably wonderful, maybe one day I'll manage to try them.

OMELETTE

The snack for anyone in a hurry. It takes less time to cook an omelette than to read the instructions. The whole process is swift and the end result must be eaten immediately. Have everything ready before starting to cook, including the other eater. For two it is possible to make one omelette and divide it between you but the whole operation is so quick I prefer to make each of us our own. Do try and keep a special omelette pan that is never washed up, just wiped at the end of each session, then your omelettes will never stick. The following recipe is for one person. The water gives extra lightness as it evaporates into steam during cooking.

2 eggs
1 dessertspoon cold water
Salt and freshly ground black pepper
Fillings: 1 large tablespoon chopped fresh herbs OR some diced ham OR diced cooked bacon OR 2 tablespoons grated cheese OR little meat or mushrooms in sauce, etc.
Small knob of butter
Garnish: Freshly chopped parsley (optional)

Beat the eggs with the water and seasoning until eggs well mixed. If using herbs, ham or bacon, add these now. If using anything in a sauce, have it heated and ready. Heat pan, add the butter and swirl it around as it melts. As soon as the frothing stops, add the omelette mixture, all in one go. Immediately start moving pan across heat with one hand and using a fork in the other to move cooked mixture away from bottom of pan, allowing the liquid, uncooked mixture to run underneath. Grated cheese or anything in a sauce should be added across the middle of the omelette while the top is still runny. Leave for a few seconds for bottom to brown slightly then flip top third of omelette over filling and shake pan to loosen omelette. Take hold of a warm plate and slide the unfolded end of the omelette on to the middle, giving the pan a quick tilt so it ends up neatly rolled on the plate. Garnish with the chopped parsley and serve immediately.

VARIATIONS: Try a SMOKED TROUT OMELETTE: 100 g/4 oz smoked trout, skin and bones removed, heated very gently with ½ teaspoon creamed horseradish, a few chopped leaves of lemon thyme and a tablespoon of cream. Place across middle of nearly cooked omelette and finish as above.

COOK'S TIP: To prepare a new pan, or one used for other things, heat gently with some oil and a generous quantity of salt. Then take a large wodge of kitchen paper and give it a really good scrub, using the salt to abrade and polish the surface. This method works for a dirty pan as well and avoids having to wash it.

OEUFS EN COCOTTE

One of the best snacks, or a good starter for a main meal. The secret to these eggs is timing and knowing your oven. They all vary so much that the first time you try may not produce exactly the right result with the whites set and the yolks still runny but make a note of whether the heat was too hot, the timing too little or too long and the next time things should be better and the third time perfect. After that you have the problem licked and will find a vast range of variations to enjoy.

2 eggs
Little butter, cream, stock or other flavourings, see below
Salt and freshly ground black pepper

Place two ramekin dishes in a small roasting tin or shallow fireproof dish with sufficient warm water to come two-thirds of the way up the dishes. Add your chosen flavouring or, for plain eggs, just a few flakes of butter or a spoonful of cream or stock. Place in an oven at 180°C/350°F/Gas Mark 4, to heat through dishes and warm contents; when warm, crack an egg into each dish and return to the oven. The preheating means they will start cooking immediately and it should now take 10 minutes for the white to set and leave the yolk runny. Seasoning is usually done after the egg comes out of the oven as the salt can leave odd spots on the surface of the egg.

FLAVOURING OPTIONS:

Left-overs when cooking for two are not usually a problem. Alternatively plan ahead when making a cheese sauce or chopped spinach and reserve a couple of tablespoons for a snack meal. Warm through before using with the eggs.

1) **MUSHROOMS:** A few chopped mushrooms sautéd in butter, a little cream added, placed in bottom of the ramekin dishes or spooned over the eggs if preferred.

2) **HERBS:** A good teaspoon chopped fresh herbs with butter in the base of the dish plus a spoonful of cream if liked.

3) **CHEESE:** Grate cheese over the top of the eggs, Cheddar, Gruyère and Parmesan are all good. Cream can also be added, put this in before the eggs.

4) **BACON:** Dice a rasher or two of bacon, sauté until lightly browned, then add to dish or scatter on top of egg.

5) **SMOKED FISH:** A few flakes of smoked trout, mackerel or salmon with a spoonful of cream.

6) **COURGETTE:** Stir-fry a little grated courgette in a couple of tablespoons of good stock, enough to make a sauce of the vegetable, season carefully. Can be added either to bottom of dish or on top of egg.

7) **ASPARAGUS:** A few asparagus, sliced obliquely and quite thinly, sautéd in butter until tender, added on top of egg.

8) **ARTICHOKE HEARTS:** As for asparagus.

9) **CHEESE SAUCE:** Not worth making especially for the eggs but a couple of reserved tablespoons from a cauliflower cheese or other dish can come in useful here. Warm first then spoon carefully over top of egg.

10) **SPICED TOMATO:** Prepare tomato as suggested to accompany scrambled eggs, season well with a dash of Tabasco sauce and a couple of dashes of Worcestershire sauce, add either to dish or on top of eggs.

11) **SPINACH:** A little chopped spinach mixed with a spoonful of cream or yoghurt, seasoned with grated nutmeg, salt and pepper, can be placed under or over the eggs.

CROQUE MONSIEUR

The classic French snack. Tasty, easy to do, calling for ingredients almost always on hand, it is ideal for most occasions.

4 slices good white bread (or brown if you prefer) cut fairly thinly
Little French mustard
2 thin slices ham
4 thin slices cheese, Gruyère is best but Cheddar will do and can be grated if you prefer
1 small egg, lightly beaten
2 tablespoons butter

Spread each slice of bread with a little mustard then make sandwiches with a slice of ham placed in between two slices of cheese, or have grated cheese on each side. Press well together. Dip each sandwich briefly in the egg then fry in butter until golden brown each side. Serve immediately. The sandwiches can be fried in butter without being dipped first in the beaten egg, either version is delicious.

VARIATIONS: To make a Croque Madame, add a fried egg on top. The sandwiches can also be toasted instead of fried. Not quite so good but less calorific.

CHEERED-UP BAKED BEANS

Sneer if you will but baked beans are extremely healthy and liked by a large percentage of the population. After all, a million housewives every day pick up a can of beans. They can't all be wrong! Here are a few ways of making them a little more individual.

REFLAVOURING: Adding a couple of dashes of Tabasco and Worcestershire sauce plus a pinch ground cumin if you have it, provides a good facsimile of chilli beans. A couple of dried chilli beans can be added to the beans for the reheating process as well (remember to remove before serving). OR add a couple of rashers of smoked bacon, diced and sautéd, OR a couple of sliced frankfurter sausages, OR some diced garlic sausage.

BAKED BEANS AND EGGS: Reheat baked beans, place in a gratin dish, press the back of a tablespoon into the beans to make two dents and break an egg into each. Season lightly (see OEUFS EN CO-COTTE on page 259), place in a preheated oven at 180°C/350°F/Gas Mark 4, and cook for 10 minutes, until the whites of the eggs are set but yolks are still runny. Bacon can also be added.

BAKED BEANS AND KIDNEY: Dice a pig's kidney, brown quickly in a little butter, add a tin of baked beans and cook gently until beans hot and kidney just cooked through, add half a teaspoon of French mustard and serve garnished with a little chopped parsley.

HELP FOR MOTHER HUBBARD

Meals from the storecupboard are for real emergencies. Those times when an unexpected guest arrives and your intended meal won't stretch. Or perhaps you had expected to go out, the plans were cancelled and shops are shut. Or something prevented you getting to the shops, or the household budget is exhausted. Then it's good to find the makings of a meal on the shelf.

A word of warning, tinned and dried products are very rarely a match for fresh or specially prepared. Some, like tinned tomatoes, which pack a real flavour punch, or sardines and baked beans, are good to have on hand for all sorts of uses, others are for emergency purposes only, such as tinned tongue or ham. So buy the best. They are not for regular use and you might just as well pay a little extra and get something reasonable.

Items I find useful to have in the storecupboard: tins of sardines, tuna fish, salmon and anchovy, Scandinavian herrings in various sauces. Tins of peeled tomato, red peppers, various pulses, beans, artichoke hearts, celery hearts, corn niblets, mushrooms, tinned fruits such as cherries and apricots. Long-life milk and cream (doesn't taste quite as good as the real thing but useful in emergencies, especially when mixed with other ingredients). Pasta of various sorts and rice. Black olives. Dried mushrooms, and dried apricots and prunes of the ready-to-eat variety. Pumpernickel bread. Plus, of course, the usual stock items such as flour, sugar, spices, bottled sauces, dark block chocolate, etc. Pine nuts and almonds for finishing touches are indispensable. (As this book goes to press, the former have vanished but I hope they will reappear next season. In the meantime I am using pistachio nuts instead.) Items useful to have on hand at any time include your own French dressing and mayonnaise. Well wrapped, Parmesan cheese in a block will keep a long time in the fridge and is a great boon. Cheddar cheese is not so long lasting but is always good to have on hand.

Fresh herbs from the garden or window-box will help immeasurably, their flavour will perk up canned items and just the look of that fresh green can transform a storecupboard item.

Other sections of this book can help as well. A well-flavoured white or cheese sauce (see SAUCY IDEAS section on page 189) can form the basis of a gratin dish, use with tinned tuna fish or on top of drained vegetables, finish with grated cheese. A soufflé omelette can be made with sliced mushrooms or flaked tuna fish.

I think one of the secrets of a successful storecupboard meal is not to try and produce too many courses or dishes. You haven't the resources for a good conventional meal so be unconventional. Accompany a vegetable salad with delicious crostini topped with olive paste. Serve a pasta dish followed by a salad. Try a soup followed by a small herring smorgasbord.

There are some reasonable tinned soups, all benefit from a good slurp of brandy or sherry when being reheated, some from a tablespoonful or two of cream if it's available. But there are also easy soups that can be made from storecupboard items. Both the following are filling and excellent standbys. With a toasted cheese sandwich, they can provide a complete meal. Or can be followed by cold meats from a delicatessen.

CORN AND TUNA FISH SOUP

This is a good storecupboard soup, excellent for emergencies. If you have good chicken stock available, it will make all the difference. If you are making do with a chicken stock cube, do watch the seasoning, you will probably not need any more salt.

½ teaspoon hot Madras curry powder
1½ tablespoons flour
15 g/½ oz/1 tablespoon butter or 1 tablespoon oil
250 ml/scant 10 fl oz/1 cup chicken stock or water or one third of a chicken stock cube dissolved in boiling water
150 ml/5 fl oz/generous ½ cup milk
Small can sweetcorn niblets, drained
Small tin tuna fish, drained and flaked
1 tablespoon brandy (optional)
Garnish: Little lemon thyme, leaves taken off branch, or chopped parsley

Gently cook curry powder and flour in butter or oil for several minutes. Then add first the stock and after that the milk to make a smooth, thin sauce, bringing to boil and simmering several minutes. Stir in the sweetcorn and flaked tuna fish and heat through. Add the brandy and serve sprinkled with the lemon thyme or parsley.

COOK'S TIP: Cooking the curry powder with the flour helps take the raw edge off the spices. If you want to add extra curry flavour to any dish after this stage, it is best to use curry paste, which has been tempered.

BEAN AND TOMATO SOUP

Another good standby.

1 standard size tin peeled tomatoes, sieved
Pinch sugar
½ teaspoon dried basil
2 tablespoons extra virgin olive oil
Salt and freshly ground black pepper
1 standard size tin haricot or flageolet beans, drained and rinsed if necessary
Little water
Optional: Parmesan cheese for serving

Place the tomato, sugar, basil and oil in a saucepan, season and heat steadily to boiling point then simmer for a few minutes. Then add the beans, stir well and heat, adding sufficient water to achieve a good consistency. Serve with grated Parmesan cheese if you have it.

HERRING SMÖRGÅSBORD

It is now quite easy to get Scandinavian herrings preserved in a number of different sauces. These can be arranged nicely in a serving dish or dishes and accompanied by hard-boiled eggs, a PICKLED BEETROOT SALAD (see page 269) and some hot new potatoes (there are very reasonable vacuum packed or tinned ones available).

PASTA

Pasta has to be one of the most useful of all storecupboard items. Ribbons of pasta, thick or thin, or pasta shapes, can be served with very simple sauces for almost instant meals. Allow 175 g/6 oz/2 cups pasta for two people. Here are some possible sauces:

1) **PESTO** – though the best pesto is homemade from fresh basil, garlic, pine nuts, Italian cheese and olive oil, it is possible to buy reasonable versions. Cook the pasta then dress in the pesto sauce and top with freshly grated Parmesan cheese.

2) **TOMATO AND SMOKED OYSTERS:** Heat 2 tablespoons olive oil, sieve a small tin of peeled tomatoes and add with ½ teaspoon dried basil (if you have fresh, tear and add a handful of leaves at the end), season to taste (remembering that the oysters will be quite salty) and cook for several minutes for the flavours to meld together and the sauce to achieve a good consistency. Drain the oysters of their oil, cut each oyster into two or three pieces, add all to the sauce and heat through. Pour over cooked pasta and serve, if possible, with freshly grated Parmesan.

3) **MUSHROOMS AND GARLIC:** Soak 15 g/½ oz dried mushrooms in boiling water for 20–30 minutes, drain the mushrooms, reserving the water, check for any dirt then slice the fungi. Melt 25 g/1 oz/2 tablespoons butter in a large saucepan, add 2 cloves garlic, peeled and crushed with a little salt, and cook for 1–2 minutes, then add the sliced mushrooms and cook gently for 5 minutes before adding a 250 ml/8 fl oz/1 cup carton of long-life double cream, season well, bring to boil then simmer very gently for 10 minutes, adding some of the strained mushroom water to achieve a good consistency sauce. Adjust seasoning, pour over the cooked pasta and serve with freshly grated Parmesan cheese.

4) **TUNA FISH AND OLIVES:** Drain a small tin of tuna fish in olive oil then shred the flesh. Heat 1 tablespoon olive oil. Sieve a small tin of peeled tomatoes, add to the pan with a good pinch of dried basil, bring to the boil then simmer for several minutes to reduce slightly. Add the shredded tuna fish and two chopped fillets of anchovy and heat through, then pour over cooked and drained pasta, toss over a gentle heat for a couple of minutes then add 10 black olives that have been halved and stoned, check seasoning and serve, if possible with freshly grated Parmesan.

5) **MUSHROOMS AND PEAS:** Gently heat 25 g/1 oz/2 tablespoons butter, add 1 clove garlic, peeled and crushed with a little salt, then a tin of *petits pois*, drained, a tin of mushrooms, sliced, and a 250 ml/8 fl oz/1 cup carton of long-life double cream. Stir together and heat to boiling point, check seasoning, pour over cooked pasta and serve with freshly grated Parmesan. If a little sliced bacon or shredded ham or salami is available, this will be a welcome addition.

SALMON MOUSSE

This is an Italian recipe, many thanks to Marcella Hazan, a simple but versatile salmon mousse made from tinned salmon. It can be served with a simple BEAN SALAD (see page 268), or as a pâté with toast or biscuits, or piled on CROSTINI (see page 268).

A 225 g/8 oz (approx.) tin of salmon
2 tablespoons extra virgin olive oil
1 tablespoon lemon juice
Salt and freshly ground black pepper
150 ml/5 fl oz/⅔ cup long-life whipping cream

Drain the salmon and remove any bones and skin. Place in a food processor (or crush with a fork in a bowl), add the oil, lemon, a very little salt and a rather more generous helping of pepper then process until smooth (or beat well). Check seasoning. Have the cream well chilled then beat in a chilled bowl until it holds its shape. Fold into the salmon mixture then chill for anything from 2 to 24 hours. The mousse can then be moulded into little "eggs" with the aid of two dessertspoons.

OLIVE PÂTÉ

Almost as useful as the salmon mousse above is olive pâté.

Black olives
Extra virgin olive oil, green and pungent
Freshly ground black pepper

Stone a quantity of black olives, place in a processor and reduce to a purée whilst adding a little green olive oil, tasting as you go to judge the result, and a good grinding of black pepper. Other additions can be capers, anchovies, garlic, herbs, etc. but it is good just as it is. Try it with hard-boiled eggs, or on toasted split muffins or on CROSTINI (see below). Or on little rounds of pumpernickel bread. Garnish with strips of red pepper dressed with a little olive oil or with split fillets of anchovy.

CROSTINI

A version of croûtons baked in the oven with olive oil and an ideal way to use up a stale loaf. The baked crostini can be kept in an air-tight tin for several days.

Cut slices of bread, remove crusts, brush with good olive oil then bake in a hot oven at 200°C/400°F/Gas Mark 6 for 10 minutes or so until golden and crisp. Top with either of the previous two recipes or anything else that takes your fancy and is available. Small ones are ideal for drinks, large ones are good for a substantial snack.

SALADS

With a good French dressing, a variety of storecupboard items can be turned into serviceable salads, particularly if you can add some fresh herbs as well. These can be served with a soufflé or straight omelette to make a complete meal, or can accompany SALMON MOUSSE (see page 267) or a CROSTINI of OLIVE PÂTÉ (see page 267).

1) **BEAN SALAD:** Small tins of three different types of beans, broad, butter, red kidney, etc., mixed together and dressed with French dressing. A chopped shallot can add extra zing. Serve with salmon mousse or cold meats from a delicatessen.

2) **BUTTER BEANS AND ANCHOVY:** Mix together a small tin of butter beans with three chopped fillets of anchovy and a few spoonfuls of long-life cream, adding a few drops of oil from the anchovy tin to taste. Serve with scrambled or hard-boiled eggs or SALMON MOUSSE (see page 267) or CROSTINI of OLIVE PÂTÉ (see page 267).

3) **MUSHROOMS, TUNA FISH AND BROAD BEANS:** Slice contents of a tin of mushrooms, drain a small tin of tuna fish in olive oil, shred fish, drain a standard tin of broad beans, mix all together and dress with a vinaigrette and 2 tablespoons cream or yoghurt. Finish with toasted, flaked almonds. Very good on its own after a soup, or with CROSTINI of OLIVE PÂTÉ for the really hungry.

4) **CELERY HEARTS AND RED PEPPERS:** Slice celery hearts obliquely across, toss in French dressing then mix carefully with sliced red peppers drained of their liquid and dressed with a little olive oil. Finish with a few black olives. Serve with grilled sardines.

5) **ARTICHOKE HEARTS, HARD-BOILED EGGS AND PINE NUTS:** Drain a tin of artichoke hearts, slice, toss in French dressing then arrange with sliced hard-boiled eggs. Sprinkle with toasted pine nuts. A meal on its own or with sliced meats.

6) **FRENCH BEANS, WATER-CHESTNUTS AND MUSHROOMS:** Drain the French beans, slice the water-chestnuts and mushrooms, mix all together and dress with French dressing. Finish with toasted pine nuts or flaked almonds. Serve with grilled sardines or hard-boiled eggs. Again, a meal on its own, especially after a soup.

7) **PICKLED BEETROOT:** Dice three or four pickled beetroot and a crisp eating apple then gently mix with two or three tablespoons mayonnaise or whipped cream. Serve with Scandinavian herrings in sauce and hot new potatoes, or with cold meats, particularly tongue.

TONGUE IN MUSHROOMS AND ONIONS

A substantial dish that is really too good to keep for emergencies.

1 tin of tongue
1 tablespoon arachide/groundnut/peanut oil
1 medium onion, peeled and chopped
1 tin mushrooms, drained and sliced
Salt and freshly ground black pepper
4 tablespoons red vermouth
Approx. 6 tablespoons grated Parmesan cheese

Slice the tongue and place in a shallow, ovenproof dish. Heat the oil and gently cook the onion until soft and transparent. Add the sliced mushrooms, season then pour in the red vermouth, mix well together and spoon over the tongue. Sprinkle with the Parmesan cheese, place in a preheated oven at 190°C/375°F/Gas Mark 5 for 30 minutes.

ACCOMPANIMENTS: Serve with pasta or new potatoes and a tin of *petits pois à la française*.

MICROWAVE OVEN: Mix oil with onion in a bowl, cover tightly with cling film and microwave on HIGH for 3 minutes. Mix together with the mushrooms and vermouth, pour over the sliced tongue arranged in a shallow dish, sprinkle with the cheese, cover tightly with cling film and microwave on HIGH for 5 minutes.

HAM IN RUM AND RAISIN SAUCE

Another simple dish in a sauce very similar to one given in the SAUCY IDEAS section on page 185. It makes a very appetising dish.

1 small tin of ham
2 tablespoons soft brown sugar
1 teaspoon cornflour
½ teaspoon dry English mustard
150 ml/5 fl oz/⅔ cup dry cider or stock or water
2 tablespoons raisins, preferably large, soaked in 3 tablespoons light rum for 30–60 minutes

Slice the ham and arrange in a shallow ovenproof dish. Place sugar in a saucepan, stir in cornflour and mustard then slowly add the cider, stock or water, stirring well. Heat gently, stirring constantly, until sugar melted, then bring to boil. When sauce has thickened and become clear, add the raisins and rum and continue stirring until fruit plump and soft. Check seasoning, remembering that ham will be salty. Pour over ham, cover with tin foil and place in a preheated oven at 180°C/350°F/Gas Mark 4 for 30 minutes.

ACCOMPANIMENTS: Pasta, rice or new potatoes would all go well, plus reheated celery hearts or *petits pois à la française*.

MICROWAVE OVEN: Place all sauce ingredients in large jug, stirring well to mix. Cover tightly with cling film, microwave on HIGH for 5 minutes, uncover carefully and whisk with a fork. Pour over ham arranged in a shallow dish, cover tightly with cling film and microwave on HIGH for 4 minutes. Allow to stand for 2 minutes before serving.

DESSERTS

Tinned cherries or apricots can be used for a APRICOT CLAFOUTIS (see the SWEET TALK section on page 206). Tinned apricots can be processed with a little rum and turned into a stunning sauce for ice cream or baked apples or used for a store-cupboard trifle with sherry-splashed trifle sponges and a few amaretti topped with whipped cream flavoured with a little vanilla or rum and sweetened with a little icing sugar. Fruit bottled in brandy or other alcohol, either homemade or good commercial varieties, will provide an instant pudding, especially if you have some homemade meringues to accompany. Instead of long-life cream, make a CRÈME ANGLAISE (see the SAUCY IDEAS section on page 196).

HOF DESSERT

A Danish friend used to serve a delicious version of this very simple dessert. All you need is to raid the meringue tin, sandwich with whipped cream, treated as above, and, at the last minute, pour over hot chocolate sauce:

CHOCOLATE SAUCE

This chocolate sauce is ideal with the meringues, or you can serve the one in the SAUCY IDEAS section on page 195.

50 g/2 oz plain chocolate
2 level tablespoons golden syrup
Small knob butter

Place all ingredients in a bowl set over a small pan of simmering water and heat, stirring from time to time, until melted into a shiny sauce.

MICROWAVE OVEN: Place all ingredients into a bowl, leave uncovered, microwave on HIGH for 2 minutes. Stir well.

DRIED FRUIT COMPOTE

If you have a microwave, this compote can be made very quickly. Even without one, it doesn't take all that long. Alcohol improves the results dramatically.

175 g/6 oz dried fruit, either apricots or a mixture
300 ml/10 fl oz/generous cup water or mixture water and wine
Small piece of lemon peel, if available, or stick cinnamon
Flaked and toasted almonds to finish

Place the dried fruit in the liquid and leave to soak for several hours if possible, then place over heat with the lemon peel, if available, or cinnamon stick. Bring to simmering point and cook gently until tender. If in a hurry, bring the fruit and liquid to boiling point, remove from heat, leave for 40 minutes, return to heat and simmer gently until tender. If using water, a little brandy or rum added just before the end of cooking adds extra interest. Scatter the flaked and toasted almonds over before serving.

ACCOMPANIMENTS: Some nice crisp little biscuits, or meringue halves. Cream if available.

MICROWAVE OVEN: Place fruit, liquid and lemon peel in deep dish, cover tightly with cling film and microwave on HIGH for 12 minutes, stirring or giving a good shake halfway through cooking.

ICE CREAM

Storecupboard ice creams are a definite possibility, very quick and easy if you have an electric maker. Even without, the process is fairly simple but will take several hours to freeze. Here are two amazingly simple ones that don't even require eggs.

COFFEE ICE CREAM

You can make this ice cream with instant coffee but it is a great deal better with fresh grounds. Best of all with filter fine grounds that are left in the ice cream to add extra texture.

150 ml/5 fl oz/⅔ cup boiling water
2 tablespoons fresh coffee grounds or good instant coffee
100 g/4 oz/8 tablespoons demerara sugar
3 tablespoons rum
250 ml/8 fl oz/1 cup double cream (long-life)

Allow the water to come just off the boil then pour over the coffee. Add the sugar and stir to dissolve. Allow to cool. Add the rum and the double cream. Pour into ice-cream maker and follow instructions to freeze.

OR pour into a metal container and place in freezing compartment of fridge or a freezer. As the mixture beings to freeze round the edges, beat well, return to container and freezing compartment. Repeat twice more.

Place ice cream in main part of fridge for 20 minutes to soften slightly before serving.

VARIATIONS: Chopped walnuts (approximately 20 g/¾ oz/3 tablespoons) can be added to ice cream if liked.

COOK'S TIP: The amount of coffee may seem high but chilling deadens taste so ice cream needs a strong flavour.

PEACH ICE CREAM

Another very quick, very easy ice cream. The better the tinned fruit, the better the result.

1 tin peaches in syrup
2 tablespoons brandy
2 tablespoons honey, preferably acacia
250 ml/8 fl oz/1 cup long-life double cream
2 additional tablespoons brandy

Strain the peaches and purée three-quarters of them, adding the brandy and honey. Mix together with the cream and pour into an ice-cream maker, following instructions to freeze.

OR pour into a metal container and place in freezing compartment of fridge or a freezer. As the mixture begins to freeze round the edges, beat well, return to container and freezing compartment. Repeat twice more. Place ice cream in main part of fridge for 20 minutes to soften slightly before serving.

Dice remaining peach slices, pour over the final two tablespoons of brandy and leave to marinate. Serve over the ice cream.

VARIATIONS: Use a different fruit: apricots, strawberries, blackcurrants, raspberries, mango, passion fruit, are all good. If they are not canned in syrup, you will need to add a third of their weight in sugar; apart from sweetening, the sugar helps prevent the ice cream freezing too hard.

BACK TO BASICS

A short section covering some basic recipes that crop up again and again plus some useful techniques.

PASTRY

Good shortcrust pastry is very versatile. Apart from the uses that spring immediately to mind such as flans, pies, tarts, en croûte dishes, any left-over trimmings can provide quick cheese straws or little tartlet cases which can be filled with any sort of fish or meat mixed with mayonnaise to serve with drinks or provide a quick light meal. For the best pastry, handle the mixture as little as possible (a processor gives ideal results), have the fat cold but not fridge solid and use just enough liquid to bind the pastry together.

The following recipe is halfway between ordinary and rich shortcrust; easier to handle than rich, lighter and tastier than ordinary shortcrust, a very good all-purpose pastry. If you follow the instructions, it should turn out perfectly every time.

---

225 g/8 oz/2 cups plain flour sifted with ½ teaspoon salt

---

140 g/5 oz/10 tablespoons butter

---

4 tablespoons ice-cold water, or 3 tablespoons water and 1 egg yolk

---

BY HAND: Cut fat into small pieces and toss in the flour. Rub fat into flour by scooping up pieces of fat with flour and flicking between fingers and thumb, don't press or squeeze, until the mixture resembles breadcrumbs. Give the bowl a shake when nearly finished, the larger pieces will sit on the top and can be cut with a knife to avoid overworking and making them greasy. Sprinkle over the liquid, stirring in at the same time, then use one hand to bring the mixture together, gently pressing it into a coherent mass. If necessary, add a smidgeon more liquid, flours vary in their capacity to absorb liquids, wholewheat, for instance, needs more liquid than finely ground white flour and strong flours need more than soft flours. Once it has come together, don't knead the pastry, just let it rest for 20 minutes or so under the pastry bowl or wrapped in cling film. The gluten in the flour, which is what gives it the elastic quality so useful for bread making, will have been stretched by the rubbing in of the fat, and needs to relax otherwise the pastry could shrink badly when cooked.

BY PROCESSOR: Add the flour with the salt, roughly cut up the fat and add as well, then process in a series of short bursts until the mixture resembles breadcrumbs. Add the liquid with the machine running and stop it as soon as the pastry starts coming together. Tip it out and finish forcing any stray bits together with your hands.

ROLL OUT on a well-floured board and flour rolling pin rather than pastry. Use short strokes always going away from your body in the same direction and move pastry round on the board to achieve a good shape and prevent it sticking. Always use the first rolling out, even if it means a little patching, the second will be just a little bit tougher. Pile up trimmings neatly rather than scrunching them all together, this produces a much better second rolling out for what is left.

TO LINE A FLAN TIN: Judge size by placing tin lightly on pastry and allowing a generous margin. Roll pastry gently round pin then unroll over tin. Lift the sides of the pastry and gently fit into the tin, allowing excess to hang over sides. Then lift this, push it in towards the centre and pinch together a double layer all round the top of the tin, making a sort of ledge or overhang over the base. Roll the pin over the tin so that the remaining excess pastry falls away. Finally ease this "ledge" up, pinching it into shape so that it stands up straight and even, effectively doubling the depth of the tin. Refrigerate for 30 minutes or so before baking.

TO BAKE: Shortcrust pastry should be baked in a moderately hot oven: 190°C/375°F/Gas Mark 5 until the pastry is set, which will take about 25 minutes for a flan or pie, less for little tartlet cases. If necessary, the oven can be turned down after that for a filling to be cooked right through.

BAKING BLIND: Flan cases, etc., are best baked before filling for the crispest result. Cover pastry with greaseproof paper that has been well scrunched up and smoothed out again (this prevents creases cutting into the dough) then add baking beans, rice or pulses to prevent the pastry puffing up. Make sure the paper covers the edges of the pastry then they won't overbrown in the final baking. Bake for 10–15 minutes, remove paper and beans and return pastry to oven to finish off. For tartlet cases, place an identical tin on top of tart tin, making the pastry the filling between a tin sandwich. A crisper case can be achieved by using a well-scrunched wad of tin foil gently fitted into the shape of the flan's interior. This will conduct heat to the bottom of the case and slightly brown it the same colour as the edges. This is particularly good for cases that won't receive further cooking.

MERINGUES

An airtight tin of meringues will keep almost indefinitely and provide the makings of a host of desserts. The basic mixture can be piped or spooned into individual "halves" or swirled into flat circles the size of a side plate to make into impressive vacherins.

Egg whites keep two to three weeks in the fridge in a covered jar, longer if the eggs are very fresh, and also freeze excellently. To use for meringues, weigh whites and use 50 g/2 oz/4 tablespoons caster sugar per 25 g/1 oz/ 1 medium size egg white.

Make sure bowl and whisk are completely clean and free of any specks of yolk or grease then start to beat whites slowly. As they begin to mount, like massing clouds, beat more quickly. When they stand in stiff peaks, beat in half the sugar by the tablespoonful, then fold in remaining half (if using an electric beater, all the sugar can be beaten in, the adding of the tablespoons of sugar should be almost continuous). Mixture should be satin smooth and thick enough to stand in stiff peaks.

Either spoon or pipe little mounds of meringue on to siliconised paper and bake in a cool oven, 110°C/225°F/Gas Mark ¼ for 2 hours or until meringue halves lift easily off the paper. It is a good idea then to let them cool in the turned-off oven. When completely cold, place in an airtight container. Instead of small shapes, the meringue can be spread into two flat circles and baked in the same way.

COOK'S TIP: Do keep a watch while beating egg whites. First they will be very loose, then become much denser and, if the whisk is lifted, peaks will form that then flop over; this is called "soft peak" and is the stage needed for folding into other mixtures such as mousses. If beating is continued, the egg whites become very shiny and the peaks will stand straight up; this is "stiff peak" and is the stage at which sugar is whipped in for meringues. If beating is continued beyond this stage, the mixture will lose its shine and look grainy. The white is now starting to break down and lose its stiffness, finally becoming watery. There is no way to resurrect the whites after this stage is reached. If beaten egg whites are left to stand, they will also start to break down but in this case a quick whisk of the mixture will restore most of the buoyancy provided the breaking down hasn't gone too far. Once sugar has been beaten in or the whites have been folded into another mixture, a certain stability has been achieved. Overbeating the sugar can also cause breaking down, or sometimes weeping of meringues.

FISH AND MEAT STOCK

A little stock can help flavour a soup, casserole or sauce. Whenever a chicken carcass or some meaty bones are available, make a stock. A pressure cooker is a great help, cutting down the simmering time. Microwave ovens can also make stock very quickly.

MEAT STOCK

Bones on their own produce a slightly gluey stock, always try and have a little meat with them, poultry giblets, other than the liver (which has a rather individual flavour), are ideal. Have bones chopped into smallish pieces then brown in a dry pan over a moderate heat or in a roasting pan in oven at 190°C/375°F/Gas Mark 5. Then add a few vegetables: an onion, a carrot, and a stick of celery, throw in a few stalks of parsley, some peppercorns and a very small amount of salt. Cover with water, bring gently to the boil, skim off the brown scum that rises just before the liquid boils, then lower heat and simmer for 2–3 hours. Strain and keep refrigerated. Boil up every two days, every day if it is kept in a cool place rather than the fridge.

PRESSURE COOKER: Place stock ingredients in pressure cooker, half fill container with water, add lid, bring up to highest pressure and maintain for 35 minutes.

MICROWAVE OVEN: Use 450 g/1 lb bones, meat and a small onion plus a piece of carrot to 600 ml/1 pint/2 cups water, omit salt and peppercorns. Place in a large bowl, cover tightly with cling film and microwave on HIGH for 20 minutes.

FISH STOCK

Use 450 g/1 lb fish trimmings, most fishmongers will be delighted to let you have some when you buy any sort of fish: bones, skin and heads (but make sure any blood is well washed out or stock will be very discoloured and bitter), add a slice of onion, a celery stalk and small carrot, both cut in chunks, a squeeze of lemon, parsley stalks, a small piece of bay leaf, a few peppercorns and a very small amount of salt. Cover with water, or half water and half wine, or water and a few tablespoons dry vermouth, or water and a tablespoon of wine vinegar. Bring to boil, remove scum that rises to surface then lower heat and simmer very gently for 25 minutes.

PRESSURE COOKER: As above, bring to pressure and maintain for 7 minutes.

MICROWAVE OVEN: To above fish trimmings, vegetables and flavourings add 600 ml/1 pint/2 cups liquid as above, place in a large bowl, cover tightly with cling film and microwave on HIGH for 10 minutes.

SKINNING AND FILLETING FISH

A fishmonger will fillet fish for you and skin them as well. But it is quite a simple process and useful if you buy trout, say, from the deep-freeze cabinet. A long, flexible bladed knife will make the job easier but is not essential. A knife with a really sharp blade is. *For a round fish:* cut off the head and tail then run the knife blade down the centre of the back, where the dorsal fin sticks out, and down one side of the backbone, then almost lift the flesh off the ribs. Repeat on the other side. Trim off the small fins. Tweezers can be used to tweak out the little "pin" bones running down the centre of each fillet. *For a flat fish:* no need to remove head and tail. Cut down the centre of the fish, along one side of the spine that sticks up in a little ridge underneath the skin, then slip the blade of your knife under the fillet, keeping the knife scraping along the rib bones, almost lifting the flesh off. Repeat on the other side then turn the fish over and do the same on the underneath.
To skin fillets: place the fillet on the work surface with skin side underneath. Using a sharp bladed knife, lift up a little of the flesh at one end of the fillet so you slide the blade between flesh and skin. Then grasp the skin firmly (a little salt can help if you find it very slippery), have the knife held at a flat angle and wiggle it underneath the flesh, almost sawing it off the skin. It is very much easier than it sounds! Skin and bones can be used to make a fish stock (see page 277).

BONING AND JOINTING POULTRY

Buying a whole bird is both cheaper and more cost effective than portions. One chicken, or duck, will yield two breasts, two legs, two wings and a useful piece of carcass for stock. The only tool required is a small, very sharp knife.
1. REMOVE LEGS: Pull one of the legs away from the body and cut through the loose taut skin so it can be bent back towards the spine. This will enable you to find exactly where to cut through the ball and socket

278

joint. Then cut between the flesh and the backbone, digging round the oyster so this succulent little nugget of flesh remains with the leg and is not left on the carcass. The leg should now be separated from the body. Repeat on the other side. Each leg can be separated into thigh and drumstick by cutting through the joint, feel with your fingers to find exactly where the ball fits into the socket, then cut through to release the tendons holding it in place.

2. REMOVE WINGS: If you want the breast whole, pull the wing away from the body and cut through first the loose, taut skin and then the joint, the same as for the leg, taking the tip of the breast with its thick white membrane with the wing. These little wing joints are ideal for serving with drinks, they can be accumulated in a deep-freeze. If you want a wing joint with a nice piece of breast attached, to use for a casserole perhaps, place the bird on its back with the wing end towards you. Remove the wishbone by lifting back the skin, cutting through the flesh over the wishbone then using your fingers to work it out of the chicken, pulling the bone back to break it away from the end of the breastbone. Then make two matching, oblique cuts, one on either side of the breast, and detach the wings as above.

3. REMOVE BREASTS: It is now quite easy to pull off the skin, though it can be left on if you prefer. The skin itself can be cut into small pieces and fried till crisp then used to garnish a salad. To remove each breast, cut down the side of the breastbone, then use small, scraping cuts, keeping the knife against the bone, down the ribcage, detaching the meat. Repeat on the other side.

If you prefer to keep the meat on the bone, use a strong pair of kitchen scissors, or poultry scissors, to cut away the backbone and sever the breast into two. Each breast can then be cut into two pieces if required, quite useful if the bird is very big.

4. THE EXTRA PIECES: The carcass will usually have odd pieces of flesh still attached to it around the backbone. These can be detached and, with the meat from the wings, can add up to a useful quantity for a risotto (see FINGER LICKIN' CHICKEN section on page 38) or soup or a SALADE TIÈDE (see SALAD BOWLS section on page 173). If you have a bird with giblets, the liver can also be used for a salade tiède, or kept in the deep-freeze until enough have been assembled for chicken liver pâté. The rest of the giblets can be used with the remainder of the carcass for stock (see page 277).

TO BONE A CHICKEN (OR DUCK OR TURKEY) LEG:

Grasp the leg by the ball joint which attached it to the main body of the bird. Using a small, sharp knife, scrape down the bone, pushing away the flesh. When you get to the joint, be careful not to leave the knee-cap in the flesh, this should be cut round so it remains attached to the bone. By the time the end of the bone is reached, the flesh will have more or less turned itself inside out. Grasp this and pull away from the bone, then cut through the thin skin at the end, detaching flesh completely. Trim out any tough sinews or tendons, turn back so skin side is outside and proceed as required.

TO BONE A CHICKEN, TURKEY OR ANY OTHER BIRD:

A boned chicken or turkey are maybe a little large to cook for two but a pheasant is not, nor are poussins, quails or pigeons. Start by cutting down the backbone then use your small, sharp knife to make scraping cuts, keeping the blade against the bone, to detach the flesh, cutting through the leg and wing joints as you go. Leave detaching the breastbone until the end and try not to nick the skin as you do so, nicks will widen alarmingly in the cooking but can be sewn up beforehand so are not disastrous. For the larger birds, the legs can be boned out as above, it's a little more tricky with the rest of the flesh attached but not really difficult. Leave the wings or bone out the first joint then sever the rest off; it's best then to push the bit of wing flesh inside itself into the main body of the bird, it makes a tidier finish. The boned bird is then ready for stuffing. With quails and pigeons, the legs and wings are left unboned.

SEGMENTING CITRUS FRUIT

Another very useful little technique that makes eating either oranges or grapefruit so much more pleasant.

Cut off the top and bottom of the fruit, stand it upright on a board and slice off the rest of the skin with downward strokes, like removing the staves of a barrel. The main trick is to make sure you take the pith with the skin without removing too much flesh. Then trim off any remaining pith.

Hold the now naked fruit in your non-knife-wielding hand and slip the blade of your sharp little knife down between one of the segment's membranes and the flesh. Repeat on the other side of the segment and lift it out, leaving the membrane still attached to the rest of the orange. Slip the knife blade down the other side of the piece of membrane furthest away from you then give the blade a little jerk so that it slips underneath the point of the segment, at the centre of fruit, and half lifts, half scrapes it off the other side of the membrane and out of the orange. It's usually easiest to pick any seeds out of each segment before you finish lifting it off the other side of the membrane.

Repeat with the remaining segments.

Do the job over a bowl to catch any juices that drip out, then squeeze the little packet of membrane that's left after all the segments have been removed to release any remaining juice. Pick out any seeds from the segments.

This is one of those techniques that takes much longer to describe than it does to do, it's a knack that's quite easy to acquire. And I promise that after your first or second attempt you will find it much quicker to release the flesh from an orange or grapefruit this way than to peel it nicely and separate out all the segments.

INDEX